OBS

"The Stain on the Other Man's Pants" by Andrew Holleran
He was handsome. He was sweet. He was sexy. He hasn't
called back in six years. And a small-town southern
loner is still pining for the one-night stand that got away.

"Love Maps" by Mack Friedman
An elusive medical text fuels an *outré* obsession for a horny
young bibliophile hungry to satisfy his ultimate erotic
fantasy: a boy, a doctor, and an exam.

"In This Corner" by Charles Flowers
It's pummeling fists and slamming flesh as a novice boxer
strips down to his satin trunks for a bareback knock-
down-drag-out with the mentor of his dreams.

"Harold Ramis's Glasses" by D. Travers Scott
Smitten by all things Semitic, a gentile finds salvation in men
who can wax Talmudic as they deliver the (kosher) goods.

. . . and other uncensored erotic confessionals.

Michael Lowenthal is the author of a novel, *The Same Embrace*
(Dutton/Plume), and editor of *Gay Men at the Millennium*
(Tarcher/Putnam) and the Flesh and the Word series. His sto-
ries and essays have appeared in numerous anthologies, in-
cluding *Men on Men 5* (Plume), *Best American Gay Fiction 1*, and
Queer 13. He lives in Boston.

ALSO BY MICHAEL LOWENTHAL

The Same Embrace (novel)

EDITOR

Gay Men at the Millennium

Flesh and the Word 4

Winter's Light

Friends and Lovers (with John Preston)

Flesh and the Word 3 (with John Preston)

OBSESSED

A FLESH AND THE WORD COLLECTION OF GAY EROTIC MEMOIRS

EDITED BY

Michael Lowenthal

A PLUME BOOK

PLUME
Published by the Penguin Group
Penguin Putnam Inc., 375 Hudson Street, New York, New York 10014, U.S.A.
Penguin Books Ltd, 27 Wrights Lane, London W8 5TZ, England
Penguin Books Australia Ltd, Ringwood, Victoria, Australia
Penguin Books Canada Ltd, 10 Alcorn Avenue, Toronto, Ontario, Canada M4V 3B2
Penguin Books (N.Z.) Ltd, 182–190 Wairau Road, Auckland 10, New Zealand

Penguin Books Ltd, Registered Offices: Harmondsworth, Middlesex, England

First published by Plume, a member of Penguin Putnam Inc.

First Printing, May, 1999
10 9 8 7 6 5 4 3 2 1

Page 237 constitutes an extension of this copyright page.

 REGISTERED TRADEMARK—MARCA REGISTRADA

LIBRARY OF CONGRESS CATALOGING-IN-PUBLICATION DATA
Obsessed : a Flesh and the word collection of gay erotic memoirs /
edited by Michael Lowenthal.
    p.   cm.
    ISBN 0-452-27999-2
    1. Gay men—Sexual behavior—Literary collections.   2. Erotic
literature, American—Male authors.   3. Gay men's writings,
American.   I. Lowenthal, Michael.
PS509.H57025   1999
810.8'03538'08664—dc21   98-50411
                                                              CIP

Printed in the United States of America
Set in New Baskerville
Designed by Julian Hamer

BOOKS ARE AVAILABLE AT QUANTITY DISCOUNTS WHEN USED TO PROMOTE PRODUCTS OR
SERVICES. FOR INFORMATION PLEASE WRITE TO PREMIUM MARKETING DIVISION, PENGUIN
PUTNAM INC., 375 HUDSON STREET, NEW YORK, NEW YORK 10014.

The names and characteristics of certain people mentioned in these stories have been changed to protect their privacy.

CONTENTS

ACKNOWLEDGMENTS

For their help and support, I'd like to thank Mitchell Waters, Arnold Dolin, and Jennifer Dickerson; also the many folks at Dutton/Plume who make me smile, especially Sarah Branham, Stephen Cipriano, and Kip Hakala; and, of course, Scott: my obsession.

INTRODUCTION

MICHAEL LOWENTHAL

In our overstimulated age, the act of reading remains, in the general view, an ivory-tower experience: quiet and clean, suitable for the library's pristine hush—or, if in bed, under the chastity of a thick comforter. Books are for the mind, we're told, not the body. And the words routinely used to commend literature—*moving, stirring, rousing*—are just that: words, metaphors disemboweled of any gutsy reality. When readers are in fact *moved* by a piece of writing—most especially if what *stirs* or is *roused* is the organ between their legs—the work in question is quickly deemed a lesser form of art, unworthy of serious attention.

Not for me. One of my greatest pleasures is reading a book and finding that I have to set it down—or can't make myself do so—because the words have turned me on, or turned my stomach. When I say of a novel "It got me stiff" or "It made me sick," I intend these appraisals quite literally, and almost always they indicate my enthusiasm.

After all, what a tremendous feat! A writer in some distant place and time has committed his thoughts to paper, and somehow those tiny marks on pressed sheets of wood pulp inspire a swell of muscles and blood. There is something so quintessentially human about this interaction, something primal and even sacred. What other animal in our known universe is capable of such communication?

Physical excitement is by no means the only stimulation I seek from literature. But it's an essential part of a wider array.

If it's appropriate to weep at the conclusion of *Beloved* (proving the emotional truth of Toni Morrison's story) or, while reading *The Grapes of Wrath,* to have my nostrils filled with the smell of California orchards (testifying to John Steinbeck's accuracy of detail), why then isn't it equally appropriate—even laudatory— to read, say, Dennis Cooper's account of a young hustler giving head, and sprout a thrumming erection? Doesn't this testify to Cooper's skill as a writer? For me, literature fails erotically un- less it also succeeds on other sensual fronts; it must be emo- tionally true, accurate in its details. Thus, writers who turn me on have accomplished as much as other writers, or more. The best literature is synesthetic, appealing simultaneously to all our senses.

I revel in the physicality of my response to powerful writing. And as a writer myself, I aspire to provoke the same full-body reaction in my readers.

Last year I received an e-mail message from a man who'd read a short story of mine in *Best American Erotica,* the story of a character who, after an unsafe sexual encounter, rushes to syn- agogue on Yom Kippur to repent. This reader had bought the book at O'Hare Airport, he told me, and began it on his flight to New York. By the time he finished my story, he was so aroused and disturbed that—in violation of the KEEP SEAT BELTS FASTENED sign—he had to retreat to the plane's bathroom, where he calmed himself and made a vow that upon landing, he would visit a synagogue.

I cheered out loud when I read this e-mail. This was the first time a reader had responded so viscerally to my writing. My words about bodies had stirred his body. I had moved him—lit- erally.

Recently I received another letter, from someone who'd pur- chased *Flesh and the Word 4.* "I was riding the commuter bus one evening," the letter began,

> sitting next to a woman, reading your book. When I got toward the end of [Kevin Killian's essay "Spurt"]—with all the blood and cut flesh and mirror glass—I passed out. . . . One thing

happens when I pass out: my bladder lets loose. When I came to I felt ill and woozy, with a clammy sweat on my forehead and a huge wet spot on my jeans and the seat beneath me. The book had slipped from my hands and lodged in my crotch, so that the bottom edge near the spine soaked up some pee. (It is now yellow and water-wrinkled.) The woman sitting next to me did not appear to notice any of this happening . . . and I decided not to tell her until just before I got off the bus, in order to minimize both her discomfort and my own embarrassment. . . . I haven't gone back to the book since, though I expect I will someday. And I'll be sure to read it in the privacy of my own home, lying down, having just taken a piss.

This account is perhaps the best review of any book I've published. (I forwarded the note to Kevin Killian, who seemed to agree.) Picturing my correspondent's yellow, wrinkled copy of *Flesh and the Word,* I know that all the work of editing the collection paid off. That single pee-stained copy means more to me than a dozen others propped on dusty shelves.

I especially enjoyed this letter because I do much of my own reading of erotic literature on public transportation. As *Flesh and the Word* submissions arrive in the mail, I save them up, and then, some afternoon when I have an appointment in downtown Boston, I take the stack with me on the no. 39 bus. It's an efficient use of otherwise lost time, but the real reason I wait for a bus ride is that I enjoy the extra thrill of reading sexy stories in the company of strangers. The atmosphere serves as an excellent editorial gauge: if a submission is powerful enough to make me uncomfortable in my seat, nervous that other passengers might see evidence of my arousal, then it's a likely candidate for acceptance.

I look for writing that physically thrills or discomforts me, that steals my breath and curls my toes. I look for writing that battles my senses—and wins.

Obsessed is a collection of twenty erotic essays that make me squirm. Like *Flesh and the Word 4,* this book consists entirely of first-person, confessional accounts—not the faked "It really happened to me!" wankery found in skin magazines, but artful literary memoirs about the nature of gay sexuality. These are reports from the sexual front lines, erotic espionage in which the spies and the spied-upon are one and the same.

These memoirs fall within the boundaries of what Edmund White has championed as "the new lyrical sexual realism" among gay writers. Moving beyond an earlier generation's rudimentary (and Tourettically repetitive) masturbation aids, such writers, White says, attempt

> a dissection of what actually goes on in the head of someone while he is having sex—all the half-thoughts and fleeting distractions, the sudden memory of a broken appointment just at the second of insertion, the unspoken rituals and uncodified etiquette that accompany every moment of the erotic tangle.

Which is not to say that the writing included here disallows the idealism of fantasy. On the contrary, fantasy fuels almost every sentence. But these authors forgo the blandly grandiose daydreaming endemic to porn scenarios ("Hi! Pizza boy! Can I suck your dick?") in favor of much grittier, more detailed, more honest imaginings.

The specific focus of this collection is obsession—in our culture, a much maligned state of being. The word evokes individuals with obsessive-compulsive disorder, or serial murderers, the Jeffrey Dahmer types whose unwavering fixations lead to acts of criminal malevolence.

Surely, any trait in excess can be dangerous. But apart from these extremes, I think that obsession—particularly erotic obsession—is to be celebrated, not overcome. What else marks so clearly our humanity? Lower animals fixate on necessity: the squirrel stocks up on acorns, the beaver dulls its teeth on trees—poor beasts condemned to striving after what's good for them. But our human passion for pleasure—for things we don't necessarily need, but *want*—is what makes us the beautifully imperfect, complicated higher creatures we are.

How wonderful that we often obsess over precisely those people and experiences and things (unattainable or abusive mates, physically dangerous acts, drugs) that we know are *bad* for us. What exquisite pleasure there is in this pain!

In a sense, every erotic attraction is obsessive: in order to hurdle all the cultural and biological obstacles to sexual fulfillment, we must be sufficiently fixated on the object of our affection as to be willing to work for the goal. All of us—from the teenager smitten with his schoolmate, to the bathhouse prowler, to the man who, after a dozen years of partnership, still finds sexy the liverish spot on his lover's lower back—are necessarily obsessed with that which attracts us.

Obsession is a particularly rich theme for writers, who, by the nature of their calling, are obsessive. To get each sentence, each word, each comma correct, a writer reads and rereads and rereads again, revisiting the same material. A tolerance for this process, for the physical act of concentration on minutiae, seems to correlate with an inclination to fixate on matters of emotion and memory. Writers also learn to observe the people around them with near microscopic scrutiny in order to get the details just right: the precise swagger of a man's stride, the exact length of pause before he answers the question "What do you like?" and what that reveals about what he *really* likes, how the smell of his sweat changes in the moment before orgasm.

When I asked writers to contribute to this volume essays about their erotic obsessions, I thought I knew roughly what I'd receive. There would be a foot fetishist or two, someone into leather, an aficionado of alfresco sex. Someone might confess his crush on Leonardo DiCaprio.

But as it turns out, there are no podophiles, no leather queens, no nature lovers in this book; and I'm the only one who wants to drool on Leo. The reality of our erotic obsessions, it seems—when we get to a deeper, more candid level than that which pornography has brainwashed us to expect—is at once more mundane and more compelling.

Almost all the contributors do write about actual people, but these individuals are for the most part not *Titanic* celebrities. They are, instead, childhood bullies and best friends, one-night stands that got away, a boyfriend's ex-boyfriends, guys at the gym, and, in two cases, the writer's brother. They are the kinds of real people with whom we interact in day-to-day life, and I think that this says something about the ubiquity of obsession and its fundamental place in our existence.

A few contributors confess their attraction to certain "types"—Jews, white guys, Chinese men—but, working against the trend of facile pornographic objectifying, they keep eyes wide for complexity and paradox; there is no such thing, their essays suggest, as simple as "having a type." Other writers explore more liberal interpretations of obsession. One finds a turn-on not so much in any particular sex act as in talking about it afterward. Another is hooked on his bathroom sink!

What the memoirs have in common is unabashed candor and yearning for truth. The writers respond to what Edmund White calls the "erotic tangle" by trying to describe in exact detail each loop and gnarl. But, of course, sexual attraction is a knot than can never be untied. Pull one thread and another tightens. The string has no ends; it's all middle.

We are all inevitably bound by our obsessions, and yet by our binding we are also freed. These writers capture that contradiction: all the joys and foibles and heartache and triumph of how intensely we desire. They write openly of being moved—metaphorically and literally—and in so doing, they dare us to be moved as well. And thus, to those who would condemn erotic writing as shameless, they defiantly announce their agreement: they are indeed shameless in their writing, because they have nothing of which to be ashamed.

Boston, Massachusetts
June 1998

OBSESSED

THE STAIN ON
THE OTHER MAN'S PANTS

ANDREW HOLLERAN

An obsession, said a friend who has had more experience with psychiatry than I, organizes your life. Another way of putting that, I suppose, is that it simplifies it. ("Simplify, simplify," said Thoreau.) An obsession concentrates your energy on one object—it marks off, out of the whole vast planet, a plot of ground *you* can cultivate. It narrows things down—like the troubadors' courtly love, the single lady a knight devotes himself to (an unattainable lady at that; the jongleurs knew what they were singing about). Or the saints' fixation on Christ.

Stendhal speaks not of obsession but of crystallization—that moment when desire suddenly focuses on one particular person—but the two seem to me like the same thing. My obsession began the night D. slept with me six years ago. I had known of his existence for seven years before that. (Later, in the depths of my obsession, I saw a biblical parallel: Jacob toiling for Rachel's father for the same period.) We lived in the same small town in rural Florida. The nearest gay bar was in a city twenty-three miles west. Shortly after I moved down there in 1983, D. was pointed out to me across that crowded bar as someone who lived in my town too. I looked at him, but that was all. He was standing with someone as handsome as he was. Tall, rangy, lean, with expensive haircuts, both men held themselves aloof somehow from the crowd around them, if by no other means than their beauty. I never saw D. again—till one night seven years later when he introduced himself at the boat ramp, a county park much closer to our town than the gay bar, a place where men gather to cruise and have sex in a public rest room.

He was thirty-four then and still handsome—in 501s and a Navy sweatshirt as he leaned against the fender of his car smoking cigarettes and waiting for me to get out of mine. (Some premonition, some warning, some gay version of street smarts that tells us Beauty is never easy, kept me sitting in my car long after he moved his hand sideways through the air in a kind of self-deprecating, comic wave.) I was so nervous that my legs were shaking when I finally got out and walked over to him and said hello. But when he introduced himself, the tension dissolved, and we bonded—as two gay men stuck in the same small town who knew some of the same families and who each knew where the other lived. It was so late when we stopped talking that we decided to get together some other night, at an earlier hour, and after giving him my phone number I was so smitten that as he drove back to town behind me through the fragrant spring night, his little car like a puppy following mine, I thought: This is as happy as you will ever be. The next night, to my great satisfaction, he called, and I told him to come over.

Our visit lasted three or four hours, during which we mostly talked in the still, lamp-lit room whose windows were open to the damp, cool night outside. Finally I glanced at the clock—it was shortly before midnight—and told him, "Stand up." He did. Then I walked over and enclosed him in my arms. I could have stood like that forever, but sex is a progress, so I led him to the bedroom, where I left him for a moment to turn off the lamps in the other room. He undressed while I was gone, so that when I walked in I found him standing naked before a mirror. He had a body that would not even interest a muscle queen: though he was tall, six foot one or two, his head and hands were in a way too large for his torso, his shoulders too narrow, his chest flat and undeveloped—more a thorax than a chest—and sprinkled lightly with dark brown hair. His scrotal sac was especially large, the red folds of wrinkled flesh flowing down his inner thighs. There was an abashed, almost apologetic expression on his face as he stood there. I was in fact the one abashed, abject, vulnerable, my sense of unworthiness intensifying when his penis grew, so long it bent halfway, as if engineering principles could not support a weight that far distant from his trunk and the second half had to be cantilevered; a penis thicker at the bottom than the top ("a lighthouse penis," a friend said when I described it). Operating on a theory I had at the time that all gay men are really bottoms and find attention paid their cocks a mere distraction, I ignored this obvious object—as if to adore the penis others had no doubt made much of would lose me his respect—until the sex was almost done, and then I briefly put my mouth on it. At that point he gasped and, jerking himself off as I raised my head, came immediately. (So that's what he wanted, I thought. All sex is a learning process.) After his orgasm, he lay there, looking at me down his long, lean torso with the expression an infant wears after being bathed, powdered, and diapered, while I continued to lick his limbs, causing him to flinch, the way highly sensitive flesh does when it's touched. "I hope you enjoyed this as much as I did," he said when he finally got up off the bed; I was too shocked by his strangely formal courtesy to reply. Still, I offered him a shower, and I was thus able to soap the back of this body I did not want to stop touching—though he was apparently indifferent to the opportunities a shower gives for further lovemaking. Then he dressed, and after darting back down the hall with the coiled grace of a cat burglar making his escape—to make sure he hadn't left his cigarette lighter behind—he said good night and disappeared.

(Months later, I was still able to replay the thirty minutes of our sex over and over again, like a conspiracy theorist viewing the Zapruder film. Or, rather, like Emma Bovary remembering the ball at the château—the one she never gets over. He was handsome, he was kind, he was grown-up, he was masculine, he was sweet, he was even better undressed than dressed, he lived four blocks away, he was all I could ever have wanted had a genie asked me to make a wish.)

The next night he called but I couldn't see him; then I heard nothing. After several weeks of silence, I called him after I

heard that a drunk driver had crashed into his house (thus I
had a pretext for contacting him). It was the first of many long
phone conversations between us, though I gradually realized
that for some reason he had no desire to have sex with me
again, that our evening was going to be of a sort I associated
with urban existence (the one-night stand), and that no matter
how depressed or highly sexed he might be, I was not going to
be the alleviator of either of those two afflictions. And so began
my wondering why I had been rejected; and so began my obsession.

I wrote letters to him I never mailed, including lists of the
things about his body and character I loved; walked past his
parents' house every night because one evening I'd seen him
sitting shirtless on a bench in the driveway there, exhausted by
his long day at the sand mine where he worked; drove past his
house as nonchalantly as I could, hardly slowing down, terrified he would see me; wondered whom he was having sex with,
if not with me; got up before dawn when I couldn't sleep and
went to the boat ramp, thinking not that he would be there but
that his car might be on the road with mine as he drove to
work; looked at the phone book each time a new one came out
to make sure his name was still there and that he had not
moved away. All of this was exacerbated, of course, by the fact
that he had *not* moved away—that we *did* live in the same small
town and that there *were* just four blocks of houses between his
and mine. It was especially awful during those long, excruciating twilights in spring, after we changed to daylight saving time,
when I knew he must be home from work. What was he doing?
Why couldn't I go visit him? I couldn't—that was all—because
he didn't, despite the depression and boredom of our separate
lives, want me to; and because one of the great unwritten laws
of human society, as obdurate and impermeable as lead, is that
we cannot force our amorous feelings onto another. "We are all
doomed to the caprices of unequal affection," a friend wrote
me in a letter at the time. Some caprice! It seemed to me more
like an iron curtain separating his home from my own, even
though the twilight was so clear; why television and radio sig-

nals could travel freely through the atmosphere above the trees into his home but I could not I did not know, and the fact drove me crazy.

Of course I could talk to him on the telephone—though I did that at judicious intervals, careful not to call him too much, and it took a certain courage and control over my breath before I could even dial his number. Our talks were always wonderful. He became a voice, a beautiful, rich, melancholy, masculine voice on the other end of the line, somewhere in the darkness of that little sleeping town. Both of us alone in our houses, both of us at home, talking for hours, the way we had the night he slept with me; only this time he didn't sleep with me—he hung up with a "Thanks for calling," and I knew, the minute I replaced the receiver, that I had been refused again. And the clock was ticking on what I considered a decent interval before I called him again.

One night I gathered my nerve and asked him if he wanted to come over, and he said, yawning, that he was too tired: "I think I'll have a glass of water and go to bed." "I'm being rejected for a glass of water!" I said. He laughed and said: "You tickle me." I was glad I had—making someone laugh is like making love to him—but I was bereft that this was all I was allowed to do. Our conversations on the phone were like the conversation we'd had at my house before I told him "Stand up" and we went to bed together; only each time I hung up the phone I was alone, I could not touch him; he was as remote, as refusing, as ever.

Of course that was part of his appeal: I told myself it was only by rejecting me that he'd amassed this power—that in fact he was just an ordinary, small-town southern queen; but this attempt to free myself did not work very well. Soon I was listing the reasons he *was* special—the looks, the voice, the masculinity, the sweetness, the dick—but my attempts to disinfect, with an intellectual bleach, my obsession with D. always ended with the reverberating certainty that no matter what the "objective" reasons for this masochistic fixation on a man I could not have, I still wanted him, so much it hurt. Yet I could not even see him.

He didn't go to the boat ramp again; he didn't have to. He was young (thirteen years younger than I) and had a boyfriend (the best-looking man at my gym in Gainesville, I eventually learned). The boyfriend, D. had told me during our sole evening together, even wanted to move in with D., but D. had refused; D. was already raising a teenage daughter ("I've brought one up and I'm not about to bring up another"). He had a daughter to raise, a boyfriend who wanted to move in, a job that left him exhausted at the end of the day, but none of this mattered; I wanted to be a piece on the side. "I'm a very sexual person," he'd said. *Who isn't?* I thought—though I knew what he meant; some people are more sexual than others, and he was one. What I wanted was that we be sexual together. And so I became obsessed, outraged by every waking hour that we were not conjoined in bed.

Everywhere I went I thought of him—at the baths (which he thought "too impersonal"), the post office (surely he received mail!), the grocery store (even he had to eat!)—but he remained invisible. I brought his name up in conversation with other people just to hear what they had to say about him. (One neighbor thought him a ne'er-do-well, the music teacher called him "sweet," another friend labeled him "a snob," though admitted he was handsome.) The whole town became a reference library with only one subject heading: D. I told myself I was being neurotic because I was so lonely and sex-starved, and that he was probably something very different from what I imagined; but this did no good. Because he did not want to see me again, was apparently able to live without me—incredible!—I could not see how he differed from my idealized portrait. That, I told myself when the pain was most intense, was the problem: nothing allows an obsession to intensify like the vacuum of a person's absence. If absence makes the heart grow fonder, it causes an obsession to catch fire and billow up into the night, like one of those oil wells the Iraqis ignited during the Gulf War.

Romantic obsessions actually give rise to similes like that; suddenly you are reading poetry again to ease your mind—

John Donne, Emily Dickinson, Shakespeare. Donne seems especially right: you *are* a tick sucking blood from your lover's arm. Yes! You *are* an oil field in Kuwait, a pillar of flame, burning in the night! And popular songs: Bonnie Raitt was singing "I Can't Make You Love Me" on the radio that spring—a song so lovely and on-target that every time it was played I leaned forward to hear each exquisite tinkle of the piano keys, feeling that amazement we all do when a pop song expresses, but exactly, what is going on in our lives and hearts.

On the other hand, nothing is so incommunicable as a romantic obsession. When you're on the receiving end of an obsessive's description of his passion, it's like listening to a drunk, or to someone telling you his dreams; you simply cannot feel what he is feeling; and I knew, even as I told my tale of unrequited love, that my friends were not enthralled. They all gave advice anyway. One said: "It's because you live in the same town that he doesn't want to see you." A second: "He just wanted to see what was in your pants." A third: "If he chooses to live in that town, then you're not the kind of person he wants to know." A fourth: "Love is an opportunity for personal growth." Finally, a bartender I knew—no one is more schooled in love than bartenders—told me to stop calling D., told me that I was only humiliating myself.

In truth, I couldn't tell what D.'s mood was: he always thanked me for my call; the nights *were* so boring in that town, surely he enjoyed talking to *someone*. But he never called me back. And he never asked me a question about myself. And though I assured myself that I was simply offering friendship, he could tell, no doubt, that I wanted more; that was surely why he told me in great detail about the hemorrhoid operation he was recuperating from the last time we spoke—to demystify, to desexualize himself. It didn't work. It simply saddened me that I hadn't been able to go visit him at home that week to keep him company. Then, when two nights in a row he did not answer the phone, the truth of what I was doing hit me, and I realized I should not call again.

At first, in the silence that now began, I hoped he would be there each time I went to the boat ramp. Then I hoped he wouldn't. I needn't have worried. Three years passed without my seeing him. Then, after my hair turned gray one summer, I became *afraid* I might run into him. Like Deborah Kerr in *An Affair to Remember* after she is crippled in an accident and refuses to show up for the date she'd made with Cary Grant when they'd fallen in love on a cruise ship, I felt I could not expect D. to want me now—the thirteen years between us had become visible. (Is that what an obsession is? The symbol on which one's personal angst, not desire, crystallizes?) Occasionally I thought I saw him, even passed him, in the post office, but he said nothing, nor did I, and afterward I was not sure if it had been he, or only a man who looked like him. D. was like a Ken doll—he looked different with each outfit. One night in the supermarket I saw a tall, handsome, skinny man perusing frozen pizzas at the end of the aisle I was pushing my shopping cart down, but his chin looked smaller, his nose longer, his mustache too handlebar, his hair too wavy, his profile too Victorian. It was not D. But I waited outside after checking out to make sure. The way this man walked when he emerged immediately convinced me I was wrong—it *was* D. Watching him get into a silver Cavalier, I realized he'd bought a new car, and I drove home behind him that rainy night and watched him turn onto his street (the clincher) as I thought: What a shame, what a waste! As if we were two convicts imprisoned in the same cell and neither would speak to the other. I thought of Zorba the Greek saying it was a crime when any woman slept alone. His gorgeous cock was going unused—this great national resource! Why couldn't I have it? Why couldn't we spend these wasted evenings together?

A year later I saw another man who looked like D., yawning as he pushed open the door of the post office while I stood in line waiting to mail something; again, I did not think it was D. till I saw him get into a silver Cavalier and drive off, and then I became so obsessed with his little yawn (had he been up all night, having sex?) that though I went to the town library afterward to read the Travel section of the Sunday *Times*—articles about Antwerp, Maastricht—I felt like weeping as I did so. Travel is hell, I thought; life has no pleasures except D. I'll stay in this town till he speaks to me. Clearly this was absurd; but it didn't matter. I was obsessed with his body. "I've got a brand-new asshole," he'd drawled the evening he told me about his hemorrhoid operation; but all this had made me want to do was reply: "Then let my tongue dissolve the stitches."

By now D.'s asshole was quite healed, of course, and we no longer even acknowledged each other in the post office, and I went to the boat ramp hoping to meet someone who'd free me of him. (The only practical advice I've ever heard for liberating oneself from an obsession: meet someone else.) It didn't work. No one compared to him. Everyone else's mediocrity only confirmed his excellence. Then one April evening—six years after our meeting at the boat ramp—I was parked there shortly after sunset opposite another vehicle, a truck that belonged to a stout, well-built, bearded man in his early thirties whom I'd followed into the men's room a week earlier (hoping to find a D.-substitute) but embarrassed myself in front of because—faced with his thick, stiff dick—I could not get an erection. ("Oh, come on!" I'd cried as he zipped up. "I'm just nervous!" But he'd walked out.) My older appearance was causing me such attrition of my self-esteem that when faced with someone really young and handsome I was impotent. Still, the man's impatience had angered me. So that April evening I was sitting there stubbornly in my car while he sat in his, the two of us ignoring each other, when another car drove up. In the dim glow of the lampposts, it looked pale cinnamon; so when the tall, slender man with a mustache got out and walked over to the truck in which the bearded youth sat, I did not think it was D. I did steel myself, however, for the inevitable envy when the two of them got together, as I was sure they would. Instead, to my surprise—and satisfaction, if I am to be honest—when the tall man with the mustache walked up to the driver's window of the truck and waved, the man inside sat bolt upright, started his engine, and drove off. Mollified, I drove away myself, leaving the tall, skinny man alone.

A few miles from the boat ramp it occurred to me that the way the tall man had waved at the man in the truck was exactly the way D. had waved at me the night he picked me up. I knew then that the tall, slender man was therefore D., and that the car was not cinnamon but silver—it was a trick played by the light of the lampposts. When I got home, I phoned him to make sure; when nobody answered, my suspicion solidified; an hour later I phoned again to apologize for not having said hello to him at the boat ramp, if indeed he had been there, which indeed (he said) he had.

He knew the man in the truck who'd driven off, he told me: he was called J.B., he had a lover, and he could be "quite arrogant." ("And I don't have much use for arrogance," said D.) Then we slipped into another of our long conversations, and he brought me up to date on the past five years. "Life's been a bitch," D. said. He was in debt; his daughter had moved out and given birth to twins; he'd broken up with his boyfriend, who now refused to speak to him (because he was still in love with D., I knew without even asking); he'd been fired from the job he hated, and from four others after that; he was working now in the drugstore in the mall outside of town. I could see him anytime I wanted, I realized, just by walking into Walgreen's. I suggested he come over for dinner, but he said, "Oh no no!" with the nervousness of someone who does not want to be obligated, or to encourage closeness. (It's not fun being an obsession.) Yet when we hung up I was relieved, elated, and touched.

I was elated, I suppose, because he no longer had the boyfriend, was living alone like me (though he'd acquired a dog, the final seal on bachelorhood), and was now working in a place where I could at least see him if I wanted to.

My only gay friend in town and I call each other whenever we see someone handsome at the boat ramp, or at the grocery store, both to alert the other person and to relieve ourselves of the pressure created by Beauty—but when Frank called this time to rave about a man working in Walgreen's, I smiled and told him that it was D., that I knew all about him, and that I did not have to go see. Still, I was pleased when Frank called me thereafter whenever he went to Walgreen's to get the pills he takes to medicate his prostate. "Was he there?" I always asked. And he told me. Then an interrogation followed. "What was he wearing?" "You know I never remember what people are wearing." "Then what was he doing?" "He was in the cosmetics department." "Arranging things?" "I don't know—he was on the other side of the aisle."

This image somehow tamed and domesticated D., reduced him to the role of drugstore manager, simply a nice man, if a bit too handsome for the job. (Imagine that as an overqualification: "I'm sorry," his employer should have said, "you're too handsome for this job. You should be a hustler.") And it seemed to me he had been brought back to earth: a constellation, an animal composed of stars, finally caged.

Of course he had been caged all along, if I was to believe the things he'd told me—how much he'd hated his old job all those years, how he felt that people who'd watched him grow up in that town were always judging him, how depressed he used to get (so depressed that his boyfriend once canceled a business trip he was to take when D. phoned to announce his sadness, told D. to come over, and was waiting naked in bed when D. arrived—one of the many little stories with which I'd tortured myself).

Sex had been his protest, his escape, all along—as it was mine—and now, for some reason, if only that he didn't have to go into the drugstore till three in the afternoon, D. began visiting the boat ramp before work. Nor was that the only change, from what Frank (who went to the boat ramp daily) told me one day. The object of my obsession—who, when I first met him, had had a handsome thirty-year-old boyfriend he went to the gay bar with every Saturday night—now went to the boat ramp to solicit men who, Frank said, were all quite elderly. One of them, Frank said, a man with white hair and a pronounced limp, had been with D. in the men's room that day for a very long time, and when the man came hobbling out and got into his car, Frank was embarrassed to see a little stain right on the seat of the old man's pants.

That stain was a triumph—of D.'s polymorphous sexual tastes, so catholic, so changing; now he was pursuing old, white-haired men and apparently poking them. (Because he assumed that at their age they must be HIV-free? Because they reminded him of his father? Because he was trying some new meat?) Still, though I kept thinking of D. and the old man together in the shadowy latrine, I was not envious. That was not what I wanted to do with D. I wanted to take him to Europe, to New York, to wake up with him on linen sheets in hotel rooms in Egypt. Instead, he was rematerializing in our own town—falling to earth in my own backyard like an old satellite that breaks up reentering the atmosphere.

One day I even spoke to him, face-to-face, in the post office parking lot. As I was coming out, sifting through my mail, I heard my name called, looked up, and there was D.—looking, as usual, not quite like D.: shorter than I remembered, with a fuller face, a closer haircut, a bit flushed but smiling, and handsome in white pants and a navy blue polo shirt, as if dressed for a date. "How's work going?" I said. "It's going," he said, as he walked away from his car and I walked toward mine. That was all we said. I laughed, and backed up, and he watched me go.

Should I have stopped and chatted? What would have been the point? After a while, obsessions become almost abstract—much more important than their objects. And yet, people are corporeal—they have voices, those voices have timbre—and though I smiled all the way home, glad the five years of ostracism were over, that he was still friendly, that he'd seen me with my silver hair, I was sad the moment I parked the car, realizing the power D. still had over me, and walked up to my front door, where, during the height of my longing, I'd always hoped I'd find taped a note from D., saying he'd been there and wanted to see me.

The next time I saw D., just two days later, he was parked at the boat ramp, talking to another man from our town, a married, closeted fellow D. had heaped scorn upon the night we met (for trying to seduce D. and, when D. refused, reporting him to the town council for not paying his garbage fee). I kept driving. Suddenly, it all looked tawdry. So, I thought as I left the park, there is D., just one more good ol' boy, sitting all morning in his car, waiting like the rest of them for some fresh meat to show up. They might as well be hog farmers at an auction waiting for a blue-ribbon sow to be brought out.

Our next encounter disillusioned me further. The following Saturday night I did not even recognize him at first in the check-out line of the grocery store until he waved to me. He was ill, he said, he'd been vomiting and shitting all day; he was leaning on his shopping cart, he was so weak; he was paste-white and, for the first time, did not look entirely handsome. A baggy blue sweater made him seem corpulent; the loafers and pressed jeans, the tired eyes in the pale white face, all gave him the look of a middle-class southern queen—from Atlanta, say. Nevertheless I walked him out to his car and helped him pack away his groceries as we talked of all the flu strains going around and the fact that it was Saturday night and neither one of us was at the bar. (He was tired of the games people played there, he said; the fake fog; everything.) I was sure as I drove off that this was the obsession's end: I even thought of the final scene in *Lolita*, when Humbert Humbert sees the object of *his* obsession come to the door, a pregnant, disheveled, harassed housewife. We were both just middle-aged queens now, going home alone on a Saturday night. I had to hand it to him: he had won. He had separated himself from my obsession—it no longer connected us.

A few nights later, the phone rang. It was Frank. He'd been at the boat ramp that afternoon, and said that D. had been sitting in his car with a white-haired man when Frank drove in, and that the two of them—D. and the old man—talked for a long time. This didn't bother me. D. really is what he said he was the night we met, I thought—"a very sexual person." Let him stain the pants of any old man he cares to. Then, as Frank and I were finishing our conversation, which had turned to other topics, for some reason I went back to the original subject and made a last request for details. "Do you think he and that man were having sex in the car?" I asked. "No," said Frank.

"I think they'd had sex in the bathroom and were just talking afterward." I felt a slight pang; D. had said, the night we met, that he liked to talk after he had sex; now he was talking to someone else. "How do you know that?" I said to Frank. "I don't," he said. "But I saw the man get out of the car with a little piece of paper, and then drive off. So I assume he had given the old man his number." And then it all shattered, and I was undone by the thing Proust claimed was the cause of obsession: jealousy. He gave him his number, I thought, so the man could call him and they could have sex together again. Exactly what he would not do with me. What was it? I wondered. Why that man, and not me? And I was back where I had started: envious of the stain on the other man's pants, even if D. was now so unthreatened by my desire that he could afford to be utterly affable when we met. When I saw him at the post office a few days later, we had the nicest talk; he honked his horn at me as he drove off. Then I went home and fell into another trough of sadness.

EX MARKS THE SPOT

BRIAN BOULDREY

My partner, Anthony, is six foot five of what can only be described as pure Dutch babeness. He has an imperious wide-faced handsomeness and black hair flecked with gray. When his hair is short, it's straight and military and he looks even more intimidating. When he grows it out, he's a boy again. I have a photo of him with long hair leaning over a calf somewhere in France. He dwarfs the calf, but he looks impish because he is smiling. Somewhere along the way somebody told him not to smile for cameras, so he always looks like your grim Great Uncle Sampson in posed shots. It's only when his guard is down before a candid camera that he grins and you can see two boyish dimples. They are rare, but their rarity is a kind of pleasure, too.

Anthony fits my every mood, give or take two, this serious and comedic man, this military boy, this top, this bottom. He's everything I want, all things to all of me. I strive, therefore, to be the same for him.

That's why I am obsessed with his old boyfriends, even the ones he dated for only a week. We'll be walking up the street and pass one of them, and I'll look. Of course there's some jealousy (Anthony is mine, you can't have him), but there's also envy (I want to have Anthony and you, too). Anthony and I have what's called "an open relationship," but believe me, all the rest are merely shoe salesmen, means of practice for the Real (big) McCoy. *What,* I want to know when I see one of his previous rehearsal partners, *did he see in this guy?* What can I learn from him and adopt for my repertoire, so that I can be more of a god, to fit Anthony's every mood?

Anthony is a pastry fan, and he won't eat baked goods from anywhere but The Cakery, a café near our apartment. Who knows why. It's part of a small chain, and though it's not bad, it's got a stupid name, and what's more, it has no specialty, no glazed pain au chocolat or marzipan-slathered tarta de Santiago, no blanc-belly-buttoned black-bottom muffin; nothing, in short, to *prefer*.

But when his birthday came up, I knew where I had to order the cake.

I went to the counter and asked for the catalog of their special-order items. I was led to the quiet end of the shop by a goofy-handsome boy, the kind with hair that needs cutting and an easy smile. He had thick forearms, probably from kneading dough and mixing batter, webbed with a layer of dark fur. He was horsey, a stick-to-your-ribs type of guy. Those hairy arms were dusted with flour; his eyes were agleam with all the chemical energy caffeine and sugar can generate. I'm told that bakers are susceptible to diabetes—not from eating too many of their own bonbons, but from absorbing sugar through their skin.

His name tag said "John." Before I could speak, he held the flat of his hand up like a traffic cop. Then he reached into his bib overalls' front pocket and pulled out a little apparatus, which he hooked over his ear and adjusted. "Sorry, I hate this thing when I don't have to listen to people."

I explained it to this hunky, goofy deaf guy: "This is for a friend celebrating his thirtieth birthday, so it has to be big. He's big."

John grabbed a pad and pen, awaiting further details of what Anthony would like. "Chocolate, vanilla, angel food, devil's food?" Almonds, I said, and ginger, big rough-hewn things, rustic makeshift stuff. Nothing garish, nothing like those little pastel decorations made of hardened frosting, those roses, those pointillist cowboy hats. Nothing plastic, none of those squiggles that curlicue out of a hose. Anthony forbids bright sprinkles on

Christmas cookies, red-hots, extruded foods, marshmallow Peeps.

But the bakery offered a gingerbread house, and I thought that denuded, it might be what he'd like. "Could you do that for me?" I asked John, aiming at the hearing aid. "Remove the gumdrop gewgaws? Skip the peppermint portals?"

John looked at me suspiciously. He knitted his brow. The look of perplexity can only be cute.

"And can you put real candied ginger into the gingerbread? He loves that."

John dropped his pen onto the pad. "This wouldn't be for Anthony, would it?"

I nodded. "I'm sure he's famous here."

John smiled. "Yes, and we dated for a while. I know how he likes plain things."

Plain things? Was that a dig at me, his current choice? They'd dated? How long ago, and when did it end, and why? John looked at me questioningly, too. Obviously I was his replacement. What did the big guy see in *me*? But no, he didn't think I was a plain thing, not the way he looked at me. He was evaluating the possibilities.

An important fact about me: I hate being scrutinized. Cruised, whatever you call it. It makes me feel, well, girlish, and I am sure that my every flaw is being noted. Also, I feel flushed out of a hiding place. I feel out of control. I would rather be the one doing the studying.

John filled out the order slip. I gave him our phone number, but told him to call only between four and five, when I was home and Anthony was not, because the cake was supposed to be a surprise. He told me it would be ready in seven days. He gave me a prolonged gaze and handed me my copy of the order slip, his traffic-cop palm flat against mine for just a beat too long. I gazed back, and then I left.

I wanted to tell Anthony about my encounter with John, but I couldn't, because that would make him suspicious: what was I doing at The Cakery? So for a whole week I bit my tongue. I said nothing until John called me.

I went to the shop. Fumbling with his hearing aid, John told another counter person to take over while he helped me with my order. Apparently, he was senior manager at The Cakery. He pulled out the gingerbread house. It was beautifully executed: not a single gumdrop, no Hershey's Kisses, just clean white drizzled icicles of frosting along the roof and chimney. John must have known exactly what Anthony liked and disliked.

On the bill, John wrote, "$32, PAID IN FULL." I hadn't.

"Is this your birthday present for Anthony?" I asked. Was he trying to co-opt my big idea?

But John said, "Don't tell him. It's a present for you, too."

"How can I repay you?"

He smiled and pointed to my phone number, scrawled on the slip. "I'll let you know one of these days," he said.

I looked down at his powdery arms. He was hulking, Italianate. When he smiled, his lips curled into an insinuating snarl.

That evening, the cake was a big hit. Anthony recognized the cake box and pulled me into his lap. "A very sensible cake."

"Your buddy John helped me," I finally confessed.

"Oh, you met John."

"How long did you carry on with him?"

He shrugged—an unstudied and unrehearsed shrug. "I don't know. We fooled around for a couple of months. But he's deaf, you know, and he'd be so loud when he came. He doesn't have a clue how loud he is. He stomped down the hall to the bathroom, he made noises in his sleep."

"You left him because he was too noisy?" I wondered: Have I been too noisy? Do I scream in the throes? Anthony is mostly silent during sex. He adheres to an unspoken belief that sex should be a perfect ballet of intuited desire, a mind-meld. This ballet, however, has to be rehearsed over several years, as good sex usually does. Mostly, between rehearsals, he just sits on my face, and I suffocate thrillingly in his giantness, his own face far, far away from my mouthful of his balls, which silence me (no, therefore, no, don't worry, not too noisy), his dick flexing on my face *bonk bonk bonk* like little drumbeats as his pelvis grinds my head.

"No," Anthony said. "I left him because he wasn't a very good listener."

It was four or five weeks later when I got that follow-up call. I had nearly forgotten the free cake. I picked up the phone.

"You owe me," John growled.

"How much?"

Mafioso, collecting. "I'm closing today. Come at five and ring the bell, I'll let you in."

As I rang, I peered through the glass door at the darkened café and saw him push through the swinging doors that divided the kitchen from the customer area. He unlatched the glass door and I stepped in. "Where to?"

He didn't speak, just led me behind the counter and back through those swinging doors. The kitchen was twice as big as the café, with two massive, wall-height ovens.

There were three worktables, all covered in brushed sheet metal. On large wheeled shelving units, bread loaves had been left to rise in the hot room, yeasty and sugary. A big mixer lazily stirred muffin batter.

On the middle table, over which hung on a suspended rack an assortment of ladles, sifters, spoons, spatulas, and eggbeaters, John had spread out an unbelievably raunchy array of his own preferred utensils: condoms, lube, dildoes, cock rings, nipple clamps, leather thongs, poppers. While I was inspecting his wares, he shucked off his clothes: apron, T-shirt, boots, socks, jeans. He hopped up on the table and went to a hands-and-knees position so that his ass, fuzzed with black hair, winked its clean, pink periwinkle hole at me while his fat, shaved balls and thick, half-hard dick dangled below. That's the triumvirate of lust. I love to reach between a man's legs from behind and grasp his cock and balls at the same time—the way I would some ripe and fulsome fruit: guava, maybe. Cradling them firmly like that, I'll run the forefinger of my other hand in a straight line connecting his pucker to the scrotum seam to the tip of his dick. I did that to John.

"Fuck me," he demanded.

I kicked off my shoes without untying them. Shirt, socks, then pants; I bunched and snarled them and untangled them in desperation. John bided his time snapping on a cock ring, lubing his hole with two thick fingers.

I leaped onto the table, my cock enraged. I was sweating already from the heat of the ovens. My head knocked up against the hanging sifters and spoons, and they made a sound like cowbells. Quiet, I said to myself, we don't want to let anybody know what's going on back here.

John wasn't worried about the noise, however. He groaned with perfect satisfaction when I sank my dick into him, which I did without much fooling around. His ass was a well-trained one, one clearly used to being worked. (Had Anthony been one of its previous trainers? Did he like extensive ass play? We'd never done that before; perhaps I needed to introduce it into my repertoire.) It was a meaty ass, and I drilled down slowly, such a pleasure to watch myself sink in as though I were seeking a core sample. I gripped his strong hips and withdrew, then sank in again.

When you screw like that, you sweat a lot. It's a good sweat, it doesn't feel dirty, it feels cleansing: every impurity purged from the system. You can feel pleasantly basted in your own juices, cooked, well-done.

"Just think of it," I mused out loud to John, over his shoulder, doggy-styling his butt while I held his tight, thick gut in my right hand and grabbed his left hip with the other for torque. "All those businessmen coming in here for their coffee cake every morning, all those scones you roll out on this table, wouldn't you just like to shoot a load of protein into them for extra energy?"

He moaned—no, *screamed*—with pleasure. Aha! He loved me to talk dirty to him. I know an affirmative-action grunt when I hear one; I'd been tuned to that by my strong but silent partner.

"Maybe I should take some of the muffin batter and drizzle it down the crack of your ass and eat it out. You'd like that, huh? Or grab a loaf of bread dough and sink your dick into it, tie it in some knots and jack you off into it?" He showed his satisfaction by arching his back, opening up more, ramming himself onto my dick.

Now and then I'd brush my hand up the runnel of hair that flowed from his belly to his chest. I could grab two handfuls of his pecs and then reach under and around his shoulders to pull him hard up on my dick, so he could feel flesh on flesh and know he'd gotten it all.

He wanted me to suffocate in the heat. He didn't talk, though; he wanted me to do all the talking. When I stopped for a moment, he'd moan for more, and I found myself creating complex narratives for him.

"I'll bring Anthony in here and have him throw you on your back up on this table and hold your legs apart while I screw you, he loves to see that, it's his favorite thing. Let you suck frosting off his dick while I pound you until you blow . . ."

That's where my mind wandered. I had to have my chance to study John, but did I look at him because I wanted to have sex with him or because I wanted to *be* him? A little of both, I think: a combination of greed and vanity.

It went on and on. He was firmly rooted on all fours on that table, not moving, while I burned myself out on him. He was exhausting me, sucking the life out of me, making me pay and pay for that cake, and the longer I fucked him, the longer he took it, until I knew that I was going to be the sore one in the morning, not him. And still he hollered for more story, more narrative.

"Did Anthony do you up here? . . ."

He suddenly glanced over his beefy shoulders with a quizzical look in his eye: "What? Did you say something?"

He did not have his hearing aid in. I'd been telling my tale to the superheated air.

That was okay by me, though. I am the listener, I am the spy, the detective, the obsessor, and I had enough information for the Baker John Dossier. Case, for the time being, closed.

*   *   *

There are those who are watched and those who watch. I am a watcher. I delude myself into believing I'm mostly invisible, or at least that I blend in. To what purpose? To spy, to collect information, to obsess. I use this information in hopes of transforming myself into Anthony's perfect counterpart.

I am obsessed with these old boyfriends of Anthony's, and if there is some shred of them remaining in his life, then I become even more interested. An intrepid traveler and amateur photographer, Anthony has managed to take a great many pictures of old boyfriends, and coaxed from them plenty of candid moments in and out of clothes. Most of these men are exotic and unreachable: the Italian fashion dingbat, the French boy with the big flat nose (who apparently hated to be in clothes, ever), the Danish redhead, the Portuguese babe with hair so slick and black he looked like a licorice reptile. Anthony lost his virginity, he revealed to me in a weak moment, to a gorgeous Dutch bodybuilder in a dark room in Amsterdam. This anecdote is unutterably hot to me, the source of a million jack-off sessions, because it is Anthony out of character: underneath a bigger man, in a sling, legs open, ass begging, doing something very nasty. What sort of man could make my normally reserved Anthony drop all his inhibitions?

Because I can never meet these men, they are bigger than life. When a man stands still, he looks bigger. When I hear stories about other people, they seem as big as legends. I see this gigantifying effect also in the pages of my favorite skin magazines: guys standing in the buff against a velvet curtain or next to a Greek column look monumental. It comes as a shock to me when I see them in porn movies and they are short, often, smaller, less important. The repetitive motions of sex, the thrusts and grunts and wanks and shots, are a blur. When I was a boy, the bathroom in our house had a spring-coil doorstop at the baseboard with a little rubber head, and I would pull it back and watch it vibrate from its fan of movement into a smaller and smaller object, until it was its ordinary, still, tiny self again. That is what sex looks like to me, that's what these seductions of Anthony's old boyfriends amount to: bringing them down from legendary magnitude to something not so formidable. Yes, call it conquering.

Meanwhile, Anthony defies this natural shrinkage, and gets bigger. With each reductive act with the ex-boyfriends, I come home to the man who is bigger and bigger in my life. The repetitions between us are part of a pattern that grows and grows; every morning he wraps his huge body around me and we listen to the news on the radio; in the evenings we each fight for space on the couch and read paragraphs to each other, now and then sliding a foot up to the other's crotch, feeling entitled, feeling absolutely together. Whomever we've gone to for extramarital sex has given us something else to make our relationship truer, bigger.

Five years ago, the first week I was dating Anthony, I met the ex-boyfriend I was slated to replace. Vadim was a barrel-chested, chest-thumping, humpy Russian muckamuck in the Department of Immigration. He had a stony, solid, handsome face with a smooth, wolfish slope to it, brown hair mixed with a little silver, broad shoulders; he was nearly as tall as Anthony.

The first time, I got to see him in all his perfection, un-draped. Vadim went to the same gym as the two of us. He was a swimmer, like me, but he usually swam in the morning before work, not after, which is when Anthony and I tend to go and when we ran into him. There was an odd awkwardness to our meeting, because we were all three naked in the steam room, Anthony making the introductions that made it clear that if you didn't think it was over for the two of us, Vadim, then here's your proof.

But Vadim was gracious and smiled easily. He was more than happy to meet me. He was articulate and charming and hot as hell. He was so charming that he almost kept my attention away from the big gnarly piece of uncut dick between his legs with so much foreskin overhang it begged you to stick a finger in and go on a hunt. Almost.

Oh, Vadim was perfect. And Anthony let me know it, too.

Later that evening, I heard all the stories (and I'm *still* hearing them). Not only was he handsome and cosmopolitan, he was smart, too, and a good person. He was on a crusade to help people find shelter in the city and get jobs, he spoke four languages fluently, his dick was even bigger than I thought, and he rode his bicycle to work instead of a smog-producing car. He was on all the fund-raising committees and he was a great kisser and the mayor called him often for advice and you could balance a martini glass on his butt.

"So why in the hell did you leave him?" I wanted to know. Why are the most eligible bachelors, well, bachelors?

Anthony grinned and whispered conspiratorially (for what is a relationship if not a conspiracy?), "When you touch his penis, he comes immediately."

It sounded like an excuse to me.

Over the months and years, my partnership with Anthony solidified, and we did all those things couples do: travel, quarrel, buy challenging yet tasteful art, shack up. However, we did not keep our relationship "closed" (whatever that means; in many ways, it's sealed as tight as a space capsule), and that's generally known among our friends. Vadim must have known it, too.

Every once in a while, it was easier on my schedule if I went swimming in the morning. When I did, I'd see Vadim. He swam in a sensible black Speedo, and I took extra special care to have my goggles defogged and to swim in a lane positioned to the left of his, so that as I lifted my head for air, I could watch him pass. There were brief, glorious laps where we swam in sync, two dolphins gamboling, and I liked to think he swam at my speed on purpose. (Normally, he was faster than me; I had his speed down to a scientific fraction: he'd pass me once every seventeen laps.)

Water magnifies, and Vadim's strong, muscled body gliding over the chlorine-blue tiles looked grandiose to me, a protector and a moose and a power that could move boulders. When his body swiveled as his arms windmilled down the lane, I loved to study his outie belly button and the structure of the six perfect muscle squares in his abdomen, like a stack of a child's wooden blocks. Sometimes he would rest at the end of the lane and smile at me, and sometimes I'd have my head in the water and see him groping himself through his Speedo. I never believed those gropes were intended for my benefit. As a watcher, I find it hard to believe I'm ever watched. Perhaps he was just itchy down there.

In the steam room, we'd sit near each other and not speak, but there was a palpable tension as we each casually massaged our own worked-out arms and legs, stretching out after the laps. Just as our minds would seem to be turning toward the lascivious— yes, that is a hard-on between his legs, I can see the head of his penis poking a little out of all that bunched-up foreskin—somebody would walk into the steam room and spoil our fun. I didn't hold it against the intruder. I was a little freaked out by the possibility that I might truly have this perfect specimen.

Each encounter with Vadim was a little more intense than the one before it. He or I would pointedly sit close to the other, even if there were seats elsewhere. We'd let our knees rub together, let a careless hand slide down a haunch. Once, his arm wrapped momentarily around my waist. We played footsie; he borrowed my swim-out shampoo. We never spoke to each other all those years, except perhaps a "hello" or a "so long." Ours was a forbidden obsession, which speech might either destroy or consummate. Perhaps, I thought, what kept either of us from making a full-on pass was the oddness of our being Anthony's boys. Anthony remained good friends with Vadim, and the two of them would have lunch now and then, downtown, where they both worked.

This went on for a long time. It was a five-year seduction, and only coincidence brought everything together. One day, we got an invitation in the mail—no, Anthony got an invitation in the mail—for Vadim's fortieth-birthday and . . . going-away party.

"Forty?" I said, incredulous. "That man is forty? He looks like he's twenty-five." He did. As somebody who has, since the age of eighteen, looked thirty, I am completely jealous of anybody who can appear so ageless. One more perfection of Vadim's.

He rides a bike, he saves poor immigrants, he has a monster uncut drooling penis between his legs, and he's forty going on twenty-five.

Not only that, he was going away. It seemed that he'd been selected for a highly prestigious fellowship to study foreign policy at Johns Hopkins University and would be leaving our fair city, fair gymnasium, fair obsession, for more than a year.

I was out of town the weekend of the big birthday–bon voyage party. Anthony gave me a full report. It was a mob scene, full of all the most important people. The mayor came. Oh, great. Vadim is handsome and smart and has a fellowship and rides a bike and the mayor comes to his damn birthday party.

"All the people from his office were there and begging him not to leave," Anthony said. Over champagne, Anthony talked to Vadim for a long time, and whenever a handsome man wished the guest of honor well, Anthony would ask, "Whoa, who was that?"

Vadim would shrug. He had a terrible memory sometimes, Anthony said, and being a public figure, he often had "friends" better called "acquaintances"—they were simply people he'd met. He couldn't keep all those names in his head.

The Wednesday after his party, I went to swim in the midafternoon, around three o'clock, an off time for me. It was quiet at the gym, the steam room was empty. I was able to stretch out slowly and had the place to myself. Then the door at the far end opened and a beefy silhouette glided through the fog and sat across from me: Vadim.

Anthony had told me that Vadim had quit his job and given himself a week to get his things packed before he moved to Baltimore; for the first time, he had some leisure.

Then, in the steam room, he moved directly beside me. Without waiting for an invitation, he wrapped his big muscled arms around me, pulled me to him, and locked his lips on mine. His tongue was all over the inside of my mouth. His blue eyes were wide open and we were staring cross-eyed at each other in the closeness. One of his hands snaked down my belly to my dick, which went hard in his grasp. I did what I had always wanted to do and slipped my pinkie under the hood of his foreskin. My other hand was holding him at the neck so that he wouldn't pull away, and I could feel his heart pulsing in his jugular.

Then a man came in. We pulled away from each other quickly, but were completely too far gone, completely too incomplete, not to finish this. Besides, it was our last chance: he knew and I knew that he was leaving town in three days. "I've got a house in the Mission," he said. Oh, of course, the politically correct, perfect Mission, the place where all good doobees live. "Want to come over?"

"Of course," I said.

He gave me the address. I was on my scooter, he was on his perfect bicycle. We'd meet up at his house.

His house was not in the state of disarray I would have anticipated for somebody about to skip town. Later he'd tell me that a friend was going to sublet it from him and that he, Vadim, was planning to return to the city as soon as he could. He had a dog, Sheila, a devoted collie, and she stayed near him, even during sex.

He threw me onto the bed. From riding his bicycle through the streets as fast as he could, there was a thin sheen of sweat all over him. The room was a little cold, so the tips of my fingers were numb, and when I put my hand between the nape of his neck and the protective curtain of his shoulder-length silken hair, they warmed up.

He was the most pleasant make-out artist, obliging and thorough without being a lip-chapper. His hands roamed my body, he wanted my body. Was he up to the same thing I'm always up to? Did he want me because I was Anthony's boyfriend?

He unbuttoned my shirt, I unlatched his belt. We stopped for a moment and allowed ourselves to step out of our clothes.

The massive arms of this guy! My mind slipped to images of him and Anthony together on this same bed, grappling for power, two big men with lust and integrity, may the best man win. But I like to be squashed like a bug beneath the weight of bruisers, I like the air taken out of me—thickness, presence, and power.

He was attentive, and loved to put things in his mouth, not just my raging dick, but my fingers and toes, too. His mouth was also warmer than the room, and the heat we generated made the coolness desirable.

His dick was obscene. Sort of like his Picture of Dorian Gray. Here was this golden man with perfect teeth and a perfect brain and a Boy Scout lifestyle, and he had a veined, downward-curving prong with so much foreskin I could grab a handful of it and stretch it, slide more than three fingers inside. It bunched like an exotic flower of the kind that grows in a climate without bees, and thus, in order to pollinate, has adapted to attract files; they look hideous and smell worse.

Meanwhile, I was determined to devour him too, but I decided not to test Anthony's description of Vadim's minuteman proclivities. Except for a few friendly gropes and yanks, I steered clear of his big raunchy dick, no matter how much I craved that flab of foreskin.

But my attraction got the best of me, and I made my first mistake of the afternoon: I put my mouth down there, stuck my tongue deep into that overhang and touched the piss hole in his glans. He uttered a head-for-the-hills kind of warning and then erupted geysers that flew and flew, over his head, onto his cheek, neck, chest, belly.

I was thrilled at the copiousness, and while I wished our coupling had gone on forever, I was so turned on I shot two seconds later, and flopped down to share a pillow with him.

We rested against each other and listened together to our two swiftly beating hearts. I rested my hand there where his was, on his staved chest, in a slick of cum the shape of Idaho.

Sheila the dog began to whimper for attention. She paced alongside of the bed, patrolling, rubbing her nose against the base of the mattress.

"Sheila, no!" Vadim commanded, and then apologized to me: "I don't know what her problem is, she's been so upset lately."

I shrugged. "She can probably tell you're getting ready to leave town."

He sat up and wrinkled his brow. "How did you know I was leaving?"

I looked at him, and the pieces of the puzzle came together, or fell apart. "You do know who I am, don't you?" I said.

He shook his head. "Who are you?"

I laughed, terrifying both of us. "I'm Brian," I said. "Anthony's boyfriend!"

His eyes widened. "Oh no. Oh God. Oh, you're kidding." These little utterances came out of him like he'd just run a mile in four minutes and was trying to recover his breath.

"I thought you knew!" I protested.

"Oh God, you can't tell Anthony," he begged me. This was his first response. I recalled how Anthony told me of Vadim's poor memory, even for would-be suitors. I'd completely misread this man, this Vadim.

After Vadim settled down, he asked me, "What's it like to be Anthony's boyfriend?" And I said, "You wouldn't believe it. All he ever talks about is Vadim this, Vadim that. Vadim rides his bike to work. Vadim had the mayor come to his birthday party. Vadim saves poor people from the gutter. Vadim has an uncut penis. Blah, blah, blah."

I saw my obsession wash over Vadim even as I was telling him this: he realized that for five years, I'd been, well, consumed with him and his perfections, watching him, reading all the press clips, listening to Anthony's stories about their casual lunch dates downtown, all of it. As a sort of protective measure, he began to get dressed. He'd let a freak into his house. He laughed, but perhaps you too have found out that a person on the periphery of your life has for a long time considered you the center of his life, all his thought, focus, desire, obsession. As quickly as he decently could, Vadim hustled me out the front door. The obsession had ended.

Vadim, like John, has been conquered: I have made them both less than legendary by seeing them in some miniaturized completion, the completion of one orgasm. But in conquering, in being the watcher who reveals himself to the watched, I inadvertently conquer something in myself. I make myself visible, and shrink a little, as well.

I am a watcher, but perhaps the whole point of these pursuits of my boyfriend's exes is to become the watched. To finally insert myself into the picture, to become visible, even if I'm more comfortable standing in the margins. To be both the observer and the observed is a kind of transformation—think of Narcissus, frozen in time, bewitched by his own reflection in a pool.

When I go home to Anthony after these episodes, I am ready to be watched by him. I am willing to be seen by him, imperfect, weak, visible. And if Anthony does not adore me, he certainly watches me—he won't let me leave the house without making sure that my tie is straight, my shirt is buttoned, and my fly is zipped (at least at first). Love is scrutiny, I'm sure of it, long and careful. I need Anthony to see that I am all the things he wants, but I need him to see all the imperfections, too, so that they might be improved upon. He makes me stand in front of him in the morning, and he stares, and sometimes he says, subtly, "Are you going out in *that*?"

HAROLD RAMIS'S GLASSES

D. TRAVERS SCOTT

Scenes of a Gentile in Heat

Recently I was trying to describe a crush:

"He's really smart and he's got these cute little glasses and most of his friends are straight and he's not obsessed with pop culture and he drives a red VW Bug and he's kinda geeky in a hot way . . ."

My boyfriend of the last eight years looks at me, confused. "Yeah, but what does he look like?"

"Oh," I say. "Well, he's kinda average height and build, curly hair, little spectacles, real sexy nose . . ."

My boyfriend rolls his eyes. "This is your Jew thing again, isn't it?"

He's one to talk. A midwestern, Protestant paragon of white-itude if there ever was one, he worked in a Chicago kosher deli for two years and knows his challah, lox, and whitefish with the best of them. A significant factor in my continued attraction to him? Well, to paraphrase Gilda Radner's *Saturday Night Live* skit advertising Jewess Jeans, a guy doesn't have to be Jewish to get in my pants, but it doesn't hurt.

How do I describe my Jew thing? Well, the actor Harold Ramis is a favorite fantasy subject (and this is the younger Harold Ramis, mind you, the brainy Ghostbuster and buddy to Bill Murray in *Stripes*). In my fantasy, Harold is usually my graduate school adviser, therapist, or perhaps a freelance writer whose apartment I clean. He's always very busy. To get his attention, I have to brush my swelling crotch against his desk and instigate insipid small talk. He's invariably peeved at the interruption, and looks up at me with bemusement. Why are you talking to me? his face asks, and he rakes his hand through his curly black hair in exasperation. I'm debased to humiliating blatancy, grabbing my crotch and asking him please to fuck me. He never acquiesces immediately. He glances back at his computer, makes a phone call, or tells me to wait while he finishes the paragraph he's working on. Finally, when he's at a convenient stopping point, he tells me flatly, "Take off your clothes, and sit on top of the desk there." The wool of his argyle sweater vest and dark pleated trousers itches against my naked skin. He pushes me away and instructs me to jack off—"I want to watch you play with it." Slowly and thoughtfully, he strips and lays his clothes across a chair. My spine presses flat against the hard wood desktop, and he sweeps to the floor stacks of Lacan, Zizek, and Phelan, issues of *Davka* and *The New York Times Book Review*. As he fucks me face-front, my legs up against his hairy shoulders, I watch sweat glisten above his mouth. He frowns in determination, as if putting great thought into each thrust and slam of his dick. His lips surround mine, bite and tease and chew. He whispers trash in my ear, but it is not of an affected blue-collar parlance. "You realize, of course," he huffs, "this could continue here for"—grunt!—"quite"—unh!—"a while." He purses his lips, scowling. His dark eyelashes rest at half mast, a studied cool as he contemplates what he will do with me next. He stands up tall, flipping me over and pushing my head and shoulders down against the desk. Knuckles pressed into the back of my neck, he announces that he's "enjoying fucking you very much." The slick hair of his chest, arms, and legs slides all over me. His crotch hair grinds against my comparatively bare ass like steel wool. And—most important—when Harold Ramis fucks me, he keeps his glasses on.

Real life is usually a bit tamer. Walking through midtown Manhattan, I pass a yeshiva academy near my hotel. A van is parked out front, either picking up or dropping off a half-dozen boys in pressed navy or black slacks and crunchy white dress shirts. They slouch in the open doors of the van and against the poles of the school awning. I eye them as I pass, and they glare back with penetrating amber eyes, furrowed charcoal eyebrows, pale skin with cheeks flushed red as if they'd just been slapped. I realize I'm wearing my skinhead-lite drag: white wifebeater, black suspenders, tight jeans, combat boots with red laces, shaved head. Maybe this has something to do with their sexy-surly glares. I sneak a peek back at them and my knees grow weak. I think: this must be how straight guys feel about Catholic schoolgirls.

My best friend, Deb, agrees. She's a straight woman who grew up in a mixed family of Jews and Greek Orthodox Christians. She's dated and/or fucked lots of Jewish men, and now lives with her gentile boyfriend in Williamsburg, a section of Brooklyn with a large Hasidic population.

"I always have a crush on cute young Hasidic guys walking through Williamsburg," she confesses. "It's like the whole 'good boy' thing, the innocence, showing someone the ropes, taking them over your knee. Plus they're mysterious, you want to know what's under the little outfits, like the Amish. Amish guys are sexy, especially when it's a young Harrison Ford pretending to be one."

I agree with her, and propose that religious garb is sexy in a manner similar to military uniforms, both of which suggest a homosocial eroticism, all that testosteroniffic social control, rigid dogma, and—the sexiest thing of all—repression. I suggest that religious garb also has an intellectual component superior to the brute masculinity of the military. She agrees, but we split when I bring up Harold Ramis and several mutual friends of ours.

"Nah," she says. "Hasids are one thing, but your average hyper New York Jewboy is a whole different thing; it's apples and oranges. It's hard for me to stereotype because I've known so many different types of Jewish guys. They're all just different people to me, not really fetishizable."

Goy on the Range

My background was quite different from Deb's. Growing up in Texas, I had no clear concept of Jews. I knew only Yankees. I saw Jewish stereotypes on TV and in movies, but to my Texan mind they were indistinguishable from Italian mafiosi, Irish cops, and Long Island beauticians—all white-based stereotypes I identified simply as Yankees or "New York people."

I remember knowing that friends were Jehovah's Witnesses, Mormons, or even Hindus, but never Jews. I read in Steve Allen's *Funny People* that many comedians are Jews, but whatever connected Allen, Mel Brooks, and Woody Allen eluded me. I learned about the Holocaust in school but in a typically American, middle-class, public-school way; it fell into the general category of Various and Sundry Incomprehensible Things That Happen in Europe, such as royalty, serving alcohol to children, having a ménage à trois, and fire-bombings.

Once, when promenading along Galveston's seawall, my mother and I passed an elderly woman and man talking in a language I'd never heard. I asked my mom what they were speaking.

"Yiddish," she informed me.

"Oh," I said, taking this in. "Where is that country, 'Yid'?"

She explained that Yiddish was spoken by Jews, who didn't have a typical country but one called Israel that was created in "oh, like the 1960s or something." However, they didn't speak Yiddish there; they spoke Hebrew. The mystery only deepened.

I figured out from Mel Brooks et al. that Jews were circumcised. But most every American male born in the last fifty years is circumcised! I never saw an uncircumcised dick until I was in my twenties. All I knew was that Jews were circumcised, like every other man I'd seen or heard of, but that somehow with them it was different. The mystery deepened further.

The one acknowledged Jew I met face-to-face was a friend of my stepmother's who came to our house for a visit (not dinner). They had met at her Christian church because he was involved with Jews for Jesus. I asked her what that was all about, and she told me as best she could. "So," I replied after her explanation, testing to see if I had things straight, "Jews are Christians who don't believe in Jesus, but Jews for Jesus are Jews who do." She nodded.

Hmm. Okay. I see.

To this day, I'm always the last person to realize anyone's Jewish. Friends always give me a reaction of "Jesus, what did you think? Fink? Cohen? Rivkin?" Excuse me, but where is this master list of Jewish last names everyone seems to have studied? Locked away with the gay hanky code chart? The physical stereotypes I have finally been able to piece together: big nose, curly dark hair, thick lips. But again, how did everybody else seem to learn this? Not to mention that none of the Jews I know look exactly like that.

Fucking with My Head

I have to qualify my rabid generalizing about Jews. Although it sounds as if I have a very fixed fetish, I don't exactly. Only in the last few years have I realized that sexy boys X, Y, and Z all have certain things in common, including being Jewish, which has led me to try to figure out if what I like has something to do with their Jewishness.

My friend and sex buddy Ira talks. And talks and talks. His talking gets me so fucking turned on, and it's not—initially, at least—"hot talk." Ira can rant on about everything, from queer theory and online publishing to the side effects of various antidepressants, with such energy and engagement that I'm riveted. His intensity, the speed of his mind and his speech, gets me so hard that I just want to slam him down and shove my tongue in his mouth. Which I do, but it has the unfortunate effect of shutting him up, and as I said, I really like hearing him talk.

Sometimes in the middle of fucking, he'll blurt out a point following up on our earlier discussion, or a song on the radio we'd left on for a coitus sound track will remind me to tell him about the *Radical Jewish Culture* two-CD set of Burt Bacharach covers I just bought. We'll start talking again. Ira will tell me about his mother, Sylvie, and her PFLAG chapter, about how disappointed she is that he's marrying an English girl for U.K. citizenship when she was so looking forward to his commitment ceremony with some nice young man. Ira talks about growing up in the Jewish suburbs of L.A., so culturally ensconced that he never experienced anti-Semitism consciously until he was away at college. " 'Oh, so *this* is that anti-Semitism I've been hearing so much about.' "

At moments like this I have to throw Ira down on the bed again. He's one of the few people I know who can maintain a sense of humor between the sheets, and it makes him so much sexier than the stony cold, porn-imitative sex partners who usually bore me to tears. When Ira cracks a joke as I'm grinding my combat boot into his chest, it doesn't lessen the intensity at all. He seems cocksure enough in his masculinity and sexuality that he doesn't see humor and intellect as a threat to them. He doesn't feel obligated to be a grunt.

Which confuses me because, as much as I've been able to decipher the stereotype, Jewish men are supposed to be sexually neurotic. Yet more often than not I've found the opposite to be true. Mitch, for instance, picked me up initially at a party on the last night of a writers' conference, stealing me away from someone else I'd been talking to, and we fucked around that night. The next day, after he'd checked out of his hotel room, he asked a female friend point-blank if we could borrow her room to fuck in. It wasn't available, and at this point I was willing to give up, but Mitch, determined, led me around the hotel until we found a temporarily empty conference room with a lockable bathroom door. Once inside, he whipped out condoms and lube and bent over the bathroom sink. My attaché bag of résumés, manuscripts, and plane tickets spilled at our feet around our bunched-up jeans. I fucked him, his face pressed against the mirror, while maids cleaned out the conference room, attendees wandered in, and panelists set up for the next session. "I was *not* going to let you leave town without fucking me again," he told me.

Now tell me, what is hotter than a man who knows what he wants and has the balls to ask for it?

Josh, another smart 'n' swarthy Semite I'm hopelessly hot for, has, from the day I first met him, locked eyes steadily and flirted with me aggressively and confidently. Is it just the dark, heavy-lidded eyes that make this seem *not* absurd? No, even his most banal message on my answering machine is still sexy-sounding enough to capture even my boyfriend's attention. How come Josh can get away with the low, throaty voice and bedroom eyes that make most WASP boys seem like idiotic porno wanna-bes?

Deb says, "Yeah, I know what you mean about Jewish men being all flirty and sexually confident. It goes with the personality, smart and outgoing. They're white guys but not really; they're different. White guys are cute but self-conscious in bed. They're boys even when they're men—more passive, slackery, don't take responsibility for themselves. You have to be the flirter, the confident one, and maybe you can bring it out in them. Jewish boys are adults already."

A bisexual female friend of mine tells me about her new boyfriend: "He's tall, dark, lanky, real handsome," she gushes. "He's thirty and in therapy."

"Mmmm . . ." I growl appreciatively. She and I are both getting old enough to be frustrated with our twentysomething peers.

"He's an architect," she purrs.

"Oooh!" Why is this so hot? No fucking clue, but we both think architects are sexy as hell (Mike Brady excepted).

"He's Jewish!" she squeals, and I slap my forehead, swooning.

"And," she says proudly, pausing for effect, "he loves getting fucked by my strap-on!"

We scream like teens at a slumber party (well, actually, we are in pajamas, on a bed, watching late-night Aaron Spelling reruns and gorging on greasy take-out, so I guess we scream like twentysomethings at a slumber party). I am so jealous. She tells me how quickly and early in their relationship he took to being fucked. I've never heard of any gentile, especially a straight gentile boy, taking quite so readily to getting plowed.

Some Porn Would Be Nice

From what I've gathered, the basic physical stereotype of Jews is a lot like that of Italians, who are frequently eroticized and fetishized. If Jews basically look like Italians, and porn is basically about looks, why haven't I been able to find Jewish fetish porn? Occasionally I come across a Jewporn story (and I am eager to see the Jewish-specific erotic anthologies currently in development), but never have I found identifiable Jews in video porn or skin mags. No porn stars have names I can recognize as Jewish (although I can't be sure without that damn master list).

I've always been a believer in the truism that if you look hard enough, there's porn out there for every possible taste. So why, in searching for a product to satisfy what seems to me a pretty simple taste that I know I'm not alone in possessing, do I consistently draw blanks? Internet searches, even with smut-specific search engines, turn up zero hits for the word *Jew* or *Semitic*. (Compare that to the avalanche when searching for *black, Latino, Asian, Puerto Rican,* et cetera.) I'm not even looking for *Horse-Hung Hasids.* I'd be psyched simply to find a description of a plain old vanilla video that read "Featuring the swarthy Semitic good looks of topman Kyle Katzmann" or "While shopping for a commitment ring set, Dirk is lead astray by the hot Jewstud at the jewelers who quickly stretches Dirk's *other* ring." Twice Blessed, the Jewish GLBT online archive, includes only this cryptic erotic listing in their voluminous film/video directory: "*Stud Me,* USA, color, video. Homoerotic video in which one actor wears a 'chai' (Hebrew for 'life') medallion." Imagine if a Black GLBT film/video directory had only one sex-oriented listing, and solely because a racially ambiguous character sported a medallion of the African continent.

I try to imagine an entire Jewish porno oeuvre. You would

enter your corner video shop and find it, in the Specialty section of the adult wing, past *Big Black Bananas, Hooked on Hispanics,* and *Rappin' Ricans.* There you'd encounter titles like *Shtuppin' That Shaygets, Kosher Deli Boy—He Delivers!* and *The Best of Long Schlong Silverman.* Think of the scenes: the story of one man's *tzahal* service could include lonely Israeli soldiers taking comfort in each other's arms, khaki uniforms peeling off to reveal stiff cocks yearning for release from the tension of military life, submachine gun straps slapping against bare chests from the thrusting of a good face-fuck inside an abandoned house in the Gaza Strip. Or in New York, a horny Hasidic guy could lock eyes with a cruising B-boy on the subway platform, sneaking to the backseat of the car to bury his *payess* against the rising bulge in the B-boy's Fila warm-ups.

Of course, I realize that sexual objectification and fetishizing raise problematic questions, but I am trying to call attention to how unsexualized Jews seem to be in porn. In a culture that can sexually objectify a traffic cone, how has a cultural group as well known as Jews escaped eroticization?

Finding a Nice Doctor

Appearances to the contrary, porn is a conservative medium. It took the Bear movement years of underground and amateur porn production to make the mainstream porn industry realize that every model didn't have to be gym-toned and well-coiffed, and that body hair wasn't just a seventies fad. The porn industry doesn't take risks because it wants to please as many people as possible. The stereotype of the intellectual, myopic Torah student keeps identifiable Jews out of porn, and also out of American gay cultural consciousness. Makers of porn fall back on traditional masculinity, forgetting that, as queers, we ditch the notion of traditional masculinity every time we suck dick.

Americans tend to value populist common sense over intelleckshual book-learnin'. We rebelled against Europe and its intellectual, aristocratic tradition. I know that during cruisy bar chat, mentioning I've written for NYU's feminist theory journal *Women and Performance* will not help me get laid as much as mentioning I've written for *Drummer*. Yet I myself would have the reverse reaction, especially in the unexpected context of a cruise bar. My ears prick up and my prick perks up when someone says "semiotics" more than "fisting." Confident intellectualism turns me on; it's something I want to know and possess. The American—particularly Protestant Christian—anti-intellectual tradition was firmly instilled in me growing up in Texas. Not until my junior year of high school did passing one's classes become a prerequisite for devoting ten to twenty hours a week to sports or extracurriculars (and guess what intellectual giant masterminded Texas's massive public education reform in the 1980s? Presidential candidate-to-be Ross "Pie Chart" Perot).

Think of the American tendency to hide intellect: being embarrassed about getting straight A's, being afraid to suggest a foreign movie on a video date, substituting contacts for glasses when going to bars ("Men seldom make passes . . ."), the quiet anxiety at brunch when someone goes off the deep end talking seriously or passionately about some subject—and the palpable relief when the conversation returns to gossip, cruising, or getting tickets for *Tap Dogs*.

Imagine if we were body-shy instead of brain-shy: books replacing porn videos in bars, guys proudly saying they were at the library instead of the gym, arranging jeans and jockstraps to hide rather than show off bulges, boasting in personal ads "I have a nice, small-to-average dick," rushing to switch the conversation back to Denton Welch novels when someone embarrasses the table by commenting on the waiter's fine ass. No one wants a culture of such Victorian sex prudes, but why should we be brain prudes instead?

I'm greedy. I want all of a man, head and crotch. It's often said that your most powerful sex organ lies between your ears. I agree, and I like men with a big one. I like a man who knows how to use it, and isn't afraid to. I like getting fucked in the head.

Which is why my fantasy Harold Ramis keeps his glasses on.

He's not merely a big 'n' stupid bohunk sexlunk. He's a hard, sexy, rutting machine, but he's also got it going on upstairs. He's thinking. He's thinking about what he's going to do to me next. He's thinking up new ways to get me off, new ways he wants to be gotten off. He's not afraid of probing my head as well as my ass. Not to mention he has a big enough vocabulary to think up something to growl besides "Suck that dick."

Thanks God it sometimes happens in real life. I remember one bathhouse trick who had both his head and his dick screwed on right. We'd met in a hallway and gone to his room, and we'd been playing around only a few minutes when he sneered at me, "What now, you can't get hard or something?" Truth be told, I was having trouble getting hard for some reason, but that's such a taboo subject that normally another fag would never comment on it immediately, much less try to turn it into hot talk. This guy did and—surprise, surprise—I was stiff in seconds.

Damn, I thought as he squeezed my nuts till they bulged and shoved his dick down my throat, this guy's *smart*. He was savvy and confident enough in fucking with my mental sex organ that he knew he could twist an anxiety into a verbal-abuse scenario and turn me on more. He was perceptive enough to know it would work on me. I never learned his name, but when I think back on him now for jack-off material, I visualize his hands gripping the base of my skull as he face-fucks me, his shaved head gleaming under red and blue lights. I look up at his face locked in concentration, the mental wheels turning, turning, behind his pensive, furrowed brow cast in shadows. He scowls down at my kneeling figure, his brain whirring away as his cock thrusts away. As this stranger barks out commands and insults perfectly tailored to my psyche, I imagine his name is Hiram. Dr. Hiram Goldberg. Fuck, to be that perceptive, the guy had to be a shrink.

A NIGGER FOR NARCISSUS

REGINALD SHEPHERD

My mother always told me, "White people, they stick together, but a nigger'll just as soon stab you in the back as look at you." But what did she know about white people, stuck in that tenement apartment until the night she died? And where does that leave me (a long way from the Bronx by now), wanting you, or to be you, to be your friend at least? You said you wanted to be mine. Watching you casually drape your arm around some other man's chair, your gray eyes smiling into his, I see my mother was right after all. The white men always leave together.

Screen Memory

I don't remember when I first noticed that all the men I wanted were white. They were just people I happened to know: boys I went to school with, in another borough. None of them lived in the two-room tenement walkup where a chunk of ceiling plaster fell on my head and Norway rats I thought were dust balls chewed through my books from the inside out, or even in the brand-new poured-cement projects with red brick façades. I thought those carefully groomed white boys didn't know where I lived, but they knew all about the place: they'd seen it on the evening news.

I believed I could walk over the polluted Harlem River water that the scholarship bus ferried me across each morning on the power of my will to be someone else: at ten years old spent Friday afternoons phoning my fifth-grade friends to ask if I could visit this weekend, calling one boy after another to see if I could come over, until I ran out of numbers and names.

Many of the men and boys I wanted, or wanted to be, were blond with blue eyes, and many were brunet with brown eyes, but my favorites were the blue-eyed brunets or the brown-eyed blonds. I liked the minor mismatch, some misplaced mirror of my own near misses. All those boys had money, Kant's thing in itself, not my corner's "I got ten cents in my pocket, I can buy me a pack of Now & Laters." Most had two parents married to each other, houses with unread libraries and basement rec rooms, real Christmas trees at the called-for season. White houses, white pickets, white roses and carnations: bloom on their softball skin, bouquet of their postgame-shower bodies. I wanted to join them in their well-dressed world, the freshly mowed and watered yards where they played friendly board games with their brothers, and for a while I thought I had.

Two Tales of Getting Fucked

1. Here is something that happened. His name is Nick and I meet him at Club Heat in Buffalo, New York. (I love the names of things.) People tell me to avoid him because he's a slut, but that seems a better reason to meet him than any. I hear he's a dinge queen too. He's wearing baggy overalls and so am I, we stick our hands down each other's pants. "We're just about the same," he says, but we're not, his white hand squeezing my hard black cock, my black hand squeezing his hard white dick. We're not the same at all. My cock's a little longer, but his has slightly more girth. I hear this is statistically typical: black men have longer cocks on average, but white men's dicks are thicker—this also on average. Brown hair, brown eyes, about my height: why do these features look so different on a white man? At his apartment we watch Depeche Mode videos and then he tries to fuck me. He has only one condom and no lube. Stupid man. It doesn't work. "Ain't got no more." I ask him if

he likes black guys best and he says yes. He tells me about the first black guy he ever had sex with: he was ten. " 'Course, so was I." Then he eats my ass for a long time while I push my brown cheeks farther into his pink face. My ass is dripping with saliva like a half-eaten ripe black plum, then he shoves in his spit-slicked dick and fucks me doggy-style, skin to skin. It slips in surprisingly easily and doesn't hurt at all. I don't get fucked that often, and my ass is usually very tight. (A blond white T-shirt jock in a blue baseball cap complimented me once on the tight fit. "Some guys' asses are so loose you can't feel anything, but yours feels really good." I sat on his dick for a long time, and smeared my spunk into the gold hairs on his pumped-up chest when I came.) I ask Nick to call me a black bitch and he says no, but I come all over his white sheets and then I make him pull it out. I never last long getting fucked, and it always hurts to have a dick in me once I've come. I never sleep well in other men's beds.

2. This also happens in Buffalo. I'm bored and horny at four A.M. I've gone out and gotten nothing, the usual story, so I call a phone-sex line and end up talking to someone in Los Angeles who calls himself Larry. It's only one o'clock in California. He likes black guys and says he's a bottom, but somehow in our phone sex he's fucking me, first on my chest with my brown legs over his tan shoulders and he's kissing me while he's pounding his white cock in and out of my tight black hole. Then I ask him to fuck me doggy-style and he turns me over, grabs my hips, and shoves his cock up my ass again and again. I'm begging him to fuck me harder and I ask him to call me a black bitch and he does. "Fuck my nigger pussy," I plead, and he says, "You like getting fucked like a dog, don't you, nigger bitch? I'm fucking your black cunt with my big white cock," he tells me, and I believe him. We both come. "Thanks a lot, that was great." Then I hang up. I sleep well, I sleep till noon.

False Fab One

This is the way it never happened. His name was Fabrizio, but that was too many syllables to call out across the street between classes, so everyone called him Fab. I called him that too, wanting to be part of "everyone." We were best friends that year.

Fab threw the best parties in town, with the latest music and the latest people wearing next season's clothes, laughing in French and Italian in the hallways. I never liked those people because their lives weren't mine, but I always loved the lilt of foreign causerie. Fab had the kind of downy, tawny skin the teeth want to leave marks on, apricot, new peach, brown hair whose tips turned gold in the sun, and hazel eyes flecked with gold. He never would have slept with me, not in a million years, not for a million dollars. He already had that.

I remember the first time I saw him, pulling up to the curb on his expensive motorcycle (everything in this story costs money), his hair falling careless yet so artful across his unlined brow. No, that wasn't the first time. The first time was at a party, one A.M. or later—who'd even worn a watch that night? I didn't know it was his party until afterward: it was one of those parties you hear from down the street and say, "Sounds like someone's having fun, I think I'll go and watch," the best kind if you're not popular. That's the way college was, standing around hoping no one noticed I hadn't been invited. He was dancing on a chair beside a speaker singing along with a song about brotherly love. "Solitary brother, is there still a part of you that wants to live?" I carried that party inside me for months, and spent months looking for that song.

The second time I saw Fab, then, he was pulling his motorcycle up to the curb with his roommate Dylan the Welsh ale heir (the biker boys, we called them, my small group of friends brought together by what we lacked, being people-who-were-not-popular), throwing his bangs back from his forehead and lightly wiping his brow with a dirty linen handkerchief. He never wore a helmet. I followed him around for weeks (he walked sometimes too, as if he were a mere mortal, sat in the dining hall and ate polenta: shat too, probably, but I wasn't there for that). One afternoon he turned and said, "What do you want from me?" He didn't mean it as a challenge. All I ever wanted was everything, but Fabrizio wouldn't even give me his ass, just an afternoon together in a café on Thayer Street before he went to photography class. (It would have been warm inside his body.) "We'll have coffee, okay? You're a strange one." Fab always meant what he said. "I like people who aren't afraid. That's why I decided to meet you." What Fab didn't understand is that I was so afraid of my needs I wore them like a winter coat in May. My fear was all outside me: I called it by Fab's name. I guess that's what he meant: I was more afraid of myself than I was of him.

This is a list of the ways in which we were different: Fab was beautiful, Fab was rich, Fab was tall, Fab was confident, Fab was popular, Fab was from Milan, Fab was white. This is a list of the ways we were the same: we both loved to ride around campus on his motorcycle (marking the boundaries of a territory, his), my arms wrapped around his waist, but not too tight.

False Fab Two

This is another way it never happened. He turned around on the street in his black cashmere overcoat, asked, "What do you want from me?" I told him, and he gave it to me on the living room rug (plush white, of course) of his third-floor apartment with PROPERTY IS THEFT stickers on the kitchen cabinets. His ass, I mean, doggy-style, pale and smooth and pulling me farther in, not far enough. We listened to Billie Holiday sing "Lover Man" while our bodies did things they'd never repeat. "Satisfied?" he said, and went into the white tiled bathroom to shit me out.

Five things he never said to me:

You like to fuck white ass, don't you? I can tell.
Give it to me, you black son of a bitch.
Make me come with that nigger cock.
Shove that big black cock up my tight white cunt.
You like it when I call you nigger, don't you, stud?

What would these things sound like in Italian? More words I
wouldn't understand.

Two Tales of Fucking

1. This happens in Boston, a small city that disapproves of
sex. I see him at a gay youth meeting, and then later at the
1270. He's in town from California for the summer, his name
is Sean: a WASP with short brown hair and a little braided tail
(it's 1984). He doesn't notice me at the meeting, but he notices me at the club. We talk; I sit on his lap by the edge of
the dance floor; we kiss and neck. "I've never been with a
black guy before," he tells me. "I never knew what I was missing." I take him back to my place and I fuck his big white butt
(he's tall, a little chunky, his ass as firm and fleshy as a ripe
cantaloupe dripping with juice; his cock is a little small for
his size, but he's a bottom so it doesn't matter). There's Vaseline all over my white sheets, all over his white ass. "Take it
home in my asshole," he pleads, but by the time I come inside him he's fallen asleep. (In the morning he says, "It felt
so good I thought I'd already come.") I don't care: my
clumping spunk is seeping from between his sticky cheeks.
We're infatuated for a while. I write his name and number on
a three-by-five file card labeled MY BOYFRIEND. Once when I'm
fucking him he comes without touching himself, from
prostate stimulation alone. Then his ass tears, the doctor
tells him it's an anal fissure. "No more fucking," Sean says,
and we go our separate ways.

2. I see him at the 1270 every Wednesday, every weekend too. He has a going-out uniform, white T-shirt, black sleeveless pullover, and a little black beret, he's one of the cool people. I see him at Glad Day Bookshop on his lunch hour, reading *Black Inches* and *Latin Trade*. One Friday at the 12, I say fuck it, talk to him, what have I got to lose? His name is Patrick, he's Irish, like every other man in town. He says he's noticed me for months (he's drunk) and tells me how beautiful I am. We make out by the dance floor while Sheena Easton sings "Come spend the night inside my sugar walls." Then he takes me into the downstairs men's room and sucks my dick in a stall. I'm shoving his face into my crotch and holding the back of his head, brown fingers digging into brown hair, but a security guard interrupts us (it's closing time) and I tell myself I'm too embarrassed ever to come back. Saturday night (I lied to myself again) I see him there again and this time we take a cab to my apartment. "I haven't had a black guy in a long time," he says. "I miss it." I wonder what "it" is but don't ask. He wants me to fuck him but he's afraid it might hurt. I tell him I'm going to fuck him whether he wants me to or not, tell him to lie facedown on the bed with his white ass in the air. "Be gentle at first, okay?" he asks, and I say maybe. He spreads his cheeks apart and I put Vaseline on my cock, then stick my black shaft in him. "You don't have to be gentle anymore. It doesn't hurt," he says. He practically begs, panting "Come in me," and I oblige: right now he's just a hot tight hole. When I pull out my cock it's smeared with runny shit; the whole room stinks of his ass. "I have a boyfriend," he'd told me before he knelt and pulled down my torn Calvin's. "If it's okay with you, it's okay with him." I've come to learn nothing's ever okay.

True Fab One

This is the way it happened. There was a boy when I was a graduate student at Brown University, learning how not to write poems. We never met, but in my mind I called him Fab.

He was beautiful, clear beer-bottle-brown eyes and burnished
olive skin. Aren't they all lovely, and don't I hate them for it?
They mean too much to me, those men and boys striding
across the too-walked-over world as if they owned it. At Brown
they did own it, had men to polish their hair and buff their
skin, had men anytime they wanted, in any position. They
shone like fool's gold in early September sun. Who wouldn't
wish to own such excellence, or break it if he couldn't?

He was one of the cool people, the beautiful who live beautifully and at a distance. I bought a pair of black suede Doc
Martens because I'd seen him wearing them, thought it would
make me more like him, someone you'd want to watch cross
the street, or need to brush against in a library doorway. *Excuse
me, I was just . . .* I imagined his thin, pale lips pressed to my
darker, thicker lips ("blow-job lips," my friend Paul once called
them), or wrapped around my black cock, my cock swimming
deep into his smooth white ass. I always imagined his ass as
smooth, my tongue lapping at it like vanilla ice cream on an
August afternoon, sweet and just starting to melt.

I wrote a poem for him, about him, the Euroboy of my
dreams and nightmares. "At him" might be more accurate.

Another Movable Feast

Tawny skin the teeth want to leave marks on, down
of peaches just past ripe, apricot, russet
and gold. He says his light brown eyes
are green. *It seemed to me then that beauty.* He sucks
the stem of his sunglasses through pursed lips, or slowly
moistens with a facile tongue the upper, then the lower
lip, head slightly tilted to the left. Why
is the eye so caught? *It seemed to me that beauty*
(scanning the room to be certain he is seen)
was the one thing everyone wanted to have
(he brushes a carefully combed fall of hair

from his brow) *or to be* (his small teeth even
when he laughs with friends, whiter
than his metaphorical skin) *or, failing
that, destroy.* And where to keep it
when he leaves the three o'clock café, what
to do with it? The teeth want to
bite into ripened fruit, to tear
the skin and let the juice run out.
                                        He rides
his foreign-made motorcycle helmetless, perhaps
into an afternoon where he'll be splayed
across the asphalt and the rusted chrome
of the car in question, a summary of all the virtues
pressed to the pavement's page. (People gather
in nervous clumps or walk more quickly, the other
driver quietly cries.) I grow hard and strange
-ly formal at the thought of it (*or,
failing that, destroy*), the ceremony
of his unperjured body tangled in corruptions, skin
sallow in late light and tinged with green, the black
and purple marks the teeth have left.
He doesn't get to keep it.

False Fab Two and a Half

Of course Fab's not dead, just on another continent. He's in
Rome for the summer with his grandparents, important people,
dating the right sort of girl, riding down to Naples to meet his English boyfriend on the sly. They fuck in narrow winding alleyways at
midnight, under what starlight penetrates the inversion layer's
haze of pollution. I graduated from Brown years ago. I'll never
pine on the fringes of that world again; I'll never walk among
those privileged terms again, a smudged blank on white paper. I
can't want him without wanting to tear his perfect skin, as if I wanted
to know what's behind it. I can't want him without wanting to be
hurt, because it isn't him I hate. I can't humiliate myself forever.

Body

This is a story about bodies: they take in food and make shit. The body stands between me and other people, my black body, their white bodies, my black body I try to make mean something different from all the other black bodies it's confused with, my black body I try to redeem with my sharp mind and good taste in shoes, blithe spirit trapped in a brown-skinned mortal coil. But the body joins me to other people: those men dancing shirtless at Manhole Wednesday night, would their white flames draw me mothlike if they gave off no visible light? (Waving hands in smoke-filled air to silly music under multicolored strobes, strolling in bike shorts through a summer street fair sucking Creamsicles like cocks, they're just mirages motion leaves behind, proximities and failed connections.) Without the body there'd be nothing to touch, so how could I be lonely? My black body I try to get their white bodies to touch, maybe it will rub off. The body means nothing, but riding on the subway with a white policeman leaning against the door I knew what this black body meant to the gun humming patiently in his holster. I sat reading a book about the bodies of black gay men, trying to make my body different from those black bodies around me. *Men make their lives, but not in circumstances of their own choosing:* Karl Marx wrote that. Only black people ride the subway in Buffalo, and white policemen think reading's something faggots do. But they know a nigger when they see one.

True Fab Two

This is the way it happened. Fab? I made him up. There was a boy named Duncan Sheik, from South Carolina. I watched him in a diner on College Street, a café on Waterman. I found a picture of him in the freshman face book: he'd remade himself since then. His tan skin I wished my white teeth could tear pales in my memory (he runs away, just like in one of his songs), but I'll always remember the party where I didn't meet him, and the foreign motorcycle he rode around campus, marking the boundary that kept me out of his world, the wall that kept him in.

Now he's a pop star, barely breathing on MTV and VH1. I bought his album, listened to it many times, named one of my poems after a song. He did an in-store performance one Friday afternoon at my local Borders and I almost went: tried to, but he was late, I got bored at Borders. Besides, I'd told an acquaintance who worked there that I went to college with Duncan Sheik, and he'd told Duncan, who was curious, wanted to meet this person, reminisce perhaps. I didn't want to be embarrassed by the revelation that he hadn't the vaguest idea who I was. I remember little hands around a glass, white smooth fingers.

SINK

MATT BERNSTEIN SYCAMORE

M y eyes rolled back and I was looking in the mirror the way I
used to look at people late late *late* at clubs when the drugs
were taking me to that planet I never wanted to leave. But this
time it was just me and the bathroom sink. That's when our relationship began. Two months and still going strong; it's the
second-longest relationship I've ever had. And this one doesn't
have *any* of the drama.

He's kind of falling apart, but he's dependable. And beautiful, in the way that only a sink can be beautiful. *And* he's got
character. This isn't some Formica mess from the seventies,
with square edges and gold glitter. And it's not one of those
sinks that look all glamorous from a distance, but then you get
up close and the drain's rusted shut, the faucets are about to
break off. This sink is the real thing, made during the forties.
You know, the golden years. Sure, he's seen a little wear and
tear, but haven't we all. I mean, I'm only twenty-four and I've
got suitcases under my eyes.

It all started one night after a trick. He wanted me to fuck
him hard, harder, and after a few thrusts it actually started turning me on. I was pounding him as hard as I could and he was
grabbing my ass to pull my dick in farther. That got me to relax.
I mean, I don't like fucking someone really hard unless I know
he's enjoying it. So I put my hands on his back and got into a
good rhythm, sliding my dick almost all the way out then shoving it back in as far as it would go. It got to the point where his
moans and my grunts were synchronized, which kind of put me

in a trance. I think I even heard my balls slapping against his ass like in some porn video.

I could feel myself getting close to coming, so I stopped and held my dick all the way in his ass, but I started spasming anyway. Usually, I don't like to come with guys who are paying me, and there's nothing worse than coming when I'm trying not to. It's like doing bad drugs, makes me tense instead of euphoric. But somehow this time I managed to hold it in, even though I thought for a second that I could feel my cum spilling into the condom. Either the trick thought I was coming too or our bodies were really in tandem, which would be kind of scary. But anyway he started gasping and then he moved forward quickly and my dick slid out. And then he came. I was covered in sweat, so I took a shower while he called a taxi.

Got home and I was exhausted. Then of course I got horny. I always get horny when I think I'm too tired to move. I couldn't stop thinking about fucking some sweaty guy with a shaved head and a firm body, pounding his asshole and digging my fingers into the groove between his chest muscles until we came at the same time. He'd reach back and grab my ass to keep my dick in his asshole longer, my arms around him, tongue reaching for the back of his throat. I got hard just thinking about it, the kind of hard that makes me think my dick might explode. Not like when I'm about to come, but like *isn't this thing too red?*

I went into the bathroom to watch myself jerk off in the mirror. My dick was so hard it was vibrating. I pulled off my shirt and grabbed my armpits, licked the mirror in circles like I was making out with someone, or maybe just to see what it would taste like. The mirror got all foggy. I spit on my hand and started pumping my dick into both my fists, trying to watch myself while licking one of my armpits, which was tastier than the mirror.

I remembered Greg calling me up one night to tell me shea butter was the best lube, so I rubbed some between my hands and then onto my dick, started thrusting my dick against the rounded top of the sink, without hands. I pulled the shea butter back out of the cabinet and rubbed it onto the sink. Felt great, but the sink still wasn't slippery enough. I opened the cabinet again and took out some of this sticky vitamin E lotion that I use as pomade. Then I went into the other room and got some Bodywise Silk, the British lube that feels like lotion, and I mixed all three together.

My dick felt harder than rock-hard (granite-hard? marble-hard?). I looked in the mirror and my face was what my mother used to call lobster-red. Started pushing down on my dick so there was more friction. Sliding all the way out past the cock head and then back toward the faucet. Each time my dick slipped off the sink, I'd jerk off until I could tell by the look on my face that I was about to come, then I'd grab the sink with my hands and start pumping faster. I wanted to come without using my hands, like my dick was in someone's ass and I was pulling him against me. I got really close and then my dick slipped off again. I started pounding the sink as hard as I'd been pounding that trick, my thighs making noise—more noise than before—because porcelain echoes.

It felt good to squeeze the sink with my thighs, balancing my weight on top and thrusting hard. Concentrating to keep my dick from slipping off. Pushing down on my dick with my hands so I'd get closer to coming. By this time I was moaning, pounding the sink and sweating. And then I slipped again. Held my dick and smacked it against the sink until it felt as stiff as the sink (sink-hard). Then I grabbed on to the sides of the sink with my hands and pushed on the front with my thighs, thrusting fast now. Hard and fast and then sliding slowly back until my cock almost slipped off, then pounding again. I was concentrating so hard that I didn't even think of fantasizing. Thrusting my dick faster and faster and when I came I felt like I'd split apart.

It sure feels sexy to squeeze my thighs up against that sink. The sink feels so strong, I can trace the rough spots where the enamel's chipped but I know the sink's not going to break. Even if there are some dark areas and the white is fading to yellow. This sink was built to last, I can press down with all my weight and it doesn't even budge. That's firmer than any guy's six-pack.

Let me tell you that the sex I have with my sink is a lot better than most of the sex I've had with other guys. My sink's not going to tease my asshole with his dick, then slide it in without a condom. Or leave in the morning before I even have a chance to say good-bye. Sure, I wish the sink were more responsive, but you can't have everything, right?

Okay, maybe you think I'm in denial about the fact that when I'm having sex with my sink, I'm really masturbating. So if you want me to use the word *masturbation,* I'll use it. Let's just call it masturbation with a partner. I mean, plain old masturbation was never this exciting. I don't always fuck the sink, that's for special occasions. But I love to press the shaft of my dick against the top of the sink while I grab my abs with one hand and my balls with the other. And sometimes I lean against the sink while I slide a dildo into my ass. I can feel the sink warming against my thighs.

I always used to press my dildo against the wall and then slide onto it, but now I've got lots of variations. The other day I put the dildo up on the sink, stood on the edge of the bathtub, and sat on the dildo. I watched myself right up against the mirror. I could see my facial muscles relax as I got closer to coming. Then when I came, I shot all over myself and almost fell into the sink, which was funny and almost romantic. Usually, though, I shoot right into the drain and then just wash my cum down. Though now the drain's starting to clog. And I can't seem to get that vitamin E lotion off the edge of the sink; even when I wash with soap it still feels a bit slimy (my friends are going to read this and they're going to want to use the kitchen sink, but oh well).

The view is one of the most important parts. When I'm jerking off in the sink, I'm right up against the mirror. Sometimes I can pretend that I'm watching that Warhol movie I've never seen, the one that's just Joe Dallesandro jerking off from the waist up. I can watch all the different expressions on my face, study my eyes. Watch my jaw clench or slacken as I come and my eyes roll back.

The sink makes me feel good about myself. There's nothing getting in the way of my body becoming my own object of desire. I look in the mirror and think, Who's that hot boy? I tease my tits until they pop up, bite my armpits, smack my chest as hard as I can and watch the red marks as they fade. That first time I fucked my sink, I realized how butch I get when I'm about to come: my face curls up almost into a snarl and I start groaning like some fuck track.

I've been working out and I can watch my body developing. Balancing my hard-on against the sink, I study my new muscles. How hard are the pecs? Are my biceps still bigger than my triceps? I stand up on the toilet so I can see my legs, bend over to look at my ass. Rubbing my hand down over my abs, feeling the hills and valleys as I move from one muscle to another. All the while grinding my dick and getting hornier and hornier. For myself.

It's funny—now I start to get horny every time I'm standing in front of the sink. When I'm shaving, I press forward and I get hard. I'm moving to New York soon, though, and I'm worried that my new sink just won't be the same. It couldn't be this good. And what if I get a sink with sharp edges?

LOVE MAPS

MACK FRIEDMAN

I did something two weeks ago that I'm having trouble dealing with. I was in the men's locker room at my local Jewish Community Center. I had just finished dunking over straight boys on the b-ball court and taking a dip. I was naked, wringing out my trunks over the garbage bucket, admiring my MACK TRUCKS tattoo in the mirror in front of me. There was a stocky boy untangling his bathing suit knot in my reflected field of vision. He was probably half my age, which would make him thirteen. I turned around to the scale and weighed myself: 162 pounds, as usual. I glanced back at the mirror and caught the boy watching me.

Hmm, I thought. I swiveled back to the mirror and contorted my shorts more. Every three seconds I'd steal a glance at the chunky dude: now nude, now eyeing my backside, now absentmindedly pulling on his dick, once, twice, three times—shaking out the swimmer's shrivels?

Three seconds later, he was behind me, on the scale, our asses almost touching. It was really very touching. Like the sky greening over before a tornado, something imminent colored our closeness: the whirling expectation of a fantasy turned real.

It all started one hazy summer afternoon when my mom got back from the bookstore and tossed me a paperback called *What's Happening to Me?* It was, of course, about puberty. I must have been twelve or thirteen; it was around the time when the boy next door—my supposed best friend—was forsaking me

for chicks. Anyway, I wound up crouching in the hallway over a
fold-out illustration of a naked youth at successive stages of
sexual maturity. I wasn't sure then if it was a photograph or a
sketch, but my guess now is that it was a meticulous illustration
based on photographs. I know it wasn't in color, and I know
that when I saw the boy I fell in love. I took him upstairs to the
laundry room mirror, to compare. We were the same, only my
dick was rock-hard. I thought, What's happening to me?

By the time I was sixteen, things were even more awry. When
I cut class or procrastinated to avoid my biology assignments, I
killed time flipping through the card catalogs at the University
of Wisconsin–Milwaukee library. In short order, I discovered
"puberty—boys—rites of passage" and "sexual abuse—males—
case studies" and "homosexuality—Greece." After I had exhausted these resources, I tried the kiosk of computer screens
near the reference desk, keying "art and boys and nudes" and
"Klinefelter syndrome" and "pederasty" and—when I got more
advanced—"intergenerational male intimacy," which yielded
some detailed Dutch research that left me contending with certain inch-to-centimeter ratios.

One icy night, when I had six weeks' worth of homework
due, I sprinted the short blocks from home to the library in my
winter coat and soccer shorts, to wake myself up. There I
tapped into a CD-ROM, the Medline, and came up with a reference to "priapism and adolescence" that promised black-and-
white prints of synthetic-growth-hormone side effects. The
journal in question was located in Compact Shelving, the elec-
tronically separable stacks deep in the basement. I found my
call-number parameters and pressed the OPERATE button on the
elevator box wired into the side of the metal bookshelf. A
green light flashed. As long as I fingered the button, the stacks
hummed to life, parting for me, acquiescent as passed-out
friends. I headed down the newly created aisle, squinting for
the 1987 *American Journal of Diseases in Children*.

Vaulted within five hundred microthin pages was a doctor,
frozen grasping teen male genitalia, like a spokesmodel displaying items up for bids on *The Price Is Right*—"It's a priapic

fifteen-year-old with delayed maturation! Start the bidding at
two hundred dollars!" My heart sank to my guts, thumped into
my prostate, and surged through my dick as I carried the book
to the back of the basement, between the last closed stack and
the blank stucco wall. I tugged my blue checkered soccer shorts
under my balls and jacked off over and alongside the fondled
specimen.

A whim impelled me back over the tracks to examine the
journal's annual indices. In the 1940s, Earle Reynolds and
Janet Wines had taken thousands of pictures of fifty-nine boys
from Yellow Springs, Ohio, some of which appeared in 1951
under "Physical Changes Associated with Adolescence in Boys."
The seven sizes of the flaccid penis fascinated me. "We have
also taken a few measurements of both stretched and erect
penises," they wrote. "In four boys, there is a history of semi-
erections at a number of visits. This is noted routinely on the
physical examination record, and can also be seen readily in
the photographs."

That night, I smeared semen on my tie-dyed boxers; over a library card slipped from its slot on the top of the rack; across old
folio maps crinkling on the black plastic shelf to my left. I'd
never seen so much sperm. Hell, I'd never seen *any;* my girlfriend was always gobbling mine up. I was confused, this first
night I successfully masturbated: what did I need Abby for now?
My shorts slapped my abs as I slam-danced through the foot-
notes, hot on the trail. My eyes flashed on one title—*Somatic Development of Adolescent Boys,* by Stolz & Stolz: Macmillan, 1951.

A whole book! I was sure that if I found the Stolzes, I'd never
need anyone else. I thought, I must have this book!

The Milwaukee libraries never had Stolz, but I memorized
its Dewey decimal number, 612.661, and thus began my obsessive quest.

From that night on, whirring stacks gave me erections. I
learned to find joy in the permanent shelves, discovering *The
Linked Ring: The Secession Movement in Photography in Britain,
1892–1910,* which included some F. Holland Day expatriate
scenes, listless surreal prints of unclad, wild youngsters emulat-

ing woodsy saints. I developed a fondness for case studies of abused kids, the only accounts I could find of boys having sex with other males. I shielded Theo Sandfort's *The Sexual Aspect of Paedophile Relations: The Experience of 25 Boys,* held it close to John Money's *Lovemaps,* let *The Sexual Offender and His Offenses* kiss *The Boys of Boise.*

Sometimes I scaled locked doors and climbed into the study rooms on the library's second and third floors; there was a gap between the wooden doors and the acoustic ceiling that I could squeeze through, muscling up and then rappelling down onto the desk, where I'd pop open a Paul Kubitschek portfolio from the 1932 *Journal of Nervous and Mental Disease.* Entitled "The Secondary Sex Characteristics of Boys in Adolescence," the article was laden with soft, fuzzy photos of cherubic, denuded guys standing side by side under such captions as "Testicular size in this group varied from small almond to large walnut." Into the trash can I came.

My personal fave was Frank K. Shuttleworth's 1949 piece in *Monographs for Social Research in Child Development,* "The Adolescent Period: A Graphic Atlas." As soon as I read the abstract— "consists entirely of half-tone reproductions of photographs of nude children, mostly serial photographs taken at different ages"—I clutched the burlap backing and bounded blindly for cover in a three-walled, cornered carrel. I thought of Andy, a freshman in my homeroom, as I obsessed over Shuttleworth's "late-maturer," a pasty kid whose face was obscured by a black rectangle painted over it. Full-frontal and biannual from 11.5 to 17.1 years, he stood anal-receptive, juxtaposed to front the taller "early-maturer," a similarly defaced skinny kid. I copied their measurable attributes into my notebook, robotic. Then I took my blue Bic and wrote on the carrel's wooden wall: "I'm 16, brown hair + eyes, 5'7", 135 lbs, sparse copper pubic hair, none under my arms. If interested," and then my pen gave out.

I yearned for the opportunity to compare myself to a real, flesh-and-blood guy. In high school I got glances from one older kid in the weight room and wanted him to ask me out, or something. I trailed him one day past rotting piers and chalk-white boulders on Lake Michigan's shore, both of us alone, awash in the stench of poisoned rock cod. But nothing came of it. Books were more dependable.

One thing frustrated my bibliophilia: when I found books I wanted, like *Control of the Onset of Puberty*, or J. M. Tanner's *Growth at Adolescence*, only to see that certain pictures had been removed with razor blades. The technique seemed so cold. I preferred to fold them over, crease them slowly, gently tear the boys away.

To exact revenge against the vandals, or maybe jealously wanting the boys all to myself, I started hiding my captives inside my official high school folder, the one they gave us in homeroom, with the sketched picture of our prison etched in blue. The ripped-out photos, musty with age, gave the folder the smell of bitter almonds. I liked to carry it down into my house's dank cellar and leaf through it, like the wind, during thunderstorm warnings.

But through it all, I was still driven to find that elusive volume, *Somatic Development*. The call number that I'd known by rote since the age of sixteen—612.661—was like a mantra in my brain. I had to have it.

When I got to college at Swarthmore, I continued my quest at Bryn Mawr, the nearby all-women's school with reciprocal library privileges. An ocher sun choked through low clouds, and tower bells were tantric, chanting six o'clock. I didn't know my way that well but I had a good map, so I navigated toward the psychology library. I acknowledged nobody. Anonymity made me invisible.

At the psych building, I tried the front door—locked. I walked around the gray, two-story stone building to the back door, which the legs of a chair held ajar. I scoured vacant corridors. There was a wing in back, housing the stacks. The lights were off. I tested the glass door: it was open. I looked around and was alone.

I flicked on one column of fluorescents, followed the arcane racking system until I hit the 600 section. My fingers raced along the bindings, up one shelf, down another. Finally, not in its place, but farther down the row, I found Stolz. I was stoked. Nobody had beaten me to it. I riffled through the pages, making sure they were mostly there, wondered if the women of Bryn Mawr would miss it, guessed not, and tucked the text under my flexed left biceps.

I scampered out the door, thinking, What an easy theft. I felt the breeze and the peace outside, the wind whipping up my shorts, and was distinct, fully myself, looking barely above the tree line at the pale, failing sun.

Sliding into my car, I placed the simple navy hardcover under the passenger seat, taking no chances, and headed back to my apartment.

I was hungry, though, so I pulled into an Amoco kitty-corner from my pad. I scrounged two bucks of unused Xerox change from my pocket and picked up a shiny lime-colored bag of something toxic. On my way back to the car, I yanked a free paper from a black box by a streetlamp that had just started shining. The masthead said, *Au Courant.*

Upstairs, I fell upon the carpet, dropped the book and newspaper beside me. I left the television and lights off. I was hoping to make this last as long as possible. I slowly opened the front cover to a photo of the backside of a naked boy standing on a scale. I knew that picture; it had been reprinted in Leona Bayer's *Growth Diagnosis,* a book I had studied and vandalized at sixteen.

I peeked again at the blond's high, rounded butt cheeks, and at Dr. Herbert Stolz by the scale, looking solemnly down to where his patient's young penis would be. I couldn't help myself. I began to rub the satiny skin on the inside of my wrist against my zipper.

It was the situation: boy, doctor, exam. I could jerk off for days on that number. As I shook and splattered, I was thinking, What does this kid look like on the other side? Is he as hard as I am? Did he ever imagine people would be jacking off to his picture? Did Stolz show him how to stroke it? Nothing has ever turned me on as much as vulnerability consciously exposed.

In my postorgasmic trance, I climbed out the window of my efficiency and dropped to the twilit fire escape with my newspaper and a Lucky Strike. The *Au Courant* was exciting and in-your-face enough to seem taboo; it was the first gay periodical I'd ever read. I was drawn to the Help Wanted listings—ESCORTS/STRIPPERS/MASSAGE. I ripped out one with the word *discreet* and felt myself up for a quarter. I placed a call, got hired, became the subject of other people's obsessions. I played the wrestler boy on the scale for any married man willing to pay me.

Five years have passed. I'm now much more interested in gay artists—Pierre et Gilles, Bernard Faucon—than in anonymous medical photographers. I thought I was over my obsession. And I was, until the locker room incident at the JCC two weeks ago.

I'm not saying it was smart. My hand brushed the boy's right ear on its way to the scale measures. "Stand up straight," I commanded. JCC Boy complied. For a second, I was Herbert or Lois Meek Stolz, or the man with the camera, or maybe all three.

I looked down. He was hard. It was sticking out. There were two straight gold hairs on either side of his penis. Tanner PH stage II, I couldn't help thinking.

It was all I could do not to swallow him whole. I said, "You weigh a hundred thirteen and a half pounds, if that scale's accurate."

"Okay," he said, trembling. I turned around. We got dressed and I masturbated, later, in the handicapped stall, which is roomy, not that it mattered—it took barely four seconds to get myself off.

I wish all of life could be like that, pure fucking adrenaline, but I'd have heart failure. I'm curious: how did the boy take it? Did this mean anything to him? Or was it fulfillment only for me? For a few flashbulb moments, I was teenaged again. Though I knew it couldn't last, it was nice to blow back there, to a time when life was so clear, when I knew what I wanted.

Now I'm thinking of going to medical school.

A PLANET CALLED JEFF

KEITH BANNER

We are on our way to see *Alien*. It's July, a Friday night, 1979.
I don't tell Jeff and his mom, but this will be my first R-rated
movie, which adds a whole other level of luxury, on top of staying all night with him. Jeff and I are both fourteen. In the station wagon is the sleepy fume of his mom's cigarette smoke
mixing in with the air conditioner's chill. A large woman who
works nights at Delco, his mom has a rule: the radio has to be
on an easy-listening station. Right now, we listen to Perry
Como's rendition of "Yesterday."

"I can't wait to see this, man," Jeff says, turning around. I
smile up at him, nodding my head in the backseat. Skinny, Jeff
has a red, chapped mouth, black hair cut Boy Scout short with
bangs just above his eyebrows. His eyes are dark and always
darting, as if they have a different kind of energy than the rest
of his face, an excitement he wants to keep secret. We don't
ever talk much in front of his mom. Right away, he turns back
around, getting into her purse without her seeing, stealing a
pack of her Winstons.

At the movies, Jeff's mom escorts us in, because of the R rat-
ing. She buys the tickets, gives them to us, tells us not to get too
scared, and then walks back out to drive herself to bingo. Jeff and
I enter the theater alone. From the beginning, *Alien* doesn't
really seem like a movie—it's more of an experience, a fever
Jeff and I share like Siamese twins.

Grim, sleepy-eyed, astronauts wake up prematurely from hy-
persleep, sip their morning coffee as they float through space,

get a distress call, land on a gas-green planet with howling wind, find a huge cavern filled with neon jelly eggs. A uni-tentacled octopus sprouts from one egg onto an astronaut's face, and slithers down his throat to impregnate him. Eventually a metallic baby alien explodes from the guy's chest, growing in ten minutes into a two-legged monster that can rip people's heads off.

All this comes at us in dream form, a nightmare Bible story, the alien a baby Jesus soon to be crucified once it's an adult. Its silvery teeth open with machinelike ecstasy when it gets victims, but its ugliness and hunger are somehow pathetic at the end, when after its orgy of murder it gets hurled into space by Sigourney Weaver.

All I know is that I want to be with Jeff, witnessing this. I keep looking over at him as the movie unfolds, his open-mouthed joy at the serious weirdness of it. *Alien* is way more important to our lives than reality. It's a religion, the images on the screen laced with the ominous silence surrounding what we are going to do later tonight. Right at that moment, I know how much I love Jeff—deeper than the outer reaches of outer space. I know that what we will end up doing in his bedroom will only make that love grow deeper, into a black hole. I will come out the other end on a planet called Jeff, a planet that will have a smell like the smell coming from the movie theater's a-c vents—chilly blue mildew being the only atmosphere of this planet, the only substance you can breathe.

After *Alien*, we walk to the mall across the parking lot, smoking Jeff's mom's cigarettes.

"That movie was *fucking incredible*," Jeff says. "The special effects were *awesome*."

"Yeah," I say, and I can't really talk about it, can't find the words to tell him what it means to me. We walk around behind the mall before going in, kicking at weeds sprouting out of concrete, lit by security lights. Rusty Dumpsters, concrete bays for semi trucks, the backs of brick buildings—all this makes me want to kiss him. By the way, I happen to be the fattest kid in the whole school. I am pure white trash too, with a Fundamentalist Baptist mom who works at Kentucky Fried Chicken and a dad who works for Indiana Gas Company reading meters, with a little sister who sometimes shits her pants on the bus. I'm sort of effeminate too, but that gets canceled out because I'm trash and nobody pays that much attention to me anyway.

Inside the mall, we go to the record store by JC Penney. We take *ELO's Greatest Hits* and *Tusk* by Fleetwood Mac, eighttracks, from the shelf, go over to where the poster racks are, hide behind them, and put the tapes inside our jeans, pulling our shirts over the lumps. Jeff's eyes seem to go back deeper into his skull when he shoplifts, like he can see backward, toward security guards. We've perfected this system over the past year, and it always works.

We inspect the tapes in the middle of the mall, by a water fountain that doesn't have water in it. Jeff lifts *Tusk* up, grinning. Even though we both ripped them off, he says, "You can have this one."

"Thanks," I say, letting him be the boss. He gets an allowance of ten bucks a week, and his mom is buying him comic books all the time, so shoplifting isn't about getting what he wants, exactly. It's about doing something he can get away with. I respect this lack of need, the suburban decadence of it.

As soon as we see Jeff's mom walking toward us, we hide the stolen tapes behind our backs. She doesn't seem to care. She never really notices anything—just wants to get stuff over with quick.

"You guys ready?" she says. Her eyes are totally bloodshot, the lids swollen. I wonder if she really went to bingo. She's been crying, obviously, and I can smell booze on her, but now she's smiling in front of us, great big.

"You want pizza?" she says, a fake, almost strangled happiness in her voice—a divorcée getting over her divorce, a workaholic trying to relax.

Back home, we listen to the music we ripped off. I get shaky, in anticipation of what we are about to do. I always do that.

Jeff's mom is in her room next door, coughing, and his older brother, the one with sideburns who works at UPS, is in the kitchen, making something to eat. Electric Light Orchestra plays "Strange Magic." I am on the floor in my sleeping bag; Jeff is up on his bed. Last year he painted his walls black, to simulate outer space. Spaceship models he glued together dangle from the black ceiling on kite string.

"You wanna smoke?" he asks me.

"Sure," I say.

He opens the window, turns on the fan. We light up, Jeff on his knees, leaning against the headboard, me next to him, standing on the floor. Outside his window are trees and Tarmac roads and other houses glowing in street and porch lights—anonymous ranch-styles with trim lawns and basketball hoops, not really rich or even upper-middle-class, but elegant, out of my reach.

The moments right before we settle down to do it, before I pretend to mumble in my sleep, are like Christmas Eve, two kids waiting on Santa Claus, or other moments when you have nothing to live for but what is going to happen next.

Jeff says, "If she smells this, my ass is grass."

The end of his cigarette glows red, mixing in with the green light shining from his stereo. In that light, he looks like somebody I don't know—and I don't, not in any real way. I wonder then why he likes me, a fat white-trash kid barely making it through school. I get it all of a sudden: nobody else likes *him*. This warms me up inside, that I'm his only friend. There's a feeling of ownership, almost, like I own a part of him, and a part of everything he owns.

"Keith?"

Typing my name coming out of Jeff's mouth in the middle of the night in 1979, just that, is an amazing thing, to me at least. In fact, typing Jeff's name, at first, stunned me a little, as I have always taken what I felt for him and sieved it through a mesh of lies, over and over, to make it seem more real. His name alone does have a sort of made-up quality, after all—like "Jeff" would have to be the name of a boyfriend you had in high school who was a closet case and who loved *Star Trek* and *Battlestar Galactica.*

"Keith?" he whispers.

I keep my eyes mostly shut, turning over to see him in the moonlight.

"You sleeping?" Jeff says.

I whisper, "Yes."

This sounds so fucking schlocky, I know. After all, the two of us doing this is just a see-through pretense so that I can wind up sucking his dick. But it's more than that, too. The setup allows me to be this character peeling from my own sleep, a dreamed-up Keith. The homosexual astronaut Keith, beautiful against the black walls of Jeff's bedroom. It is Jeff desiring me, pulling me out of the dead Keith, that allows me to forget what I am. He doesn't want to know anyway. He wants the sleep to be a part of him too, so that he can wake up the next day and wash off what we did and go on.

There he is, up there, floating on his water bed, holding his hard cock, which isn't that big. I'm shaking really bad as I crawl up to the bed from my sleeping bag.

Automatically Jeff sits on my face, and I lick up into his asshole, thinking of the one-tentacled octopus in *Alien,* thinking too of how much I love Jeff. He knows how to do all kinds of sex stuff. It's like he's teaching me, and this makes me wonder now, as I type this, if his brother had fucked around with him, or maybe his dad, and that's why his folks got divorced, maybe his mom caught them—but that night all I can do is lick and taste him. His flesh, both inside and out, smells and tastes like onions and mildew, softened with soap. I take it in. This is the closest I can get to him, through his asshole. Then he makes me stop. He sits up, cross-legged, before me on the bed.

"Come here," Jeff whispers. "Keith, come here."

I half-crawl to him. He pushes my head down so that I can suck his dick. The next morning, we will be just like anybody else on earth. You need this to be in control of yourself the rest of the time, though—to know there is someone else, some other way to be, inside you, and it comes out while you pretend to be unconscious: you have his dick in your mouth, and he is moaning. He never moans outside of this. The rest of the time, he is tight-lipped, sitting with glassy eyes and an open mouth in a movie theater.

But now he is Jeff-and-me, this conglomeration. I bite into his hard, small cock, and then I stop and lick him down under, my head burrowing until I feel like I might smother. I lick whatever I can, until he directs me to suck on his dick more. I keep flashing on random images from *Alien:* the way the octopus-thing jumps from the egg, the way the baby alien screams when it first pops out of the guy's chest, like it's lost and wants to go back in.

Jeff whispers, "Keith, hey, get on your stomach. Come on. Now."

I do. He loves me, I know right then, because he asks me to get on my stomach. My face is pressed into the vinyl of the mattress. He is on top of me, finding my asshole with his fingers, using spit, massaging it in. I feel like somebody. There is purpose in the world, like I've finally crossed over, away from my white-trash family and the nasty little house on the fucking prairie we live in with the bathtub and its rust stains corroding the enamel until little flecks of it float in your bath water and stay on your skin, and my fat ignorant mom telling me to get up and get ready for church, and my tall crooked-nosed dad coming in from work and telling me I'm getting fatter get out and shoot some hoops Keith for Christ's sake Keith; I am escaping the trash we burn in the backyard in rusty barrels, the smell of what we think might be a dead cat under the floor in the crawl space, all of it, escaping it right when Jeff puts his dick up inside me. I'm right there with him after all, in his big, suburban house, on the expensive water bed his dad bought him for Christmas.

Jeff fucks me. Almost all the time, I am outside of this region of getting exactly what I want: 99.9 percent of the time there is no real pleasure in the world, just anticipation. At least that's the hyperbole I get going in my mind. I am asleep but not, he is fucking me but not, and in that confusion is this blissful few moments when he stops fucking me and lets it stay inside. He kisses the back of my neck, maybe accidentally.

He comes inside me. He pulls out. I lean away from it, swim back onto the floor like a seal diving back into the water. I jerk off while he gets up and goes into the bathroom to clean himself off. I come before he walks back into the room. He throws me a couple of Kleenexes, possibly knowing my face is covered in spit and his shit, my ass leaking his sperm. "Possibly knowing" is like a door ajar: the Kleenex comes from the waking world. The fact that after we fuck I have to clean myself up—for Jeff to know that—means he also understands that this is real. Which gives me hope.

The day after, Saturday, Jeff has to get to his afternoon karate class. I tell him and his mom that my mom's on her way to pick me up anyway. Looking clean and angelic in his white pajama-like uniform, Jeff waves at me from inside the car, then looks away. His mom tells me, "You're always welcome here, kiddo." She slams her door. I smile, sitting on the steps next to my grocery sack of dirty clothes, watching the station wagon disappear.

Inside the house, Jeff's brother is playing his stereo, Led Zeppelin's "Dancing Days." There's a hypnosis to it, and I just want to crawl back into Jeff's bedroom and hide there, wait for him to come home to me. I always get into this desperation the day after, afraid I will never feel as beautiful as I do at night, pretending to be asleep and getting butt-fucked, pretending to be a part of his life he can't live without.

When Mom does arrive, it's in the Vega without the muffler. You can hear her a mile off. She pulls up the driveway, in her red polyester Kentucky Fried Chicken uniform, my little sister beside her, wearing pink sunglasses she got at Kmart.

I get in the car, smelling the fumes from the missing muffler. In the rearview I see my sister in the backseat, clapping her hands for no reason. Her sunglasses piss me off. They make her look stupidly innocent, like she's grasping for something glamorous in the backseat of a shitty Vega, grasping but not knowing she's grasping.

"You hungry?" Mom says, putting it in reverse.

"No," I say, not looking at her.

My little sister says, "I am."

I look up as Mom backs out, the engine ringing in my ears: that big brick house, Jeff's, there in my vision, all I can really see, as we go down the hill backward, back out onto the road, back home.

VILLAINY

KELLY MCQUAIN

Today my bedroom, tomorrow the world.

As a child, I planned to stop at nothing short of global domination. For I was a supervillain as menacing as the Joker, Penguin, or Riddler, intent on dominating not only the muscled heroes of my imagination but all the boys and bullies of my neighborhood.

Headquarters for this nefarious plan was a tiny second-story bedroom in a small town in West Virginia. Twin beds—one for my older brother, Michael, and one for me—lay tucked in opposite corners and separated by a window that looked onto the street. Farrah Fawcett pinups and KISS posters covered the walls on Michael's side of the room; Shaun Cassidy and Abba decorated my side in the few spaces not thumbtacked with plastic-bagged copies of my favorite comics.

Once, in the aftermath of a fight, Michael and I had stretched masking tape across the floor of our room, separating our shared world into private hemispheres. Our mother had long since balled up the sticky line to vacuum the carpet, but demarcation remained. Ever since our squabble, Michael had grown increasingly finicky, carefully alphabetizing his record albums, tucking his bedcovers into perfect corners, racking up brownie points with our parents—he became a goody-two-shoes I couldn't possibly live up to.

On my side of the room, entropy ruled. That summer before seventh grade, I was obsessed with superheroes. Hundreds of comics filled my closet; dozens of eight-inch Mego superhero dolls stood posed in spectacular dioramas on my desktop and

wall shelves: Batman rushing to free a twine-bound Robin from
a gloating Joker; the Human Torch (suspended via thread)
swooping down to flash fireballs (Mercurochrome-dyed cotton) at a grimacing Green Goblin; Superman and Supergirl
dramatically bursting through a cardboard wall. Even though
I'd be entering junior high in the fall, some nights I still
sneaked a few action figures to bed, flying them around in the
dark till Michael began to snore.

My bed hugged another window that looked onto our neigh-
bors' house. I'd quietly scoot my head near the screen to spy on
the Caulfield boys' room across the way, waiting for their light
to flick on. I was eager for a glimpse of high-schoolers Mack or
Sam patting themselves dry after a shower or stripping down to
Jockey shorts for bed. Most of the time I only spotted their
younger brother, Gary, scratching his ass before climbing into
his bunk. But if I could stave off sleep long enough, every once
in a while I'd be rewarded with a glimpse of the older two. Both
had bodies as muscled and lithe as a superhero's.

As a stiffy rose between my legs, I'd slip my Batman doll
under the elastic waist of my pajamas and force him to wrangle
with a new nemesis, the Poker.

Mornings, the summer light hit the Caulfields' house full on,
hiding the boys' room in shadow. I'd push Mack and Sam from
my imagination, grab some comics and superhero dolls, and
start my day with a brain-rotting helping of fantasy.

If it was Saturday, I'd fly Captain Marvel and the Mighty Isis
downstairs, prop them on the arms of the sofa, and let them
watch their own cartoons. More often than not, a battle royal
erupted between my sister, Gloria, and me when my *Super-
friends* was scheduled opposite her *Speed Buggy*. If Gloria had
sneaked downstairs before me, I'd tuck Isis and the Captain inside my T-shirt for protection, seize my sister's Barbie and
throw it behind the couch. When Gloria scrambled to retrieve
it, I switched channels. As Speed Buggy's stammering *putt-putt*
gave way to the Wonder Twins' chirping, "Shape of an eagle,
form of an ice jet," Gloria's voice would rise from behind the
sofa, hollering, "Switch back! Now!"

An evil grin spread across my face. I was glad Captain Marvel and Isis, still wadded in my shirt, couldn't see. Ignoring my sister's cries, I pushed the couch back to the wall, then slid Dad's vinyl recliner tight against it, trapping Gloria with the dust bunnies. When she whined, I turned up the volume.

Yet most of my battles were waged with myself. I wasn't sure why. All I knew was that in the last year or so I had begun to look at my superhero dolls in a different light. I had grown tired of their endless adventures and now longed to get to know them in the penetrating way Phil Donahue got to know his talk-show guests. I began staging my own shows, hosted by Gloria's Ken doll, whom I "borrowed" when my sister was out roller-skating.

"Tell us, Batman," I'd make Ken say. "After fighting crime, how do you kick back on days off?"

Batman winked at an offstage Robin.

Ken pressed harder. "I want answers. What's it like to get out of that suit?"

The Caped Crusader grinned enigmatically.

I knew Batman would never answer. The Dark Knight's mask was a permanent part of his face, molded and painted in a factory far away. He could never completely become Bruce Wayne. And he could never make good on his lascivious wink, either. I had once stripped him down to his plastic skin in order to wash his uniform. Between his thighs, Batman remained noble and neutered. He had no worm, nothing to offer Robin.

I too wore a mask. It tightened my features when I passed the Caulfields' front porch. "Queerbait," Mack called. "Pussy," Sam added, as they looked up from their airplane models.

What was the source of my defectiveness?, I wondered. Mack and Sam picked on me far more than they did their own little brother, Gary, who seemed a much easier target. Born a year ahead of me, Gary was nevertheless scores of IQ points behind. He was always trying to impress my sister with misguided derring-do, like climbing a tree so high his epilepsy kicked in, or snatching flies on a hot summer day and popping them into his mouth like Raisinets. Yet somehow the defect I possessed was far worse.

I felt guilty and dirty night after night as I fell asleep to images of the two oldest Caulfield boys climbing into bed dressed only in Jockey shorts. In my dreams, I lured them onto the imaginary talk-show set and did awful things to their bodies. Lashed them tight with cord so snug it would leave red marks for weeks. Pulled the set's lights down close till the boys' pupils shrank and beads of sweat broke out on their brows. I tangled my fingers in their hair—Mack's blond, Sam's a dreamy dark—jerked back their heads, and screamed, "I want answers!"

Answers to what, I did not know. But it sounded good. Perhaps I was seeking answers to why they bullied me. To why Mack stole my bike, returning it mud-splattered and with tits drawn on the superhero stickers covering my handlebars. Answers to why Sam once threw a rock at the back of my head, his subsequent, parent-prompted "I'm sorry" unable to dull the throb of seven stitches. In dreams, I tortured them for all that and more, especially Sam, the most beautiful boy in our neighborhood. Smoky-eyed and wide-shouldered, he had an easy grace, was full of qualities I thought I'd never possess. I liked having him helpless before me. As I demanded more answers, I would watch Sam struggle in fury, his hands bound behind his back, as helpless as Robin in my favorite comic books. The smooth planes of Sam's face were so perfectly assembled I couldn't help but smack him, rip his clothes, eager to see his muscles straining against the rope that held him. I felt energized by my villainy.

On Sundays, after church, Mom and Dad sometimes allowed me to visit the Bookmart, one street over. I forwent the customary after-service handshake with the preacher and slipped out the church's back exit, cutting down an alley and racing to see what new comics had arrived that week.

The Bookmart was a front for a betting operation run by Mr. Capelli, the owner. If my parents had ever seen the stream of men placing their bets, even on Sunday, they might not have been so eager to let me go there. Bad enough that Mr. Capelli sold porno magazines, displayed on the top shelf of the magazine rack, corruptibly close to the comics aimed at kids my age. Sure, I snuck a peek from time to time, just to seem normal. And if I had any money left over from buying my Batman and Robin comics, I'd also buy a racy, oversize issue of *Vampirella,* which I knew my brother might cop if I didn't hide it well. I liked Vampirella not so much because her tits were big but because her go-go boots were kick-ass leather, and her fuck-off attitude cut as deep as her fangs. All the wrong reasons, of course, but at least when Mr. Capelli slid *Vampirella* into my bag it balanced out the rest of my purchase, made my Batman and Robin obsession a little less incriminating.

After all, I needed to remain inconspicuous. My body was going through embarrassing changes, and the public mask I wore to hide my villainy was an increasingly bad fit. Soon I would start junior high school, where, my brother told me, boys had to change clothes before gym class and shower after. In preparation, I had borne the humiliation of going to Grant's department store with my mother to buy a jockstrap. Lately Mom was tucking into each basket of folded laundry she set on my bed some new little item marking my journey toward adulthood: my very first roll-on deodorant, a bottle of Old Spice, a toy razor with no blade and a note that read, "Practice." I rubbed my still-smooth chin and wondered whether Mom feared that if given the real thing I'd slit my throat.

With reluctance I incorporated these items into my morning routine. My father was always gone early and home late, constructing a building across town to use as headquarters for his auction business, so he couldn't advise me whether to run the razor up or down the curves of my cheeks, or how to navigate the spray of acne that had cropped up along my chin. My brother was no use, either, always hanging out with the Caulfield boys next door, who thought it was cool he had finally mastered "Freebird" on his guitar.

I tried to discuss the changes our bodies were going through with Lyle, a friend from school who lived a short walk away. But I could never find the words. Afternoons, when Lyle had finished his paper route, I'd go to his house to play with his superhero dolls. His collection rivaled my own. We'd stage fights between his action figures and his massive, robotic Shogun Warriors. Lyle had followed a do-it-yourself blueprint from one of his mother's crafts magazines, cutting up refrigerator boxes with a utility knife, then assembling the pieces with a hot-glue gun, creating a superhero city perfectly scaled to our dolls' eight-inch height.

When we grew tired of orchestrating onslaughts of mayhem, we'd focus our play on the soap-opera aspects of our dolls' lives. Mr. Fantastic and the Invisible Girl would ride a pull-string elevator to the top of the Baxter Building, where they'd shed their blue uniforms and bone down in the buff. The Mighty Isis would have one martini too many in the lobby bar, kick off her braided boots, and hike up her skirt so Aquaman could cop a feel. In a dark alley, Captain Marvel and Captain America would soften up Supergirl with a chunk of Spanish Fly Kryptonite, then pull a train like a couple of frat boys. Even *Dynasty* wasn't this debauched, though sometimes we did make Wonder Woman and Batgirl catfight like Joan Collins and Linda Evans, falling into a reflecting pool made of tinfoil before stripping off their uniforms and lezzing out.

Lyle didn't care that his action figures had no naughty parts. Just grinding our dolls' plastic bodies together got him so worked up that sometimes—when his father was still at work and his mother was out running errands with Lyle's sister—he suggested we play Truth or Dare. The first dare to pop out of his mouth was always "Strip off your clothes and run downstairs in front of the windows!" I think he was trying to give Miss Bradshaw, his septuagenarian next-door neighbor, a fatal coronary.

Her heart attack would have been a small price to pay for the sudden freedom I felt on those occasions when I gave in to Lyle's request. My last streaking session had occurred right before a summer storm. I scurried naked from room to room, blue shag carpet pushing up between my toes. Cool air blew through Lyle's house, whispering between my thighs and tickling my crotch. Glancing out a living room window,

I could see the sky darkening and the wind picking up. Next door, Miss Bradshaw had already shut her windows and was nowhere in sight. I did a little dance anyway, flexing my penis so it slapped hard against my belly. I whirled around to find Lyle watching from the staircase, rubbing himself through his cutoffs. I blushed, a surge of blood coursing through my body. Behind me, a breeze whipped up the window curtain, brushing it against my butt and starting a shiver that rose from my feet. The two feelings met in my middle and swirled together like hot and cold air forming a twister. I watched Lyle, wondering if he felt the same way. But outside a sudden bolt of lightning crashed, shocking me back inside my shame.

One day Lyle decided to raise the stakes of Truth or Dare. He brushed his brown hair from his forehead and stared wickedly at me, the devilish look in his eyes magnified by his thick Coke-bottle glasses. He leaned in so close that I could smell the sour milk of his breath. His voice fell to a whisper as he added one final rule: "But today the only way we can end the game is to butt-fuck."

I felt the way I had when Sam Caulfield hit me in the stomach with a football. Though I had never heard that expression before, I instantly knew what it meant. Doing it would make you a cornholer, a name Sam and Mack sometimes called me. The idea of my best friend and me naked and pretzeled together flashed through my mind. I reeled at the image, nearly smashing into Lyle's cardboard metropolis. I caught myself against his bed and sagged down on top of it. I wanted a thunderclap to break my stunned silence, a lightning strike to recharge the moment. I wanted to transform into someone unafraid, but I couldn't say "Shazam."

Lyle noticed my shocked expression. "Just kidding," he said nervously. "Don't have a conniption." Already he was gathering up his naked superheroes and unstacking the tiers of his cardboard buildings, putting everything away. Lyle's voice was low and faraway when he spoke. "Maybe you should go."

*   *   *

I believed back then that if I had done what Lyle asked I would have crossed into another world, another life I wasn't sure I wanted. Adulthood loomed before me, complicated enough. I was learning that the line between good and bad was never as clearly demarcated as in comics or cartoons, where it was easy to tell who was a member of the Super-friends, who a member of the Legion of Doom. In real life, the line was redrawn all the time. It wouldn't adhere like a line of masking tape stretched across a bedroom floor. And it was growing harder and harder to tell on which side of the line I was supposed to be—which was the bad half, which was the good.

How easy it was to be nudged over to the side I tried so hard to avoid. All it took was a single view of Sam Caulfield: a swipe of his tongue over the beads of sweat collecting on his upper lip, one day late in August of my thirteenth year.

I was heading to Lyle's in hopes we could ignore our recent unresolved tension and play superheroes as usual. As I cut across Vine Street, a noise drew my gaze to a tangle of over-grown holly bushes in front of the Snelsons' fancy brick house. In a flash I saw Sam Caulfield. His eyes burned through the greenery as he jerked his head my way. He jumped off the Snel-sons' fence, tearing through the holly to lunge at me. I wanted to run, but my feet had turned to concrete. I stood frozen as Sam's muscled arm shot out and seized me by the shirt collar.

"Where you think you're headed, queerbait?" he snarled, hand tight around my throat. He lifted me up till I tippy-toed the ground.

"None of your beeswax," I choked out.

"Little shit. You spying on me?"

For once in my life that wasn't the case. "I was going to a friend's."

Sam let go of my shirt and I dropped to the ground. "Well, if you wanna pass, you gotta pay the toll," he said.

Oh great. A shakedown for my comics money. Junior high sure had started early. I swallowed hard and lied. "I don't have any cash."

"I don't *want* no cash," Sam said. The mean look on his face turned down a notch. His eyes unscrunched, and I could see the brown circles of his irises, the color of melted Hershey's Kisses.

Then Sam worked his tongue over his upper lip, licking the sweat away. He traced the full circle of his mouth as he collected his thoughts. I still felt shaky from being held in his grip, and I knew I would do whatever he asked.

He glanced at the neighboring houses, then peered down at me. Light flickered in the dark centers of his eyes as he calculated my measure. He sucked in his cheeks and said, "You be my lookout." He punched my shoulder. "Or else."

Before I could say anything, Sam scrambled back to the Snelsons' fence, raised his foot to the first slat, and hoisted himself up. Behind him, their fine home bulged with opulence.

My heart sank. Was this high school boy who looked like a superhero really just a common house thief? I surveyed the other houses down Vine Street, hoping someone might come out and scare us off.

There wasn't the slightest stirring.

Turning back to Sam, I followed the beeline of his gaze with my own, not to the house but to the Snelsons' grape arbor. It stood in their backyard near the driveway, next to where their camper van would have been parked if they hadn't left a few days earlier for an end-of-summer vacation.

I breathed a sigh of relief that it was only grapes Sam was after. Still, his thieving was not without danger. Several bees looped in lazy circles around the fruit, the grapes so heavy that many had already fallen to the ground. Three different kinds of grapevine laced through the arbor's latticework, producing clusters of green and glossy red among the more generous distribution of purple Concords.

Sam straddled the fence and dropped over. He glanced at me, his sidekick in crime. A thirsty smile slid across his face before he turned back and stalked toward his target.

For years Mrs. Snelson had been chasing the neighborhood boys away from her grapes. She claimed to have barely enough for the jellies she entered each year in Forest Festival competitions. Lyle, who delivered papers to her door, had told me her mantel was covered with blue ribbons. She had once given him a jar of jelly as a Christmas bonus. Lyle rationed the delicious treat for weeks, sharing with me only a fraction of a spoonful.

Sam was right to covet the grapes. Mischief and desire painted his face as he brushed away the bees and snaked his hands under the dark leaves, plucking weighty clumps of fruit off the vines. He circled the small arbor, filling his wide palms and grinning. He gleamed at the stolen grapes as though they were a first birthday cake, a new bike, a prom date who wouldn't say no.

I couldn't believe how good Sam looked stealing those grapes, so happy and alive. He felt the sun on his back and the thirst in his throat, and was unafraid to do something about it. He didn't think too much. He didn't hate himself.

Grapes slipped between Sam's fingers and fell to bounce off his sneakers. I almost laughed. Even his wide hands couldn't loot all the bounty. He untucked his dirty T-shirt, stretched it out, and dropped in his haul. I caught a glimpse of his smooth belly, watched him pop a handful of grapes into his mouth, closing his eyes as he drew the sweetness over his tongue. When his shirt grew heavy and stained, he strode through the bees and back to me, somehow clambering over the fence without spilling a single grape.

He looked at me and smiled. His big hands moved close, not to hit but to share. His muscled arm arced over my head like something out of a painting, his hand dangling grapes just for me. I could see the fine brown hairs that feathered his forearm and flecked his knuckles. A gnarled twist of vine laced through his grip. Sam's sweaty musk mixed with the sweet odor of fruit, surrounding me in a tangy cloud I breathed deep into my lungs.

My mouth stretched wide to receive stolen bounty. Sam's thumb flicked a red one free. Onto my tongue it fell, seedless and sugary beneath its tender skin. Then a green-yellow one dropped down, its juice squirting the roof of my mouth as I bit deep. Several Concords followed, smaller and sweetly sour, just now ripening.

I drew my tongue across my lips, wanting more, wanting Sam to bend his head to mine. Bright sun backlit his wild brown curls, and I thought I caught a glimpse of affection in the shadowed recesses of his eyes. I arched my neck, biting into the cluster of grapes he held. My lips brushed Sam's knuckles.

He flinched, pulled back, told me that was enough. I closed my eyes, trying to hold on to the taste. By the time I opened them again, Sam had stolen away somewhere, taking his loot with him.

Later, when I spied on Sam through my bedroom window, or lay restless and thinking about him after he'd gone off to college, I would replay our little crime in my head. Though I felt bad stealing from Mrs. Snelson, I felt strangely good at having been so close to an older boy I always thought hated me. I no longer wanted to make Sam my prisoner. I wanted to lock my fingers behind his neck and pull him close, touch his mouth with my own, taste again the sweetness of those grapes.

In the years that followed, the memory of that taste, my villainous communion with Sam Caulfield one lazy childhood day, helped me persevere. Later, in college, I would recall the taste of that fruit when I got drunk on cheap wine and came out tearfully to friends. I'd drink up and confess, drink up and fumble naked with any gay man I could find in that small college town only thirty miles from home. I hoped that each newcomer's skin would feel like Sam's might feel, that in the dark their eyes would be the same melted chocolate as his.

While I made slow but steady progress in accepting myself, Sam went on to play football at WVU and marry his college sweetheart. They produced two darling girls, I heard, and often took family drives through the mountains to the farm near town where Sam's parents finally moved.

One winter when I was off at grad school in Philadelphia, Sam fell asleep at the wheel driving in with the girls to surprise his parents. It was Christmas Eve, and his wife had stayed home, sick with the flu. I know the road Sam took and how

precariously its winding turns hug the mountainside, how
headlights at night don't always mark the line where the road
ends and the berm gives way to gravity. His daughters, asleep in
the backseat, survived with bruises and broken limbs. Sam
Caulfield died.

I am grateful to Sam for helping me appreciate the worth of
my villainy. I have come to see my sexuality not so much as
stigma but as distinction. When my lips brushed Sam's knuckles I knew love existed inside me.

Sex, sin, and Sam—my superhero dream. "Holy trinity, Batman!" I can hear Robin squeak as I give thanks to what rescued
me from the foolish standards of my small-town childhood.

I began thinking about this after college when I started working as a freelance comic-book artist. In my penciled pages, I
shot flames from my hands, breathed underwater, flew through
the air. The assignments the company FedExed me from
Chicago were standard superhero slugfests, as well as a few "Sex
Specials"—adults-only issues where the heroes got it on like the
dolls Lyle and I used to play with. I enjoyed bringing my furtive
childhood fantasies to life, but the novelty wore thin when the
company went belly-up and refused to pay me. My only reward
thereafter came in Lyle's smile of satisfaction one Christmas
when I returned home and gave him copies of the issues I had
drawn. Lyle would soon be leaving for two years' service in the
Peace Corps in Africa. I didn't know it then, but his time in
Mali would help him answer questions about his sexuality in
the same way that Sam Caulfield had helped me answer questions about mine.

Although I quit drawing comic books, I would later write stories like this one and others, about superheroes and sex and
the connection they still have for me. This is the one power I
have to bring Sam back, to smell his sweat again and taste the
grapes he held above my mouth, to make real what he meant
to me.

In the next room sleeps the man I live with, and I will soon
go to him. I will quietly slip into bed beside him, feeling his
heat against my bare skin. My arms will snake around him,

and my body will mold into his curled shoulders and the bend of his legs as we sleep like spoons throughout the night. And tomorrow morning I will kiss him the way I could never kiss Sam.

THE END
OF BEING KNOWN

MICHAEL KLEIN

The two mysteries I couldn't solve reaching puberty were (1) who I was (outside of my knowing I had a twin brother named Rex), and (2) why my mother (never mentally stable) didn't want to be herself at all. Two mysteries pulling me in two different directions. It seemed to me that what my cock and balls were up to was far too concrete a thing to worry about when I had much more baffling things to deal with. My body would take care of itself, I reasoned. What was I going to do with my mind?

Or my mother.

"How could you not want to be who you are?" I asked my father one day while we were waiting in the barbershop. *(Why does the barber flash the blade on the leather strop? Why do combs float in blue water?)*

"Well, if you get sad a lot . . . that would make you not want to be yourself all the time."

"Am I myself, without Rex?"

But my father didn't answer me. He looked at me with a strange mixture of sadness and confusion. My father was probably the wrong person to ask about my brother—or my mother, for that matter. I don't think he knew my mother very well at all (not nearly as well as I did), because he wasn't a creative person like she was and couldn't have understood the frailty of her ego.

I knew all about fragile egos. Everyone on my mother's side of the family (theater people) died of a fragile ego. My ego was sitting on top of fear, which—before puberty brought on its own terror, of other boys—had to do with war. I was terrified of nuclear destruction (China, Russia, it didn't matter), and when this felt silly or miscalculated, I narrowed the fear in my mind until it went personal. I was convinced that my mother and father were trying to poison me.

Nuclear fear or fear of being poisoned were soon replaced by my mother's betrayal (she divorced, had a breakdown, remarried). She actually *needed* someone other than Rex and me in her life. My new stepfather was brooding and adolescent— like a troll in the book I was reading the day she decided to marry him—a man, I was to learn, who used marriage the way Dr. Jekyll used serum.

The early days of their marriage were carefree, but they'd met during a time when both of them were battling an assortment of mental disorders, so I could never tell if their happiness together was authentic, a fluke, or the result of an array of psychotropic drugs. What was authentic were their awful fights, which were easy to hear because we lived in a one-bedroom apartment in those days and my parents slept in the living room. I couldn't for the life of me figure out the subject of their arguments. All I knew was how they appeared to change the valence of my mother's love, which now seemed as though it had to pass through my stepfather before it could reach me.

I tried to think from which psychological abyss their arguments shot forth and came to believe, finally, that my stepfather simply never wanted to be the father of my mother's children. I guess he couldn't see us in his mind before actually encountering us for the first time that cold day at the Central Park Zoo: two blond and talkative creatures trying to squeeze through the bars of the lion's cage.

I turned up the radio whenever they started in on each other and got lost in the show music that played on the AM station. Rex and I could hear the anger reverberating off the walls in the living room and feel it shaking under our beds.

"I'll never get married," I said to Rex. And saying it then, when we were children who didn't know how we'd later drift apart from each other and into families of our own devising, I felt that he and I were already in our own kind of marriage, which would always protect us from having to make a choice in the real world. It comforted me knowing about our marriage, but it terrified me, too, as though being known by Rex signified the end of being known.

By the time we had moved into a bigger apartment, with separate bedrooms, puberty raged in us until we let it push us toward each other and into the fire of sex. The first orgasm I ever had was with Rex—the summer we turned twelve—and we came to it like hoodlums, circumventing authority. It was only after the luminous thread of semen went clear on Rex's chest that I consulted authority (my stepfather). I informed him of the *what* of the orgasm—that I had had one—but not the *how*. I didn't tell him how in a seemingly timeless ripple of ecstasy, I came down on Rex and Rex came down on me. I told my stepfather about the orgasm, the clinical aspect of it, because I needed to hear from an adult what it meant now that the world could go from feeling physical to feeling more physical.

Eventually, for about a year, Rex and I were doing it once or twice a week. He'd come to my room, or I'd go to his, and one of us would just linger in the doorway a minute—the sign that we were about to have sex. There was barely any conversation, and all I could feel was my heart beating in my chest, but I also felt it in my head.

Of course, I didn't want to think. I wanted Rex to come to me in the night's early darkness and start by kissing me.

We kissed.

And then I wanted him to sit to the side of me on the bed and run his hand slowly down my chest and stomach until it reached a cock so hard it was a third heart beating.

He did that.

And then he kept his hand on my cock a minute, which was always when I'd come out of my temporary coma and start reciprocating. I'd grab him by his shoulders and pull him to my mouth, which was dry inside but moist at the lips. And we'd kiss again, the second time, and that would be his cue to start climbing up on me, to stay tethered to me by his tongue inside my mouth but also to move his legs on either side of my body so that he'd be straddling me. We didn't know what fucking was, or we would have fucked.

And so, we were oral lovers. And when we sixty-nined (the last in the series of sexual moves, because by then we were close to coming and we each wanted to come in the other one's mouth), I always saw us as a snake swallowing its own tail. We were exactly the same size, and the only thing distinguishing Rex's cock from my cock was the cum shooting out of it, which was thicker than mine.

Coming was the fourth beating.

And hearing my heart on top of Rex's heart beating in exactly the same time, it didn't feel like having sex with another person. It felt like an extension of my own sex, and every move toward Rex was a move toward someone inside me made only of sensation, someone I couldn't reach physically without Rex being there. I knew Rex was another body, another cock, another heart, and I knew that he was thinking different thoughts than I was, but all the differences seemed to be forgotten the more we forged ahead through the sexual world.

We were in puberty together and we always came together, and in that miniature heartbreak I felt just after orgasm—when I went back to seeing Rex as just another person, as everything *other* than sexual (someone who got up five minutes later than I did and didn't have friends in school, someone lost in books and classical music)—I was rife with something I might now call regret.

At some point I understood that Rex and I shouldn't be doing this. He came to my room one night, and I had to tell him that I didn't want to have sex anymore. It wasn't a decision based on anything except how I felt. I didn't *think* that what we were doing was wrong or bad, but I had started wanting to break away from Rex in thinking, in feeling, and to be whoever I was without him. The sex had begun to feel like an animal we'd been feeding, and I wanted to let the animal go.

Deciding to move on into whatever the rest of our lives would be brought on a whole new set of terrors. Who were we now, now that we'd broken a kind of seal and become known to each other the way only lovers are known to each other? And what was this feeling of breaking up all about? Because I hadn't broken up with anyone before, I didn't know if this was the same feeling you had when it happened with a civilian, someone you met outside your own family.

"Rex, it doesn't feel right to me anymore."

"Why not?" My brother wanted more, which made him instantly undesirable to me.

"We should be having sex with other people—not each other. With girls or something."

"Girls?" (As if I'd said "gorillas.")

"Yeah. Don't you like girls?"

"Well, I think about them. But I don't know if I like them."

"Well, maybe you need to think about them harder. Maybe we should try it with girls from now on."

"I wouldn't know where to start."

"By talking to them, for starters. There are plenty of girls at school who really like you."

"It's you they like."

"That isn't true. I just talk to them more than you do."

"What if we like boys?"

The thought set off a wave of light inside my stomach. Butterflies, I guess. "I don't think so. It's different when it's us. I mean, I don't think of you as a boy, I think of you as my brother."

It's funny what you actually remember about the things you say you'll remember all your life. I remember the sex with my brother, of course, but more than that, almost clearer than that, I remember the smell of corduroy sunflowers—a swath of fabric my mother had used to cover an old toy chest I had under the window in my bedroom. Those big flowers smelled like butter—the smell of our sex.

A few years later, out from under the wing of our sexual secrecy, Rex and I came up against our first outside erotic force, and, like the sex we'd shared, there was something about Larry, the swimming counselor at the local YMCA, that was outside the norm. Larry walked around the locker room one day with

an erection and sat down by Rex and started massaging his
shoulders. Of course, this was the seducer's hand making its
first contact, but what tilted the picture—from my point of
view, anyway—was that erection.

What was Larry doing with an erection and standing there like
we-the-people in front of all of us? Despite my already skewed sexual perspective, I knew that erections were private affairs. I was
fascinated and unnerved by Larry's moves on Rex, and as "over"
as I might have been about the sexual component of our relationship, seeing Rex move away from our peculiar light (which
felt poured) into the light (which looked aimed) of another
human being, another male, made me fearful and jealous—two
emotions that when shaken together sent shivers down my spine.

And Larry was attractive—tall, lanky, with a shock of black
hair and soft body hair like an afterthought. He had the kind
of body that looked capable only of receiving another body, not
entering one—not strong, but not underdeveloped either. His
eyes were gray and they looked a bit frightened, but that didn't
make me think he was afraid. I saw the other thing you sometimes find in someone's eyes: he could hurt someone.

Unable to bear watching what I knew was about to happen,
I told Rex I'd meet him outside. I waited for almost an hour,
and when Rex finally appeared he was washed out—as white as
the sun.

"He made me have sex with him."

"*Made* you?" I said, finding it hard to believe it wasn't con-
sensual. Suddenly, in the real world of negotiation and despair
and danger, sex was currency.

"Yeah, I didn't want to do anything."

"Well, what did he make you do?"

"Suck his dick."

It was the first time I ever heard Rex say that, and it shocked
me for a minute before it entranced me. Sucking a dick—anybody's dick—was such an extraordinary thing to do, an extraordinary way of being in control. I had always heard of
having someone by the balls—but having someone by the dick
was friendlier.

Larry had apparently suggested to Rex that he come along on a sleep-over in the Catskills the swimming group was having the next Saturday. And to bring me along. Larry wanted to have sex with me, too. But Rex said "No way" and ran out of the room with just enough time to pull up his pants. What if Rex hadn't said no and we had all ended up in those mountains?

I could see it all in my mind: the campfire, the pretending to be asleep and waiting until everyone else was asleep before I'd watch my brother find Larry in his sleeping bag, or watch Larry find Rex in *his* sleeping bag. The night bodies crawling in the grass. I'd watch my brother to know how I should approach the situation, to see how to touch Larry, to see how Larry liked to be touched. I would watch my brother unzip Larry's sleeping bag from the bottom and crawl between his legs and then just be a head moving up and down in the dark.

And Larry would groan and cough to keep the groaning from the other boys. And while I was watching I would think that the only way I could have all that was to get involved with the two of them there having sex in the dark. But I wouldn't want to have both of them. I'd want the one I never had. And the whole weekend would be a failure because I couldn't figure out a way to get Larry alone.

None of it would ever happen. Rex got scared and spilled the beans about Larry to my parents in a burger joint on the East Side where we all went, as a family, on Friday nights. My parents, of course, were horrified and told the Y administration, whereupon the swimming counselor was fired.

I looked Larry up in the phone book a few weeks later but never called him. For some reason, it was important to me to know where he lived—to make him more real, I suppose. And for months, after everything had started to be forgotten and my brother and I settled back into the confusions that were more familiar and had more calculable outcomes, I liked to imagine that Larry had his old job back just for a day and was smiling as he walked down the street on his way to swimming class.

I wondered, too, and always closed the curtain on my

thoughts of him with this: What boys were treading water in his hungry mind now, and how long had they been treading there?

I never told Rex about looking Larry up. It was my secret, the way all my crushes on boys in those days were secrets—things I needed to have in order to live but didn't need to share with anybody. And as the years went by, and Rex and I got further and further away from what we ever saw in each other sexually, I used to think about my brother standing there in the doorway, waiting to make the next move. What I loved about the sex I had with him was that it never had to be filtered through any of the feelings we already had for each other.

When the sex stopped working, I hoped there would eventually be someone else waiting for me in the world I would inhabit as an adult. I could sometimes see that person in my mind—tall, blue-eyed, curly-headed—or dimly imagine him pushing Rex out of my bed so he could get into it.

We're in our forties now, and sometimes when I look at Rex today—heavier and, because his life has partly been a process of suppressing those features that resemble mine, a bit chaotic-looking—I can't imagine I ever touched my brother's body. I don't get along with him as well as I did in that old erotic time. But seeing him now, I also know that part of who I am, and part of what I do in the beds of other men in the 1990s, comes from what I learned about sex with my brother. It was Rex instead of war.

IDOLS OF THE BROTHERLY PLANET

KEITH PIERSON

We planned to run away together, disappearing into the woods that spread across and beyond the army base, our exit curtained by fast-moving kudzu. Living on stolen canned foods and snared rabbits—our father had made Randy attend a wilderness survival course where he learned to remove a rabbit's skin like peeling a fuzzy sleeper off a baby—we'd sleep in thatched shelters and swim naked in a stream.

Our mother's religious fervor had calmed after we moved away from El Paso and Mountain View Baptist Church, where she and I both had crushes on Brother Bob Bratcher, whose inky mustache and piercing blue eyes, black suits and cowboy boots, gave him the erotic charisma of Edgar Allan Poe at the OK Corral. Still, she insisted that we be driven to Sunday school each week before the bland service at Fort Rucker's Protestant chapel or at one of several Baptist churches in the nearby town. There, among strange and usually hostile peers, Randy and I, sweating in neckties and tight shoes, were subjected to the evangelisms of huge-bosomed matrons or their football coach mates. They grilled us with Bible-verse flash cards or read sanctimoniously from the kitschily illustrated quarterlies that, like pornography, depended on the same dozen or so plots: the Flood, the loaves and fishes, the lame man who got lowered through the roof on a stretcher for one of Jesus' scintillating recitations. Randy would meet my desperate glance as we parted at the doorway to join our respective Bible groups: "We'll run away," he'd mouth. "Soon."

One Sunday, when we were let out in front of a new off-base church while our parents went to park the car and attend their adult classes, Randy grabbed my arm. "Wait—we're not going," he said. We milled around till classes began, then searched out the blue Plymouth and hid hunkered down together on the backseat floor, Randy recounting science-fiction plots from the piles of Ace double-deckers he read. Two hours later, as worshipers began to spill from the church, we raced up and casually merged with the throng. We found our parents already waiting in the car.

"I couldn't see you in church," my mother said.

"We were way in back with some kids from Sunday school," Randy lied.

"Where're your quarterlies?" our father said, looking suspiciously in the rearview mirror. "What was the lesson?"

"There weren't enough to go around. Loaves and fishes," said Randy, kicking my foot.

"Yeah, we talked about whether they had to clean all the fish, or whether it was already chopped up, like tuna fish. Anyways, I'm awful hungry," I said giddily.

"You goddamn little liars! It was 'Suffer the little children!' We sat behind Lieutenant Tarpley's boy and he hadn't seen either of you." He stretched one arm, slapping and grabbing over the seat as he backed the car out of the lot; we yelped and ducked.

Randy was older, so he got the worse punishment. Back at our base-housing duplex on Eagle Loop Way, I sat on my bed looking at the pale blue-green wall, shivering in the icy gusts of air-conditioning blasting from the vent over the door. I could hear the murmur of our father's stern voice from the next room, then the sound of the swinging belt, Randy's first indignant shouts turning to panicked shrieks, a chair being knocked over as he scrambled around the room trying to evade blows. If I concentrated hard enough, I could hear him beaming me the words: "We'll run away."

We hated our father, Hank, whose relationship to us was more that of a spiteful and jealous sibling than a wise and heartwarming TV dad like Fred MacMurray on *My Three Sons* or Carl Betz on *The Donna Reed Show,* and I didn't object when Randy said he wished Hank's helicopter would get shot down on one of his Vietnam tours.

When we were very young, we played a game called Ruff-ruff. Ruff-ruff was a dog, always portrayed by Randy. I was the lady of the house, walking Ruff-ruff with a bathrobe sash tied around his neck. Being a dog, Ruff wore only pajama bottoms or, if we were alone, underwear. I heartily punished the mischievous dog when he was bad, and he was always bad, that was the point—hiking his leg on the drapes, thrusting his snout into his mistress's crotch, or rebelling and wrestling her to the floor. I smacked the naughty dog's butt, or beat him with a broom; sometimes I'd have to pull up sharply on the leash, choking him so he'd heel. "*Ruff*-ruff!" I'd shout as I pummeled him. "Ruff! Ruff!" he'd bark, pawing me back.

In those days we still shared a bedroom with twin beds lined up side by side, and he'd wake me during the night with stories of the giant, all-seeing eyeball. It rose up looming over your bed the moment you shut your eyes. By day, it hung just over your shoulder, out of view. If you got out of bed in the night and tipped a slat in the venetian blinds, you'd discover it right at the window—but of course I didn't dare get up and look.

"It knows whatever you're thinking, so you can't fool it, and you can never get away," Randy told me. For months I woke everyone with my screaming nightmares. My parents took me to the pediatrician, Dr. Weiser, a dark-skinned young man with jet-black hair coiled on his wrists and forearms, five o'clock shadow staining his jaw blue, and thick black eyeglass frames. I was afraid to shut my eyes in the dark, my father told him.

Dr. Weiser examined me alone in his windowless office. I sat in my underwear on the edge of a cold metal table while he questioned me about school, what I liked to eat, and, finally, the nightmares. He turned out the light and we plunged to the bottom of a black sea. The air-conditioning hissed, and I shivered as he reached inside my Jockey shorts and cupped my testicles, squeezing them slightly, then harder, till I whimpered;

with his other hand he clicked on a bright penlight and peered
into my pupils. The bloodshot eyeball bobbed obscenely at his
shoulder.

> *John Dennis again left the window and approached Rhoda Kane.*
> *She was wearing a housecoat, a brassiere and panties underneath.*
> *"Take off your clothes." Rhoda unbuttoned the housecoat and*
> *slipped it off. That strange excitement showed in her eyes now. The*
> *android pointed.*
> *"Take those off." He touched her and noted the sudden jerk and*
> *quiver of her response. He became grotesquely, academically inter-*
> *ested. He touched the same nerve surface again and studied her face*
> *for the response.*
>
> —Ivar Jorgensen, *Ten from Infinity*

We lay on our backs in the shallow plastic wading pool in the
far corner of the backyard, churning the water with our feet—
Randy, Shelly, and me. July 1962: I was six. Shelly was thirteen;
she'd only recently moved in down the block, and so far she'd
made friends only with younger kids like us. We kicked to cir-
culate the water in the hot afternoon sun, to shoo away the hovering bees from a neighbor's stacked hives, and to obscure our
voices. My mother, who didn't like Shelly and thought it odd
that she should spend so much time with two little boys,
twitched aside the curtains at her bedroom window to check up
on us from time to time. Merely donning swimsuits engen-
dered a guilty excitement: our parents regarded the naked
body with unease and a kind of anger. The family word for
penis was *pottier*. "Be sure and clean your . . . you know . . . pottier . . . real good with soap," Hank would say, ducking his head
into the bathroom when my brother and I shared a tub. In our
long baths together, Randy's penis was a lady with a helmet-
shaped hairdo—a Cyclops on a cliff to be encircled and attacked by my toy rowboats. Now, compressed in my tight red
swimsuit, my pottier was stiff and poking up; Randy's tented his
red plaid boxer trunks.

"I've been there plenty of times spying on them, but they've never seen me," Shelly said, her voice low. Many afternoons that summer, lying in the pool or squatting in the secluded dirt strip between our house and the next, we listened to Shelly's tales of The Place. The Place lay somewhere out in the scary desert that stretched into the heat-shimmering distance a few blocks beyond Milagro Hills, our relatively new housing development (where the only hill in sight was the occasional sand dune). You could be grabbed off your bicycle, blindfolded, and taken there by the older boys who ran it, Shelly said. You might be stripped and tied spread-eagle to a hot metal slide, while clothespins pinched your flesh. Bound and naked victims were whipped with belts and the stinging branches of tumbleweeds. Others, trapped in pits, were urinated on by their laughing captors, who stood overhead, legs apart, silhouetted against the baking sun. Day after day we lay spellbound in the tepid water, almost ill with excitement, listening to Shelly.

She wanted to see our penises. She'd show us her pussy, she said, if we'd go first. I always followed Randy's lead, and all summer he'd steadfastly refused. But one day, crouched at the side of the house behind a cedar bush, Shelly halted her storytelling. Either we showed our dicks, then and there, or we'd be hearing no more of The Place and its troubling pastimes. Randy grudgingly lifted the leg of his trunks and proffered a brief glimpse of puckered scrotum. Shelly peeled back one side of her swimsuit and pinched out a plug of pink flesh. I was standing with my clammy suit around my ankles when our father swooped down screaming and dragged Randy and me into the house.

We had done something so horrible it couldn't even be named. We'd been slapped occasionally for back talk or misbehavior, our legs and arms flailed at (by our mother) with the fly swatter, and, for the most serious crimes, subjected to the elaborate ritual of punishment with our father's belt. You had to unzip and pull down your pants, leaving your underwear in place. My father, six foot four, would loom above as he unbuckled and swished his tooled leather cowboy belt out of his belt loops. He'd begin with the belt doubled over, but if you tried to straighten up or block the strokes with your arm, he'd become enraged and use the full length, which could mean getting hit with the buckle.

This time, shut in the next room and sobbing with fear, I heard the belt ritual escalate quickly to something more violent, with my father shouting angrily and my brother screaming with surprised pain. Even my mother was frightened, slapping her palms on the locked door and crying, "For God's sake, Hank, stop it!"

"You'll be next," I'd been told. I lay huddled, trembling, in the closed room for the next several hours, expecting my beating each time footsteps approached the door. But when my father finally came to get me, it was for dinner. "You've had your punishment," he said smugly.

We'd always played together, Randy and I, only three years apart and isolated by the frequent moves that separated us from any friends we made. This camaraderie continued for the first year or so after we'd moved to Fort Rucker; we spent long weekend days and evenings exploring the woods, or riding our bikes till late on warm summer nights. Around age thirteen, though, my brother began to turn his back on me, refusing to play board games, watch TV, or take off on bike rides with me. He assumed a Heathcliffian glamour, locked in his room at the end of the hall assembling and painting plastic models of Camaros and T-Birds for hours on end as dizzying glue fumes hung outside his door. Hank signed him up for a marksmanship course, and though he went sulkily, Randy quickly took to firing off rounds at the silhouetted torsos and brought home a trophy to prop up his paperbacks. He consumed these at a rate of two or three a day—the adult-looking Ace and Del Rey science-fiction pulps jamming his bedstead shelf, with their lurid cover illustrations of glass-domed cities and rockets, sprawling nebulae and half-clad space temptresses, and expansive titles like *The Stars Are Ours* and *The Pawns of Null-A*.

"Give me the binoculars." Linc raised the glasses again and looked closely at the approaching flight. It was coming fast, and an-

*gling down toward the stadium. He thrust his incredulity aside and
faced the facts as he saw them. They were eyes! Visible, bodiless eyes!
Revulsion and disbelief rocked through him and he got to his feet,
swallowing back sudden nausea. He watched them with an awe that
was so close to terror that he couldn't turn away. They sailed in, the
sunlight reflecting bright from their centers, their lashes closing
quickly in monstrous blinks.*

—J. Hunter Holly, *The Flying Eyes*

Even as Randy withdrew from me socially, a less visible side
of our relationship blossomed with his puberty. For this voyage
to a distant planet, he required my company. A detail swims up
at me from an old color snapshot of us seated on the ancient
daybed in his room: that blue-gray hound's-tooth fabric covering the cushions. Its exact, musty odor tightens a general memory into sharp focus, and I'm watching Randy as he straddles
one of the two long, torso-like bolsters and thrusts his hard,
scary, red dick against it. His cold, white ass flexes, low-hanging
purplish balls swinging in and out of view; harsh light from his
gooseneck desk lamp illuminates the spidery black pubic hair.
I can smell his damp privates, a smell I oughtn't to like but am
excited by unbearably. He looks around to make sure I'm
watching. I'm supposed to watch, it's doing it in front of me
that fires his excitement. He hunches faster, sucks air through
his teeth, gasps, as if in pain—shudders, then lies motionless. I
inhale the sharp odor of his sweat, the cloying smell of his co-
pious sperm.

He stands up, penis still fat and swaying. "Now you." I take
his place, rubbing my own smaller, tingling dick in the cooling
spill of his semen.

Weekends, when our parents announced a shopping trip to
the Sears in Dothan, which would mean several hours' absence,
Randy and I would both decline to go along. Shortly after the
car backed down the driveway, Randy would appear at my bedroom doorway, visible erection (boner, he'd say) showing
through his cords, a pained, half-embarrassed look on his face.
"Want to come to my room for a while?" he'd ask. He'd rush

around, closing all the venetian blinds, making sure every door was locked, shutting and locking his bedroom door behind us.

Randy didn't believe in God, and I believed in Randy. But he used a Bible to swear me to secrecy each time we had sex, placing my hand on a zippered, reeking Leatherette New Testament. "Swear on the Bible you'll never tell anyone, ever."

"I swear," I'd repeat. Later, this was streamlined to a sort of Masonic password.

"Swear?"

"I *swear.*"

First we stripped to our underwear, sometimes modeling our Jockeys twisted into Tarzan-inspired loin-pouches. Then we'd have a pillow fight; being bigger, he'd quickly pound me to crouching submission with his doubled-up pillow. His dick was swollen, angry-looking, jerking upward in front of him like some third presence in the room. I could smell his acrid sweat, the tufts of black hair in his armpits wet and flattened, and the rank odor of his icy white feet. I had an unfamiliar feeling of power or status; I might be his creature, but he put himself at my mercy by making me so. He seemed almost to avert his eyes, regretting I was witness to his naked urge. I knew that what we were doing I wanted to do, whereas he, though it was his idea, wished he did not. I loved him.

His dick drooled with precum, a long strand of it swinging from the reddish tip. He quivered with excitement—and guilt?—purposefully moving me into positions he'd meticulously sketched out in the back of a spiral notebook. I lay on my back and he squatted over me, bending forward so that our dicks bobbed in each other's faces, against nose and mouth. "Smell it," he said. The soft, damp, sticky pelt of his asshole brushed my lips. When I put out my tongue, he ordered me to stop—overt oral contact was forbidden. "That's what queers do," he said.

Sometimes I'd steal into his room when he wasn't around, to heft the drying model hot rods or browse the paperbacks. Mostly they bored me, too dense with hardware and the algebra of light-years and rocket thrust—I wasn't intelligent enough to appreciate them yet, Randy had told me—but one held my interest: *Ten from Infinity.* The cover depicted a lineup of identical green-hued, stony-faced men diminishing to the horizon. The story involved the infiltration of humankind by ten aliens in human form. I was mesmerized by a passage in which a woman unwittingly takes one of the invaders to bed and is overwhelmed by his rough, insistent lovemaking till he enters her, his penis like cold steel. He thrusts interminably, mechanically, painfully, and she realizes when she opens her eyes and sees his pupils gone flat and red: *she's fucking an alien.* Afterward, she feels as if a stake of ice has been driven through her vitals. She packs a bag and flees in terror, but later, as she stands at the airport ticket counter booking her flight, she hears a cold, uninflected voice in her head: *Put down the ticket. Pick up your bag. Come this way.* Her alien lover glares at her as he appears atop an escalator.

We'd started planning to run away during those first long treks through the miles of nearby woods. We'd seen Disney's *Swiss Family Robinson,* the Tarzan movies—and *Gilligan's Island.* Subsisting deep in the forest seemed a reasonable possibility. Back in El Paso, we'd been trapped on the infinite, flat chessboard of the hot and waterless desert; the Alabama forest seemed friendly in comparison, transforming and all-enveloping. *We'll run away* was the mantra with which, for a time, we countered each new bullying or fit of temper from our father. Probably it was never more than a game to Randy, but I believed we would do it. I was ready to pack my bags and elope with a man who had no intention of being my lover.

In the beginning, we drew up maps, floor plans for huts, and lists of provisions; later, I had to remind Randy to keep up his end of the canned goods pilfering. "When we run away . . ." I'd often start my sentences. My brother would look at me and nod absently, settling a plastic Mustang onto its chassis.

More often now he was locked in his room alone, or out with new friends from school—stealing cigars and cigarettes from the PX, staying out late and shouting back at our father, who'd

retreated from administering the belt but shook his fists and
threatened more adult violence. The motorcycle license age in
Alabama was fourteen, and after Randy conducted a long cam-
paign of begging, cajoling, and promising, our parents bought
him one. He'd disappear all day on it, meeting up with older
motorcycle-riding buddies. Occasionally, he'd take me out riding. He wouldn't allow me to ride with my arms around his
waist; instead, I had to hold on to the seat below me, terrified
of being flipped off, as I often was, when he roared away from
a stop sign. After one of these spills I'd get up, rubbing my ass
and sniffling, and refuse to climb back on. He'd roll slowly
along behind me, racing the motor, halfheartedly apologizing,
and snickering—"All right, okay, I'm sorry. Don't be such a
baby—c'mon, get back on."

His voice still broke in screaming confrontations with our father, whose only recourse now was to take away the motorcycle
keys, but to me, at eleven, he was a menacing, swaggering
teenager whose worn jean jacket exhaled tobacco and motorcycle exhaust. Summoned to his room, I lay naked on my stomach while he stretched himself on top of me, inserting his
dripping erection into the crack of my ass. With his full weight
on me and my heart pounding, I could hardly breathe. His
arms locked under my chest and his legs snaked around mine,
he'd rub up and down, thrusting between my cheeks. He'd jab
the head of his sweat-slicked cock right at the spot, always stopping just short of pushing inside. When he came, gripping me
tightly, his sticky semen flooded my asshole and ran between
my thighs.

The Big Eye seemed to hypnotize them. They pressed their noses
against the glass wall and stared at it mutely, as though somehow it
could rectify what it had done, as though, by merely stirring itself, it
could make amends for its crime.

"What have you done to us?" the staring eyes on the other side of
the glass said. "What have you done to us?"

But the monstrous apparatus was silent. It stood there, unmoved,
vast and massive and triumphant. It seemed to leer back at the white

faces malevolently, as though it were well aware of what it had done,
as though it knew the havoc it had wrought.

—Henry Ehrlich, *The Big Eye*

Our parents drove off early one Saturday on an excursion to some distant relatives; they wouldn't be returning until late evening. We were allowed to stay behind. Randy and I had often talked about just such an opportunity. "Should we do it? I've got my Christmas money. I could get my stuff ready fast," I said to my brother, following him around the house as he walked from window to window pulling blinds. Each room fell into shadow.

"What are you, an idiot? That was just kidding around. Do you seriously think we could go and live in the woods?" I followed him down the hall to his room, where he was already folding his white cords over the back of a chair. "Swear?"

"I swear." We stripped without another word. I lay across his bed, and he got on top of me and thrust his dick between my cheeks till he ejaculated.

The sporadic, drunken phone calls would come many years later—Randy bragging about his guns, his young immigrant wife: "Man, I fucked her till she couldn't walk, and I still didn't come. . . . I know what she's thinking before she even thinks it—I can control her thoughts!" Then he shot her. Both coked up at the kitchen table, a gun to swear on instead of a Bible. "Go ahead, I dare you—" she said. He's in prison now, the world shut out for twenty years and the eyeball rising each night at his window.

A cold, insistent voice says: *Pick up the phone. Call.*

I ran away, disappearing into a distant city, my exit blurred by the multitude of others headed the same way. I slept in the shelter of other men's arms, swam naked in a dangerous and thrilling sea, surfaced to find I hadn't gone far.

HANDBALL

ADAM LEVINE

In sixth grade I began a secret list of all the boys I thought were cute, and the notes after most of the names included the simple description: "Nice butt." Gary made the list after a class trip to the Bronx Zoo, during which I followed him as close as I dared while we shuffled slowly through the dark, crowded reptile house, casually bumping the back of my hand into his soft, corduroy-covered butt. Mark made the list because I imagined that his pretty round butt, clearly outlined by the tight bell-bottom pants that were fashionable in 1969, would feel as soft as his silky, long brown hair.

When we swam in a neighbor's pool, a sexy guy named Raoul wore a red, white, and blue Speedo that made the Stars and Stripes forever memorable and gave me a fetish for those butt-hugging bathing suits that persists until this day. Raoul not only made my cute-boy list, he was one of several boys about whom I wrote pornographic essays, describing what I wished to do to them or, in the case of my two best friends, what we actually did.

I did these friends separately, not together—threesomes had yet to enter my consciousness, let alone my fantasies—and what we did would barely qualify as foreplay for me today. We never kissed—of course not, we were straight; or at least they are today, if wives and children are any evidence. And though I sucked one of their dicks one time, none of us ever came. I don't know about them, but I always saved myself for later, writing up the encounter objectively, as if it were a book report for school, then jerking off while rereading it as the pornography it really was. One time—I swear this isn't just wishful thinking, or something I read in a Philip Roth novel—I really did hit the ceiling.

Back then, what inspired me to such great heights was when a naked boy, lying face-to-face on top of naked me, let me squeeze and fondle and fall in love with the feel of his musky adolescent butt.

We did it ten times total, these boys and I, and every time it somehow just happened, without words, none of us ever daring to give voice to our desires. Even in the midst of it—with warm boybreath on my neck and my sweaty, mauling hands soaking up memories as if it might be the last chance they ever had—we never said a word about how good it all felt, a shameful silence that served to cement this butt-love onto my psyche.

In the almost thirty years since then, I've managed to widen my repertoire somewhat, becoming a devoted admirer of necks and backs and balls and legs and faces and ears and, except for toes, most other parts of a man. But when I flip through a magazine or walk down the street or wander through a locker room, it's still the butts I stare at first.

Of course, I like dicks, too: how could I be gay if I didn't like a juicy hard one hanging in my face? But compared to a statuesque classical butt, most dicks look to me like dangling evolutionary afterthoughts, tending toward the primitive with their bulging veins and slithering reptilian demeanors. My favorite dicks are big, maybe because mine isn't; and maybe because I've always thought my own butt too large I prefer my partners' butts to be on the small side, pliable pairs of gluteal grapefruits that I can fit my hungry hands around. I love pawing them, prying them apart to reveal the port of entry, the manbud, which looks like a red peony bud just starting to open, the petals still tightly puckered together but the potential blossom evident to anyone who knows. In my backyard garden, ants climb the stalks of real peonies, sucking the sticky sap off the buds and helping them open up; with men, it's not ants—thank God!—but my fingers and tongue that bring them into bloom. Licking the hole of a beautiful butt—a well-washed hole, mind you; I'm not as stupid as my dick—is what I love to do most in this life. Nothing else gets me so hard, so fast.

Earlier today, at the YMCA, a sweat-soaked, luscious young man I call Handball appeared in the locker room. He's one of my favorite types: short and solidly built, with blue eyes, curly brown hair, smooth white skin, and, of course, a gorgeous round butt. As pretty as he is, he might not have seemed so special if I'd spotted him elsewhere—say, in a college locker room crowded with dozens of young bodies of equal or greater beauty. But at my gym, home base for an ever-expanding gaggle of sagging and overweight men, visitations from such well-toned beauties are a rare and much-welcome diversion.

It wasn't the first time I'd seen Handball, but the other times he had always been ten or twenty feet down the aisle, half-hidden behind flabby old bodies I'd cursed each time they'd blocked my view of him. Today, however, I hit the voyeur's jackpot: his locker was right next to mine, and though I was dressed and ready to leave when he appeared, I suddenly found other things I needed to do. I sat on the bench beside him and pretended to look for something in my gym bag, I recombed my hair several times, I reached into my pocket and counted my change—all the while stealing glances at the sweet and sweaty young thing undressing to my left.

I saw him kick off his sneakers, peel off his socks, yank his wet T-shirt over his head, then stretch his arms to the ceiling and groan. Off came his baggy gray shorts, revealing a pair of silver Lycra shorts underneath, and watching him peel that skintight fabric from his sweaty thighs reminded me of removing a condom: one moment it's stretched full of delicious firm flesh, and a moment later, its mission accomplished, it's dropped on the floor in a damp, limp heap.

Underneath the Lycra, at the core of his outfit, Handball wore a pair of sweat-soaked white Jockeys, and at this point I gave up pretending not to watch and stared at him through lowered eyes, afraid that if I turned away for even a second I might miss the unveiling. He stood still, as if girding himself for this climactic moment, which gave me time to memorize the delicious butt-curve beneath his briefs. Then he hooked his thumbs under the waistband, slid the underwear down off one leg, and with a quick, well-practiced maneuver flipped them up into the air with his other foot and caught them in his hand.

Applause! Silent but thunderous applause, for the deftness of this move, for the beauty and fullness of the white skin that lay beneath his underwear— But the show wasn't over, not yet: Handball was doing an encore! Before wrapping the little white towel around his waist and disappearing into the showers, he grabbed a liter of Evian out of his locker and, in a moment straight out of an advertisement, tilted his head back to drink. My eyes nibbled the Adam's apple that flickered on his beautiful neck, gnawed the sweaty white meat of his arms and chest, gulped at his dangling balls, and wolfed down the clenching muscles of his butt.

Bravo! I whispered. Bravo! And after tossing the empty bottle into his locker, Handball finally took a bow, bending at the waist to fish a bottle of shampoo from his gym bag, his butt cheeks parting about eight inches from my lips.

"Great butt," I say, softly but loud enough for Handball to hear, and I see his entire body stiffen as he straightens up and stares down at me. Many women have told him the same thing, I'm sure, but it seems to embarrass him to hear it from a man.

"Sorry, but I'm not gay," he says, politer than I might have been if our roles had been reversed.

"Too bad," I mutter.

"Whaddaya mean, too bad?" he asks, so sharply that all the flabby men along the aisle spin around and stare at us. Each one of them wants Handball just as much as I do, and they'd stick around for the upcoming seduction if I let them, but I wish them away and they all disappear—to the sauna and the showers, to the washroom mirrors to adjust their toupees, to the TV lounge, where they pretend to ogle *Wheel of Fortune*'s Vanna while really checking out the dirty boys in Tide commercials.

"All I mean," I explain, "is that it's too bad that God wasted such a pretty butt on a straight guy."

"I don't know what you're talking about," he says, glaring at me while he cinches the white towel tightly around his waist.

"By the way," I say, holding out my hand—knowing he won't refuse such a manly gesture, even though it comes from a man who would like to see his ass in a sling—"my name's Adam."

"I'm Handball," he says, shaking my hand and avoiding my gaze.

"Sorry if I was a little forward," I say with a shrug. "Most of the guys here aren't worth a second look. That's why I got a little carried away over you."

"Thanks," he mumbles, and then corrects himself: "I think I mean, No thanks." Against his will, a smile full of teeth as white as his skin flits across his face.

I love smiles. They make a man seem vulnerable, available. I love smiles almost as much as I love butts, and the two of them together create a synergy that makes my dick harder than either one alone. I love it, when I'm messing around in the butt of a beautiful man, if he looks over his shoulder and flashes me a smile. He doesn't even have to say a word—in fact, I prefer that he doesn't, since those overused lines we all seem to pick up from porno always sound fake to me.

I stare adoringly at Handball and tell him, "You're one of the superstars here, you know."

He snorts and shakes his head, but thinks, So that's why men follow me everywhere here. And they do: upstairs, downstairs, all around the Y. They wander in and out of the gallery whenever he plays handball, stare at him in the mirrors as he grunts though his sets in the weight room.

"Look, I got to take a shower, okay?" He seems to be asking my permission to leave, but I'm not ready to let him go. As he starts to walk away, I reach forward and rip the towel from his waist.

He turns back and glares. "Man, you are too fucking much! Give me my towel."

"Don't leave yet, handsome!"

He reaches for the towel, but I sit on it and smile.

"Just let me look at you a little longer, please?"

"What do you want from me?" he asks, throwing up his hands, his voice rising in exasperation.

"I think you know what I want."

"But I said I'm not gay!" he exclaims, wondering why I don't succumb to this irrefutable logic. He holds out his hand and says, "Come on, give it to me!"

"Ooh," I coo, "that's more like it, baby! How do you want it?"

Handball scowls, leans forward—for a kiss? could it be?—until his face is right next to mine. Then I feel his strong hands on my chest as he pushes me backward off the bench. My head resounds against a locker door, and when I look up his beautiful butt and his linen have disappeared

This script needs a rewrite, but which way should it go? I'm fifteen years older than Handball, but still, I'm bigger than he is, half a head taller and stronger, too, and if I wanted I could throw him onto the bench, have my way with him, then call the old men out of hiding and let them have him, too. Or even better yet: what if I make him a little less straight, a little more ambivalent? When he stands before me without his towel, what if he isn't angry but simply confused? Maybe he can even find it a little exciting, being desired by a new person, in a new way. . . .

"What do you want from me?" he asks, throwing up his hands, his voice rising in exasperation.

"I think you know what I want."

"But I said I'm not gay!" he exclaims, wondering why I don't succumb to this irrefutable logic.

"I never said you were—just forget the gay thing, okay?" I say. "All this is about is feeling good, and you like feeling good, right?"

"I don't know," he says, shaking his head. But as I slowly lean toward him, he doesn't back away, and his dick belies his uncertain words—pulsing, reaching out to me.

I look up into his pretty eyes and can almost read his mind: *Will it make me gay if I let this guy blow me?*

My face is a whisper away from his crotch, my exhalation rustles his pubes like a balmy breeze.

I smile and assure him, "It'll feel good, I promise."

With a long sigh and a slight shift of his hips, he moves his twitching hard-on until it almost brushes my lips—but *almost,* I know, is as far as this one will go by himself. I watch him gasp as I reach between his legs and cup his balls. I wrap my fist around his dick, lick the head, and whisper:

"Turn around."

"What?" He looks down at me, confused again.

"Turn around," I say. "I want to see your butt."

"But I thought you wanted to give me a blowjob?"

"We'll do that later. Just turn around."

"What for?"

"Just do it, okay? You'll like it, I promise."

"I don't know."

I lap at his dick again, stroke it a few more times, and then say, in my best little boy's voice:

"Please?"

He shrugs his shoulders and sighs, and I put my hands on his waist and help him, almost force him to turn. He looks over his shoulder and watches me, wide-eyed, his butt flushing pink from embarrassment, or lust, or both.

"This is what I want," I whisper.

I feel heat rising off his delicious skin, lean my cheek against his, tiny blond butt-hairs tickling my face. I see a ridge at his waist where the seam of the Lycra dug into his skin, and I nibble on its redness, tasting sweat and salt, rubbing my nose in his handball funk.

"How does it feel?" I ask him.

"Okay," he says uncertainly, and I know I need to move quickly, to go for broke before he bucks me and gallops away to the showers.

I spread his cheeks with both hands and dive into his butt-hole, nose first. He flinches in my grasp, I hear him suck in a sharp breath. His back arches as he tries simultaneously to pull away and push himself into my face.

Until this moment, all of his sexuality has been up front, centered on his dick. He can't believe that anyone would put his tongue back there, on this body part he's never seen, never even touched without first protecting his fingers with soap or toilet paper.

"How does it feel now?" I ask, as I lap like a bee at his quivering, nectar-filled flesh.

Above me I hear a hiss and his answer, barely a whisper:

"It feels great."

It feels so great that, almost against his will, he begins to wonder if other things he could do with me might also make him feel this great. He reaches back with one hand, raking his fingers across his butt, and I grab his wrist, lead his hand down the crack until his fingers flicker on his hole. Goose bumps prick his body, I hear a gasp as I guide his index finger in, half a knuckle at a time. He can't believe it goes in so easily, and like many before him, he's angry at the lifetime of lies that have kept him away from this pleasure until now; angry at the world—and then suddenly grateful, to me, for finally teaching him.

He wants to learn more, I can tell. He'll do anything I want, but I won't make him learn it all too quickly. I have a plan in mind, and for now I'm content to stick to Lesson 1: The Care and Feeding of a Butt.

I stand up, throw off my clothes, and my hard dick coils up out of my crotch like a miniature cobra—yes, I said *miniature;* I'm not ashamed of my size. In fact, since I often deal with beginners like Handball, I use it to good advantage. Sure, the virgins in porn always take monster cocks up their butts with only a momentary whimper of pain, but we all know that's not how it works in reality. As small as I am, nobody ever gets scared when I whip it out, which doesn't mean it's so small that they laugh, or that it's not big enough to make them feel good. My older brother, who is just as small as I am, taught me a line he claims our grandfather taught him: "It's not the size of the ship, it's the motion of the ocean." If I hurt my partners at all, it's not for long; my compact model needs a minimal break-in period: I slip it into gear and soon we're off and running, full throttle.

"Bend over," I say to Handball, and he does, straddling and bracing his hands on the bench, arching his back as I drill my tongue as far inside him as it can reach. My dick head whimpers for a piece of the action too, so I nuzzle it against his spit-slickened hole. He reaches back and tries to guide me inside him; to ease the way I slip my thumb in first, and he joins mine with one of his.

While we thumb-wrestle inside his butt, my free hand rifles through my gym bag, searching for the bottle of lube and three-pack of Trojans I usually keep there for encounters just like this one. In my younger days I was a trustworthy loyal helpful friendly courteous kind obedient cheerful thrifty brave clean and reverent Boy Scout whose motto, drilled in by various scoutmasters and worn proudly on my badge, was "Be Prepared." And prepared I was, especially on our many camping trips, carrying a waterproof container for matches and a flashlight with extra batteries and enough sweaters to outfit the whole troop and a special hypoallergenic pillow and my stuffed dog Dukie that to this day I sleep with—and most important, easily accessible in a side pocket of my knapsack, a small tube of Vaseline for those intimate late-night moments that every gay Scout dreams of—

But I haven't been a Scout for years, and today I find the lube but no condoms, having used all three a few days ago after I picked up a frat boy in the 7-Eleven along with a pint of Chunky Monkey that we ate in ways that would make even Ben and Jerry blush.

So I'm not going to fuck the luscious butt perched invitingly before me, but Handball doesn't seem to mind. It's all so new to him that anything we do feels fabulous (my word, not his: vocabulary comes in Lesson 2). I do put the lube to good use as I jab a three-fingered Boy Scout salute up his butt, making him sweat and tremble and moan so loudly that a few of the bolder old men come out of hiding for a look, flapping liver-spotted but surprisingly stiff hard-ons—not exactly a turn-on, and I'm

about to drive them out of my sight when I remember my Boy
Scout slogan, "Do a good turn daily," so I pass them the lube,
let them stick around and watch.

With my free hand I reach down to Handball's dick, stroke it
a few times before he bats me away.

"I don't want to come yet," he moans.

"When?" I ask.

"Soon!"

I grab him by the waist, rub my dick up and down his slippery
crack until finally I can't resist anymore: I let it slide into him,
which I know isn't right but I just tested negative and he's a virgin so we're probably safe and it feels so good that I don't last
more than four or five strokes before I have to pull out, and
just before I come I hear a voice.

"What are you doing?"

"Nothing," I say, as Handball flies away to the bedroom ceiling, hovering there like the phantom he is, watching us.

"You woke me up," Jack says.

"I'm sorry," I say, resisting the urge to wipe imaginary butt
slobber off my face.

A pause, and then he asks, "Were you jerking off?"

"Uh-huh," I admit. After nearly ten years with this man I
know not to indulge in even tiny white lies. They all come out
soiled in the wash.

"Who was it this time?" Jack asks, and though it's dark I know
he's smiling, maybe leering a bit, as I tell him, "A guy from the
gym."

"Does this one have a name?"

"I just call him Handball."

"What's he look like?" Jack asks, and I tell him.

Jack doesn't care how often I jerk off by myself as long as I
have something left for him, and in all these years that hasn't
been a problem. I do go overboard sometimes, spending hours
or even days away from home, lost in my head, but I always
come back in the end. I know where my bread is buttered, or
my butt is breaded, or my buns are kneaded, or needed—you

know what I mean. My fantasies may seem three-dimensional, especially in the moments just before I come. But I have yet to find a single one who will send me flowers or remember my birthday or cook me dinner or make our bed or do any of the many other little things that make a real man worth the work.

As I talk about Handball, I realize that Jack's right hand is in motion, stroking his dick to the beat of my story. I lean over, we kiss, and I end up straddling Jack as he lies on his back, stroking both our dicks in my slippery hand. We've done this many times before, and I know just how to hold us and the right place to rub, and it doesn't take too long before he asks me, "Are you ready?"

"Yeah," I grunt.

"When?" he asks.

"Right now!" I say, the first splurt of my Handball-primed load slapping the wall behind Jack's left shoulder, the rest of my cum, and his, splattering the hair on his stomach and chest.

I flop down on the bed beside him, in a daze. Jack goes to the bathroom to clean up, and when he returns to bed we spoon together, my face to his back, his butt to my groin, my arm across his chest.

A few hours or maybe only a few minutes later, we've rolled apart. Jack snores happily, but I'm wide awake again. I lie on my back, looking at the ceiling, and Handball drifts into view. I smile, and he floats down and stands beside the bed, a little miffed and very horny after watching what I did with Jack. He says he won't leave until we finish what I started before, and he slouches across my frontal lobe, moaning and playing with his dick.

I reach down and feel that my own dick is soft, resting, sated; and though I know it wouldn't take much to rouse it from this catnap, I decide to let it be.

To show me how badly he wants it, Handball bends over inches from my face, slips three fingers into his butt, and whispers, "Fuck me, please!"

His desire is so potent that I swear I can smell it in the air, taste it on my tongue. I swear I can feel his beautiful butt-flesh in my hands as I push him away.

"Later," I tell him. "I'm tired, I need to sleep."

"Maybe I won't be here later," he says as he slinks away to the showers. But I know it's a lie; I know he'll always be here for me, whenever I need him.

I hope that Jack will always be here for me, too.

SCHEHERAZADE OF THE DOWNSTAIRS OFFICE

PATRICK BARNES

PROLOGUE

Listen.

In the mid-late eighties, when I was still relatively new to New York, I was a waiter at a charming, airy, bistro-ish kind of place on New York's smart East Side. We were a small, happy staff, with a smaller, happier clientele and three owners, two loud and one silent; the silent partner, Brook Hanlon, was the one we, the happy staff, saw most, as he spent a large amount of time in his office downstairs next to the pay phone, which was cunningly housed in a converted confessional (the pay phone, not the office).

I was working one or two lunches each week and had to arrive at the restaurant by ten-thirty in the morning, but since I was an early riser (then), I usually got there by ten at the latest. I'd start a pot of coffee in the kitchen, take the chairs off the tables while it brewed, and then carry a cup downstairs, past the confessional, to join Brook in his cramped little office for a lazy chat. Brook was cute, shy, and soft-spoken, and I was shy and soft-spoken, and I hadn't yet learned that two shy and soft-spoken men equal trouble. In those days, I was single and dating heavily; Brook was in an on-again, off-again relationship with a remarkably handsome adman by the WASPy name of Monty Forsythe, and we both perceived the grass as greener. The thought of a comely, slim, tightly muscled, accomplished boyfriend like Monty, who wore Armani as naturally as a baby wears placenta, made me slobber. Figuratively. And the idea of

a new man every week (at least), all that *variety*, made Brook
quiver. Literally.

I

"Guess who I went out with last night," I began one morning
in the office.

"Emilio Estevez," guessed Brook, pushing aside a stack of
bills and sitting up straighter.

"Very close. David Linde." David Linde was one of our bartenders, hired while I was away on a two-month leave, a real
charmer, a man for all seasons. David had just moved to New
York from Los Angeles to be an actor/model or model/actor
or celebrity/spokesperson, and he was working as a physical
trainer, aerobics instructor, and bartender to afford a one-
bedroom on Riverside Drive. His girlfriend, who had moved
with him and worked at some sharky moneymaking sort of
thing, had just dumped him.

Brook was clearly confused. "But he's . . . Went out? Like
how, went out? Went *out* went out, or just went out?"

"I'll let you judge. Remember yesterday afternoon, David
and I were both here to get our paychecks? As we were leaving,
he asked what I had planned for the evening. I said I wasn't
doing anything, and he said we should go to a show, because he
hadn't been to any theater in town yet. So we went shopping,
we had a bite to eat, we half-priced that Bill Irwin show, and it
was short, it was over by nine-fifteen, so it was too early to call
it a night, right?"

"I'm still with you."

"So he says, 'Let's go to the eighth-floor lounge at the Mar-
riott and have a drink.' And I thought, Sure, because he's really
fun to be with. Have you ever gone out with him?"

"Uh . . . no."

"Well, he is, and we get there and the waitresses are about
ten feet tall, wearing long, tight black skirts slit up to *here*, and
they have to sort of squat to give us our drinks, and unlike most
straight guys, he doesn't fall off his chair to stare at them, he

keeps the conversation going. A real charmer, right? And the conversation motors along and he says, 'You know, my girl-friend left me because we had a fight and she walked out, so I called my friend Ricardo, and he came over to talk and ended up staying over, and she came back in the middle of the night and we were sleeping in the same bed, because he's my *friend,* and she started calling me gay and everything and walked out. Can you understand that?' Which of course I took at face value. Why not?"

"*Why* not?"

"And pretty soon it's midnight, and he's had maybe six Ab-solut martinis, up, in really big glasses, and he says, 'Look, don't take this the wrong way, but I know you're living in Brooklyn, that's really far, why don't we split a cab and you can stay over with me tonight?' And I thought, Hey, that is *such* a nice thing to do, he knows I have to work in the morning, that's really sweet. And when we get up to his place, it's an incredible one-bedroom with a view of the river and a loft bed with no lad-der. We got undressed down to our underwear—"

"What kind of underwear?" Brook interrupted.

"We were both wearing white briefs."

"Okay." He closed his eyes for a second. "Okay. And then?"

"We had to climb up onto the windowsill and jump about three feet up and over into the bed, and that's hard to do after that much drinking. He let me go first, and then when he jumped, he landed on me, and it was uncomfortable for a few seconds, but after a brief pause, he rolled over onto his side of the bed, and we just lay there for a few minutes, recovering from the exertion." I took a gulp of coffee.

"Why are you pausing here?" said Brook peevishly. "That's bad storytelling technique."

"I needed coffee. Okay, so we lie there, like I said, and I sud-denly thought, There's this big, humpy, hot straight guy lying almost naked next to me. Oh! I didn't tell you how he looked in his underwear, did I? You want to know?"

"If you're offering."

"You know how you open a Christmas box, a *big* one, and it's something you never really knew you wanted but you can't believe you have it now? That's looking at David in his underwear. His body made my sinuses open. All I can say is *chest. Stomach.* His thighs are naturally hairless, I think—not a trace of stubble. And his arms are the size of some guys' legs, but you've seen his arms, never mind."

"No, you can tell me."

"And I was thinking, How can I pass up this opportunity? But he's straight, and I never tried to get anything going with a straight guy before, and I thought back to situations like this in porno films, and remembered something, and I rolled over to him and said, 'I'm really horny, man. You wanna jack off together?' And he smiled a tiny smile on those kissy lips, and looked away, his hands at his side, and then looked back, still with this shy-little-girl smile, and I said, 'What?' and he smiled more, and then in a really quiet little voice he said, 'I'm very passive in these situations.' "

Brook was very alert. "What does *that* mean?"

"I wondered about that, too. So I thought for a little bit, and then said to myself, Why not? and grabbed his face in my hands and kissed him. With tongue."

"Did he freak out?"

"He turned into a sex animal. I have never seen anything like it before, he must've been saving it for a long while. He pulled his underwear off so fast it ripped in the seat, and while I was trying to get my shorts down he jumped on me, the whole time keeping our mouths together. And while he humped me like a bull, I kept grabbing his ass, because it's perfectly hard and very full, not a bubble butt, really, more like a Superdome butt. Etruscan burial mounds minus the grass."

"He was enthusiastic?"

"Times ten. I thought I might get hurt. I mean, that didn't worry me, but, you know. At one point, he clearly needed a rest and he sat up on top of me. His head almost hit the ceiling, but it was a well-planned loft bed, and he ran his fingers through his hair with his upper arms at a ninety-degree angle from his body, which made his biceps a religious experience. I was stunned, but I recovered enough to reach up and slide my hands down his slippery chest (from sweat, he sweated a lot), which was just as hard as his ass was. Is. His tits did not yield one millimeter! I could've been in bed with Michelangelo's David Linde. I squeezed, I pushed, I pummeled, but it was like bullets off Clark Kent. And the whole time his dick was standing at the same degree from his body as his arms and—don't interrupt, I'm about to tell you—it's probably just shy of average, according to my observations. But pretty. Very pretty, it goes with his balls very well."

"All right, I was just . . . curious, I guess," admitted Brook. "What happened next?"

"Oh . . . just more of the same, I suppose. Huffing and puffing, licking and kissing and rubbing, and then we both came at once, luckily. And he came a lot, I was drenched all over my chest and stomach, and I thought, Well, that's it, he'll roll over and sleep, and never mention it again. But no, he wanted to keep smooching—do my lips look chapped? they feel rough— and we did the same thing a few hours later after dozing a bit, and this morning of course we both had huge hangovers and he seemed embarrassed finally, which I thought he would. Straight boys. You know."

"Well . . . actually, I don't."

"Don't worry, I'm sure you will someday. As long as there is vodka in this world, there is no such thing as an entirely straight boy."

II

Brook was at a place that many mated people get to, where he felt that his spouse might not be the most interesting thing to put at the center of his life. He tried to remedy this by breaking up with Monty and getting back together, breaking up and getting back together, which is the marital equivalent of flipping the switch up and down when the lights don't come on. For me, I found that I enjoyed *telling* about my sensual escapades more than I enjoyed the actual escapading, which I enjoyed plenty. But always, toward the end of an adventure, I'd start organizing the way I would tell the tale to Brook when next I worked lunch. I became less shy and soft-spoken; since I now realized that I was providing an essential service to one of the owners, I acquired a wry and blithe persona with the customers:

"You say your sole is *ice* cold? Aren't we exaggerating just a bit, dear?"

"If madam didn't want the potatoes with madam's tuna burger, perhaps madam should have asked for no potatoes at the time madam ordered, yes?"

"Your coffee tastes like *douche water*? When have you tasted douche water before?"

And so what if I arrived at the restaurant a bit earlier each morning I worked? So what if I started finding Brook waiting and watching the door to his office instead of working like he once did? So what if I taped Brook's phone number to my refrigerator so I'd be ready any second to call him? So what if I was the first one he called if another waiter called in sick? And so what if I always came in when he called?

"Good morning, Brook."

"Hi, what have you been up to?"

"I went to see *Legs Diamond* on Wednesday."

"With anyone?"

"No, I went alone. It's terrible, you know, from the very beginning—"

"Have you had *any* dates this week?"

"It's funny you should ask," I said. "Just the other night someone I've had my eye on for a while asked me to dinner."

"Anyone I know?"

"The gentleman's identity will remain a mystery," I demurred. "Although it hardly matters as I'm sure we won't go out again."

"That bad, hmm?"

"No, no, on the contrary, great fun, but you'll see. Just wait. This guy, let's call him . . . um, Herb, okay? This Herb called and said, 'How about dinner?' At which point I restrained myself from putting the phone down my pants and said, 'Sure,' very, very casually, which is as close to hard-to-get as I can come."

"So they say—"

"Shut up, please. I met him that evening in front of his apartment building. He showed up a few minutes late, but he looked terrific. He was coming from work, and he looks amazing in a suit—have I ever told you what men in suits do to me?"

"They spank you?"

"Oh, I'm sorry. I thought I said *Shut up.* Anyway, he gave me a tired I've-been-working-all-day-and-you're-going-to-unwind-me smile, and we went up to his apartment. Nice place, a bit small, but subtle and masculine and here's the best part: no bedroom door!"

"Which is good because . . . ?"

"Because I got to watch him change out of his business clothes into his play clothes. There's a great power in being fully dressed with a guy you haven't slept with yet, and seeing him strip before you, especially when he could do it in the bathroom or around a corner but he knows that he would seem afraid of being seen naked, which is sissy-ish. A real man will be proudly and defiantly naked in front of anyone. I say. So, first off was the suit coat, onto the bed. Then the tie, ditto. He pulled his shirttails out, then bent down to slip his loafers off, unbuttoned the shirt and let it slide to the floor, so I got a good, slow revelation of his torso. Sleek? Yes, that's a good word for it, sleek. A tan waterspout. Now, at this point he could have pussied out and put on his other shirt and *then* changed pants, but no, he won my admiration by undoing the belt, unfastening the pants, pulling down the zipper, and stepping out of the pants one leg at a time, and there he was in nothing but red bikini briefs and socks. These red cotton briefs clung to his butt and basket like Saint Veronica clung to the cloth that wiped Christ's face. I use the artistic image intentionally. He didn't give me a tawdry show, lingering over a selection of jeans and shirts like some Eighth Avenue stripper—no, at a normal, neither hurried nor dawdling pace, he dressed in a very J. Crew casual kind of getup—"

"This is the first time you've told me about anyone who sounded like my type," said Brook.

"And then he went into the kitchen to mix martinis."

"Oh no. Not martinis again."

"*Yes.* Why do you suppose men need to get drunk before they let their hair down with me? Don't answer that. We had two drinks apiece, and I mean the big kind, before we even went to dinner, which luckily was just around the corner, and then we had wine there, too. I know people drink like this regularly, but I'm sure I'd be sick if I tried. I don't even remember much about the dinner itself now. I couldn't possibly tell you what I ate, my memory is a pretty thick fog up till the point we got back to . . . to . . . what's his name?"

"Herb."

"Yes, till we got back to Herb's place. Why did I pick 'Herb'? But we got back, and I *think* we even had one more martini, is that even possible? I think I remember that. And I think we were on his couch, having an indirect, desultory conversation about physical attraction and relationships when I just got tired of it all and put my glass down and got up and knelt between his legs and put my mouth on his."

"You mean you kissed him?"

"My face was a little numb to actually kiss; I just put my mouth on his. But he performed a little lip massage, and I got some feeling there again. We had one of those great, slow, quiet lip-licking-biting-sucking-slurping sessions. I played with his hair and unbuttoned his shirt so I could stroke his chest with one finger. I went lower and took his left nipple between my front teeth, very lightly, he arched his back and let out a long sigh, and I suppose that's what made me lose all control. I sort of raped him."

"I didn't know one could 'sort of' rape anyone."

"I picked him up, bodily, I just scooped him up like a groom carrying the bride over the threshold and headed for the bedroom, and he suddenly opened his eyes wide and started squirming, saying, 'No, no, no, this isn't right, stop, don't,' that sort of thing, but all the blood had rushed to my ears, so I didn't

SCHEHERAZADE OF THE DOWNSTAIRS OFFICE   131

put him down, and he was trying to hold on to the wall, trying
to grab the paint as we went toward the bed, but I got him
there, dropped him, and started pulling off his clothes. It was
a . . . a scary kind of thrilling, you know? I only had to ask a little more from my body and I got it. I was so much stronger
than him, it was almost effortless to hold him down with one
arm, and with the other pull his sweater over his head, undo his
pants and then push them down to the foot of the bed, leaving
my mouth free to bite his bare neck, his armpits, his nipples,
his stomach. I had some picture of myself as a wild animal,
crazed by blood or martinis, eating him. And then I saw,
through his underwear, that he was *hard*. He was enjoying this!
So maybe it wasn't really *rape*, but I think, looking back now,
that he was putting up a pretty genuine struggle for a while."

"Do you feel guilty?"

"I was raised Protestant—we don't feel guilt, only shame. So
I ripped his underwear off and made him lie still while I just
looked at his nakedness, touching or licking him in certain
places as I undressed. He would try to reach up to pull my
clothes off, but I would push his arms away, wanting total control. But once we were both naked, I have to confess, it was a
bit anticlimactic. He seemed tense—I mean his body was naturally very taut, he runs or swims or something—but he was
clenching a bit, which felt good at first, nice and hard, and it
went well with his hard-on, which was long and swoopy, made
me think of a knife or a machete . . . There's a lot of violent im-
agery in this story, isn't there? I don't know what I'm working
through. But as sensual as I tried to be, he stayed slightly formal. I think I was just expecting some moment when he'd go
'*Whoo-hooo!*' and throw his long legs up in the air and start
doing Liza routines or something. But it never happened. I
licked him from head to toe, and he had a nice little orgasm
and then politely jacked me off, after which we observed a
proper interval of afterglow. Afterdim? Then he said, 'You can't
stay here tonight, but you can sleep on the couch.' I tried not
to be huffy; I put on my best dignity and said, 'No, thank you,
I'm going home.' He was the one who felt guilty then, clearly

not a Protestant, objecting, 'No no no, I don't mean to throw
you out,' la la la, et cetera, and then he finally insisted on giving me cab fare, and he took me to the corner and forced
twenty dollars on me, and the cab was only ten, so I got a ten-
dollar profit out of it. Does this make me a hustler?"

"I'm not getting near that question. But I'll admit this guy
sounds like someone I'd like to meet."

I was mysterious. "It's entirely possible . . ."

"Tell me who he is."

"No, I'm going upstairs to make money for you. Good
morning."

III

Have you ever felt that you're cheating at life? That you're
playing someone you aren't? That you have to mark yourself up
so that the buyers won't think the merchandise is too cheap?

I know it's hard to believe, but I'm not addictive-compulsive.
There were nights in my life with no sex at all, nights in which
I read a book in my living room, watched a double feature at
Theatre 80, walked alone in a crowd. But after a night like that,
if I was working the next day, I would be gripped by a vibrating
apprehension when I passed through the service door to the
restaurant, a senseless dread, a swift descent of self-esteem, as
though all I had to offer in exchange for a livelihood was the
telling of true dirty stories. I never considered that maybe I
needed to feel a little *fatale*, that maybe I needed to see Brook
breathing shallowly and quickly with his tongue just peeking
through his moist lips, that maybe I was a crazed storytelling
dominatrix who wanted a world of men at my feet, listening. I
did consider that Brook was using my stories (and so, *me*) as orgasm boosters. I liked that. All right, I *needed* it. Before I'd go to
sleep, I'd thrill myself, thinking how I was making someone
come a mile away. That's a fantasy that never fades. So as determined as I might be some mornings to just sit with Brook
and chatter about a movie I'd watched, instead I'd find myself
making up some appeasingly titillating fabrication—woven

from actual events, stories told to me, obscure fiction, and pure imagination.

"You know, it's very odd, I was walking down the street night before last . . ." I trailed off, lost in thought.

"That doesn't seem odd to me, not really," Brook encouraged.

"Not that part. I heard someone behind me singing the first part of 'Rocket Man.' "

"What's that?"

"The Elton John song, remember? But it goes really, really high at the chorus. I mean, *really* high, but this guy behind me wasn't doing that part, he just kept singing the first part over and over again—you know, 'And I think it's gonna be a long, long time,' yadda yadda yadda, like that."

"Was he crazy? He sounds crazy."

"He wasn't shouting it or anything, but he wasn't just humming it to himself either. He sounded like some guy who'd had a good day and had maybe just done a bit of Ecstasy. I enjoyed listening to him, and I wanted to see what he looked like, but it would've been too obvious to turn around for a look, because I could tell that he was only a few feet behind me. At the next DON'T WALK light, I stopped, and he stopped to my right, so I looked for traffic to the left, and pretending to look for traffic to the right I looked at *him,* and he was looking right at me and smiling really big."

"Cute?"

"Very, in a scruffy kind of way. Probably around twenty-five or so, curly brown hair, sleepy eyes, perfect teeth. Little ears, which I really liked, little pink curvy-shiny ears. I've never been an ear man before."

"Did he say anything?"

"He said 'Hi . . .' in a kind of indirect, stoned way. I said 'Hi' back and we just smiled at each other for a bit and the light changed and we began to walk together, humming 'Rocket Man' in unison, and then we were at an apartment building on Washington Square after a while, which I thought was odd, again, because I thought he'd be the East Village type. You never can tell, can you? And without even discussing it, we went in and took the elevator up, just holding hands and humming, and he let us into an apartment, but I can't tell you what it was like, because he didn't turn the lights on, he kept it pitch-black and took my hand, leading me through like a blind man in a maze. I bumped into a few things, but nothing broke."

Brook was looking at me sideways, which I'd learned meant he was nervous. "You're right, this is odd."

"*This* is nothing. We got to what was his bedroom, I guess, and he lit one candle, which didn't light the whole room—it was a big room, I could tell, with tall stacks of boxes and things all along the walls. A bicycle, some lumpy stacks of fabric, what looked like a length of chain-link fence. And we sat on the floor and he showed me a bunch of pictures he'd taken of himself and a girl named Claire, who he said was his best friend. Pictures of Claire reclining in a black bra and this boy's arm reaching into the shot and pointing at her left nipple. Artsy."

"What was his name?"

"I never asked, he never told. I was thinking of him as 'Mark' by this time, he looked like a 'Mark' to me. After looking at these pictures, we started touching, fingering hair, stroking fingers, smelling. And then we began to pull at each other's clothes—he got my shirt and pants off, and I started to pull his T-shirt over his head when he turned his back to me. I got the shirt off, and he sat there for a bit with his arms folded across his chest, then he leaned back into me and whispered, 'I'm always a little shy the first time I take my shirt off . . .' And I said, 'Why? Have you had open-heart surgery?' And he sighed and nodded."

"Get out, he did not."

"No, he did. When he was eight, can you believe it? He said he'd always been sickly, with a weak heart, and after he got home after this surgery, the first thing he did was run down the steep hill behind his grandmother's house because he'd never been able to do that before. And he had a long pink scar the same color as his nipples right down the middle of his chest. I kissed it and licked it, and that's when things got weird."

"Got?"

"He gave me a pair of Lycra bike shorts and asked me to put them on, and then got the bike that was against the wall and put it on one side of the room, slid a big chair to the other side, and said, 'Okay, you're a guy biking in the park, and you get a flat tire by this bench and stop to fix it, and I've been mugged and they stole all my clothes and I'm hiding naked behind the bench and ask for your help and instead you rape me, okay?' And then he got down behind the chair."

"You like this sort of thing?"

"I'll try anything, you know that. I wheeled the bike around the room a few times, and then said, 'Shit! I've got a flat, man,' in a tough sort of voice, playing the type of biker who would rape a poor defenseless naked boy, and stopped by the chair— or bench, as it was supposed to be—and made noises like pumping a tire and stuff, and then 'Mark' whispered from behind the chair, 'Psst! Sir? Could you help me? I've been mugged and they took all my clothes.' And I said, 'Come on out here where I can see you'—very butch-daddy—'get out here, boy!' And he came out, covering himself with his hands. 'Drop those hands!' I commanded, and he did, beginning to cry, and said, 'Please, sir, don't pull on my balls or anything,' so I did. Then he snuffled, 'Please, sir, don't tie my hands together with that piece of rope you have there'—which threw me for a second because there was no rope anywhere, but I improvised with his underwear. Then he picked up a bottle of lotion and said, 'Please, sir, don't grease up my ass with that bottle of chain lubricating oil there.' And after I did that, he said, 'Oh, please, sir, please, don't fist-fuck me—' "

"Please don't tell me any more," Brook begged, leaning forward in his chair.

"Just the high points, then. After my hand had been up inside him a few minutes, he pulled away, extricating himself, and jumped onto the bed. 'That was fun!' he chirped. 'Now, do you get into balloons?' I thought he meant rubbers, he wanted me to fuck him, so I said 'Sure!' But he was being more literal than that: he got out a bag of blow-up balloons."

"What are you talking about? Like circus balloons?"

"Exactly, in assorted colors. He threw a blue one to me and said, 'Don't blow it up too fast, all right?' I stretched it out a few times, and he gasped, and I put it to my mouth and blew into it. Now, here's where it gets *really* weird—"

"Here?"

"He started moaning and writhing as he watched me blow up this balloon, like it was the hottest thing in the world. I'd let a little air out and blow some more and he would whimper. The first one got out of my hand and farted across the room, and he sort of screamed. I didn't know if it was a startled scream or an ecstatic one, but he threw me a yellow one next, and I did the same routine, blowing and letting air our, blowing and letting air out, continuously amazed at how erotic it was for him as he bucked and flailed, until I reached my saturation point. I tied off the inflated balloon, then slammed it between my hands, making it explode."

"Did he scream again?"

"Not exactly. He made a strangling sound in his throat, arched his back, thrust his pelvis up to the ceiling, and, without touching himself, shot all over the bed and the wall behind the bed, getting it in his face and hair too. I don't think I've ever seen so much cum go so far. He lay there panting and moaning and whimpering for a minute, and then opened his eyes, looked at me, and held out his arms like a little boy wanting to be picked up. So I got into bed with him and all his cum, and we fell asleep."

Brook looked confused. "When did you . . . ?"

"I didn't. It was all too odd, I didn't feel comfortable enough for an orgasm."

"But you slept there?"

"Well . . . I can sleep anywhere, you know."

"Oh." He stuck his pen in the pencil sharpener, then jerked it out. "That's some . . . tale . . ."

"But you haven't heard the best part yet!"

"What could possibly be better?" Brook seemed a bit ill.

"When I woke up, I heard this vaguely familiar voice asking,

'Do you prefer coffee or tea?' I couldn't open my eyes right away, they were crusty—"

"Please don't tell me why."

"I wasn't going to. But this voice said again, 'Do you prefer coffee or tea?' And when I looked up, I realized it was Teresa Stratas talking to me."

"The opera singer?"

"The only Teresa Stratas I know."

"What did you say?"

"I said, 'Coffee, please.' "

"But what . . . Why was *she* there?"

"She's his *mother*! And I wanted to tell her how much I loved her in *Dialogues of the Carmelites,* but her son's cum was crusted all over me, so I didn't think it was the appropriate moment, and I didn't get to see her again after I got my coffee, and 'Mark' was nowhere to be found, so I ended up just letting myself out of the apartment and walking home."

EPILOGUE

I figured that one would hold him for at least two weeks. I wasn't very good at work that day—making that much up had taken a lot out of me—but it didn't matter, because it was the last story I got to tell Brook. The next time I visited the downstairs office I had a small cold and was in a goddamned bad mood, and Brook was in a goddamned bad mood because he was broken up again with Monty Forsythe, and I just knew I'd have to make up another story. But as soon as I sat down, Brook looked sideways at me and said, "I want to ask you something."

"What?"

"That date you had with someone who you 'sort of' raped."

"Yes?"

"Tell me who it was, I can't stop wondering."

"It doesn't matter."

"No, it matters to *me*. I'm not the type who lives well with idle curiosity. It grows and grows and grows and nags and interrupts my sleep, and I need, I *need* to know."

"Okay. I'll tell you because it doesn't matter. It was Monty."

"Monty who?"

"Umm . . . your ex. Monty Forsythe?" There was a pause—not long, but longish. Brook looked at me straight on, which was so unusual I didn't know what it meant.

"And this doesn't matter *why*?"

"You weren't together, this was in June, you'd been broken up for several weeks. You were broken up, remember?"

He put his hands, palms down, on his desk and looked at the blotter. "Well . . . we weren't."

You might not believe it, but I kept my job. And from then on, Brook and I were just like two lovers who both know that the other one has cheated, but don't want to be the first to talk about it. Friendly. Wary. Dull.

That's when I started calling the sex lines.

Are you still listening?

PATRO'S REVENGE

TOM BACCHUS

Pan
Teiresias
Hermaphrodite
The Myrmidons
Apollo & Claros
Orestes & Pylades
Bacchus & Ampelus
Bacchus & Polymnus
Achilles & Patroclus
Poseidon & Pelops
Hercules & Hylas
Hercules & Iolaus
Damon & Pythias
Zeus & Ganymede
Zeus & Chrysippus
Apollo & Branchos
Apollo & Hyacinthus
Theseus & Perithous
Narcissus & Himself
Talos & Rhadamanthus
Prometheus & Hercules

It was the time I was raising Hades about the heterosexist bias of a lecturer in Greek and Roman Mythology by stapling the above flyer, black with white lettering, to every bulletin board in *that* university, where, after a certain point, I pursued the fucking degree only out of cold vengeance against those pompous asses.

It was the time I'd date a man about every two months, and even that was too much for my body and my heart. They kept making me sick in unusual and scary ways.

It was the time when, with just about all my friends with AIDS quite dead, sex, strangely, felt better than ever. It was the time when I craved uncircumcised cocks, and the beautiful hypnotic men attached to them always had Spanish accents and pot. It's the real thing: cock. Uncut men were on the vases I studied as a boy. My first porno was two thousand years old.

It was the time when I was as wrathful as Achilles, who, you know if you read your mythology, lost his lover, Patroclus.

So, in the middle of studying this, I met a guy named Patro, short for Patroclus.

He appeared to me at the COKGLU. The Castro is no longer the center of the gay universe, which has seismically shifted to the apex of Noe and Market and Sixteenth—a hexagram, a six-pointer, the Center of the Known Gay Love Universe.

Meeting someone at this crossroads is auspicious.

Through a blessing of good timing on a night that had left me, thankfully, snubbed by just about every habitué of the De-tour, and under a full moon, I met him.

Patro has the beauty of a man whom, later, you can recognize from fifty feet away and know that his smile under the black wisp of a mustache means Slow Kisses Only. He is impish, yet the way he wears his jeans has a potential . . . What is that Spanish word for a sharp gunman? *Pistolero.*

We traded numbers. Days later, I asked to meet him at the same place. COKGLU. We had dinner at Pasta Pomodore, where people wait for an hour to eat spaghetti.

After dinner, we walked up the hill to his tiny basement apartment, filled with skulls and mildew, candles and books. We smoked pot ritualistically.

I was already hooked. On him. His body was tight, smooth. Of course I adored his cock, and the way he presented it to me, in stages.

He had told me that at the gym, he boxes. He told me this while I caressed his chest with my lips and met hard muscle. He was not as flexible a man as one would hope. His muscles tightened at odd times. The threat of a punch loomed. I did not have a problem with that.

As we began to have sex, though, he transformed himself into several very different men. His face contorted into, I don't know, masks according to each position, each part of him. He could also finger my ass as if it were a pussy. As the flavor of his cock collected in my spit, I savored it, and swallowed.

He told me, afterward, that his first sexual experiences had been with his father and each of his four brothers; he told me this as if it were some casual period of family history that was not abuse, but "just experience."

He has a son back home. He sends postcards to Peru.

I loved the way he spoke and tasted.

As I had, under his instruction, sucked down the single thin joint he offered, I sucked his cock to the core. As I had let the smoke settle in my lungs, I let his cock nestle in my mouth. He pet my head and hissed Spanish curses of adoration.

We settled down to sleep, but he said his back was hurting so we would sleep on the floor. I think he was insulted when I pulled away and crawled into his bed. I think he thought I had yet to deserve his bed.

I think he was strange. I still wanted more.

In daylight, when I see him, usually at the COKGLU or from a distance at a street fair, we barely say hello.

I wrote this in my journal after our first time:

Patro is a nice guy.
Patro is excellent in bed.
Patro doesn't sleep in his bed.
Patro collects skulls.
Patro is Peruvian.

Patro is a daddy, a real one.
Patro is Italian.
Patro lives on a hill.
Patro is a coffee bean.
Patro is approaching divinity.
Patro's "weakness is men."
Patro is shy.
Patro is a vampire.
Patro is a puppy dog.

The second time, we had sex at my house. I had prepared all evening: cleaning, arranging objects I hoped would fascinate him.

While I was gulping down one end of him, he lapped at the other end of me. With a finger twirling around in my ass, his hand milking my cock as I hovered over him, he made me come too soon. I squeaked. I never squeak.

I came a bucket, lapped one glob from the valley of his sternum, and promptly fell into a state of shivering ecstasy. I mean it. Movement breaks that tingly flight where all that exists is the warmth from him, the thudding of our hearts, a squishy glue between us.

Later, he removed himself from my bed in an awkward way. He said he felt uncomfortable in my house, so he left.

Have you ever jacked off to what just happened? Weird.

Two days later, I got an infection in my penis, the discharge of which smelled of him. I thought maybe I was just allergic to smegma, that what I'd always wanted, preferred, adored, had turned on me.

Twenty-six dollars and one agonizing week of waiting for test results later, it was not gonorrhea or chlamydia. Chlamydia. Sounds like Antigone's sister.

It was "unspecified," said the health-care professional. We discussed my elusive symptoms. She wondered if it had something to do with my fears of well-we're-not-sure-if-it-is-safe sex activities.

Psychosomatic STDs?

Home, I pulled a stunt I have often done, with consistently disastrous results: I poured my rage into the phone machine of a man I could have loved just because he was a part-time jerk.

Patro returned my call, outraged that I would accuse him of spreading a disease. He vowed never to speak to me.

It was the last time I would try to open up to anybody for a long time, bodily or otherwise. Closed for the season.

Months later, another full moon.

Hours after a small herd from a fun AIDS benefit exodused to the home of a fabulous queen of our town, I realized where I was, descending rickety back stairs to see a familiar setting, but with a new entrance and way different lighting.

I ended up invited to a party that spilled into the back entrance of Patro's apartment.

I do not plan these things. People who think I do fear me.

While the first time I'd stepped out onto the porch at dawn, eating breakfast, fresh out of a shower, this time I shivered under aquatic green hot-tub lights.

Only in San Francisco can a basement flat have a yard, a hot tub, and a view.

The way Patro . . . regarded my presence from an awed distance while my bobbing hosts chatted away with him from the tub, I felt like Patrick Duffy in *The Man from Atlantis:* slightly alien, gorgeous to thousands of men, yet the object of fear and revulsion. One of a dwindlingly few men on the planet I could love forever was lost, because I, too, am a part-time jerk.

Wrapped in a towel, I shook his hand. Behind him, his apartment's windows glowed like those of a magician's cottage.

I shivered.

You have been given another chance. Don't blow it.

I memorized his cadence, his mustache, his glow. I was transfixed, bluish marble. I realized this was the last time he would ever allow me to be that close to him. But nothing would obtain his forgiveness, so I said nothing.

*   *   *

The next day, I gushed out an apologetic letter. Courier 12-point. Looks more sincere. In pouring rain, to feel even more contrite and pathetic, though I was really just impatient, I rode my bike up that hill, the swerve of Market Street, and dropped the letter in his mailbox.

I don't know why I'm so morbid now. Gods die. So do their kids.

I'm writing this at two in the morning, when I should be sleeping, because I start a new job tomorrow, interviewing men about unsafe sexual behaviors.

After finishing this story, I move on to my usual session of jacking off to pictures of Latino men. Hoods of skin fall over their penises like droopy eyelids.

Ejaculating into my cupped hand, I freeze, shiver, then bring my hand to my face, check for the traces of blood, the swirls of red in white that have begun to show up.

It smells of Patro. I lap it up. It tastes of him.

I don't care what the doctors say. I know what happened.

Achilles got it.

Patroclus won this time.

IN THIS CORNER

CHARLES FLOWERS

The first time I saw him was in the inaugural issue of *Sí*, a glossy magazine aimed at Latino readers. Fashion, language, food, music, bilingual education—all the concerns of middle- to upper-middle-class urbanites of Nuevo York, Miami, Houston, Los Angeles. And in the midst of all this culture was an eight-page spread of somebody called Oscar de la Hoya, a young boxer on the cusp of fame.

Oscar looked at me with his deep brown eyes and I felt my heart shudder: trouble. His face was pretty, with small features, lashes curling up toward his thick eyebrows. He wasn't a Tyson, some massive body of violence; he had a lean torso and a scattering of hair across his pecs, which were small but firm, human.

The first photo featured him in a deep purple satin robe, shadow-boxing an imaginary opponent, the gym outside the ring dark and moody, broken by shafts of skylight. In the next shot he wore a midnight-blue satin shirt, open to his flat belly, his face wet from a spritzing. Another shot displayed him shirtless, leaning back a bit, his face lifted toward a fan circulating the sweaty musk of the gym, his hands thrust into linen trousers. I imagined him suited up, cruising Ocean Drive in Miami, wearing sunglasses, his face inscrutable, until a sudden burst of light: his smile, a crescent of white above his unshaven chin.

Transfixed by his stare, I was disappointed to find no real text to accompany the photographs, just designer names and prices. I didn't even know then if he was really a boxer; maybe he was just a model. Surely this perfect face had never been punched, bloodied. Boxers were brutes: Rocky, Tyson, Spinks, huge, ugly mugs of sneers and sweat, streaked with cuts and swollen with bruises.

But this boy was different.

Oscar. Not the most romantic of names. The Grouch. The Odd Couple. Oscar Mayer, aha, at last a pun, Oscar's meat, a phallic lunch-punch. But *de la Hoya* is another ball game, and my mind plays with the music of all those syllables, my toya de la boya. Delicious de la Hoya. All Day de la Hoya.

Once I began to look, Oscar was everywhere. His face was plastered all over town on posters advertising an upcoming bout. I'd come up out of the subway at Times Square to find an HBO billboard with DE LA HOYA emblazoned six feet high in golden letters. His fight face—no smile, concentration defining his brow—was fierce but still stunning: the same deep brown eyes, his slicked-back hair the color of asphalt wet from rain, sleek and shiny. I wondered what his fuck face was like. Framed by the wings of my legs, would he grunt and grimace as sweat dripped from his nipples onto my chest? Or would his face remain a mystery as he bit his lower lip to keep from smiling?

Cruising by a newsstand, I stopped when I saw him on the cover of *Men's Fitness.* As the reigning Welterweight Champion of the World, he was elected "Boxer of the Year" for 1997. The article gave all his career stats (27–0, 22 knockouts), which bored me, but then I started to stiffen at a photo spread of Oscar's workout tips.

After throwing money at the cashier, I raced home to draw a hot bath, my favorite place to masturbate. Soaking in near-scalding water, I fed myself images of Oscar working out in his gym, his chest straining to lift a military press, his hands a blur as he worked the speed bag. As I licked at the sweat streaming down my biceps, I could taste the salt of his body, each bead of water wrung from his golden brown skin. I threw the magazine off to the side, then lifted my legs to my chest, clenching my knees as I sank back and down to the bottom of the tub. As I held my face up to the surface of the water, my lower back loosened, opening my ass to Oscar's liquid heat.

When I finally emerged from the bath, I found the magazine ruined, Oscar's body like mine: wrinkled and puckered in the steam. I resolved to buy another one the next day for a keepsake; in the meanwhile, though, at the end of the article I found a golden glove: *www.oscardelahoya.com.*

I logged on, dripping at my desk, and Oscar's home page flashed before me: a photo collage of Oscar, fighting, relaxing, smiling, sweating. I gorged myself with details from the interviews: a native of East Los Angeles, he was the only American boxer to win a gold medal at the 1992 Summer Games in Barcelona. Born in 1973, he lost his mother to breast cancer when he was eighteen. His father was a professional boxer in Mexico who pushed his young son to fight as early as five years old.

But a tenderness emerged that sounded all too familiar. When he first tried boxing, one of the profiles shared, he would cry and run home to hide in his room because he didn't want to fight. "A handsome young man with no steady girlfriend who is focusing all his energy on his boxing." His recipe for "Golden Blintzes" appeared in a Tito Puente celebrity cookbook. He rebuilt a run-down boxing gym in his old neighborhood, giving inner-city boys a chance at self-esteem and a career like his. And again, "A bachelor who dates often but has no steady girlfriend."

Cooks, does volunteer work, no steady girlfriend: sounds like the stories I told my family when I was in the closet.

That night I joined Team de la Hoya, his fan club, and for $39.95 and four weeks later I received a black baseball cap, a poster of Oscar dressed out in an electric-blue sweatsuit, a license-plate frame (too bad I don't drive a low-rider), and a steamy, autographed portrait of him in black and white, wearing a black satin robe, his hands gloved and held up, the hollow of his chest a dark thicket of hair.

This lasted me for a while. Soon every Latino boy I passed on the street was a stand-in for Oscar, and I'd sniff as they passed

to catch a whiff of cologne. My head would turn at every salsa
tune drifting from a passing car. Riding the subway, I'd stiffen
at the sight of a gold chain on a brown neck next to me, and I
began to wish I were a crucifix to nestle in the black, wiry bram-
ble of a Mexican boy's chest.

But it wasn't enough. I'd become a boxing junkie and a
Latinhawk. When the Blue Velvet Boxing Club opened a few
blocks from my apartment, I knew what I had to do.

I spent a couple of days walking by the plain wood storefront,
trying to glimpse the shadowy figures within. I wanted to know
what it felt like to box, to enter a ring with a man who wanted
to hurt me. What would that do to my body? Besides, Oscar had
inspired me. He'd given me an idea for a novel, an Anglo-
Latino homo thang, like a gay *West Side Story. Oscar and Charles.*
Boxer and editor. I wanted our lips locked in Latin rhythms,
our tongues to tango across our borders. How could I write a
convincing boxing novel, I rationalized, without training at a
boxing gym?

I practically fell into the place. The door was old and creaky
and jammed, so when I forced it open, I lost my balance and
stumbled into a guy who looked like a manager.

"Whoa, buddy, what's up?" he asked.

"I wanted to find out about some boxing lessons."

"You've come to the right place. I'm Geno," he said as he offered his hand and then put a brotherly arm across my shoulders. "Let me show you the place."

His arm was heavy on my neck, but sexless in a straight-guy
way, graceful and unconscious. His skin was smooth, pale olive,
his dark hair oily. He smelled like fresh-baked bread, doughy
and warm. He walked me around the ground floor, where a
boxing ring sat majestic beneath the room's single skylight.
Downstairs was a weight area, a locker room with showers,
nothing fancy.

I nodded and tried to butch it up a bit, walking stiffly and
deepening my voice, talking in monosyllables: "Cool." "Great."
"Tough." The language of the enemy.

I signed up for a three-month membership and a set of ten training sessions, beginning the next day. I walked home exhilarated and terrified. I'd never thrown a punch in my entire life.

That night, in another hot bath, I thought of Oscar and wondered if my boxing lessons might lead to a chance encounter. Maybe I'd enter an amateur boxing contest and he'd be the judge. And I'd impress him, despite my rough skills, with killer determination. My will to triumph would inspire him to take me under his wing, and he'd offer to let me work with him in his training camp. Working out with him, running trails in the woods near his camp, sparring with him alone in a dusky gym, we'd grow close. He'd mentor me with his body, and ever the willing, grateful pupil, I'd offer my heart in exchange.

When I walked into Blue Velvet the next day, my chest fluttered, like the first time I dared to enter a gay bar. Geno threw me a towel and told me to pick out a locker downstairs. Undressing felt unreal. Whenever I'm naked in a new place, I get hard. When the air hits my skin, instead of getting goose bumps I stiffen, as if at any second I'm gonna get stroked. Undressed, my body became alive, expectant, even though the locker room was deserted. The newness of the place and the rhythms of the gym above made me feel even more naked and alien.

Upstairs was sexy, disco music and testosterone pumping at equal levels. There were a couple of guys working out in the ring, their bodies aflame with speed and sweat, throwing punches in time to the George Michael tune blaring from the speakers. I kept wanting to dance, but I was afraid I would move my hips too much.

"Yo, Charlie," Geno yelled as I walked up the stairs from the locker room. "Did you bring your wraps?"

"Wraps?" I had no idea what he was talking about.

"Never mind. Here, use these." He handed me two rolls of cotton material. "This is Ness, your trainer."

Ness was big—bigger than Oscar, who's only five ten and a welterweight (147 pounds). This guy looked like Tyson, a real heavyweight. His arms were massive hammers, and his navy

T-shirt strained against his chest, the white Blue Velvet logo taut between his pecs.

"Hey, what's your name again?" he asked as Geno walked away.

"Charles."

"How 'bout I call you 'C'?"

"Sure." I thought, *Whatever*. "And you, your name . . ."

"Ness, as in Eliot."

He walked me to an empty area in front of a huge mirror that covered almost the entire wall. Off to my right was a Latino guy who looked about fifteen. He was boxing his reflection, moving and throwing punches to the beat pulsing from the speakers in the corners of the gym.

"First, you gotta warm up," Ness instructed as he led me through a series of squats and jumping jacks. Then he handed me a jump rope. "Do two rounds of rope, and then we'll put on some gloves."

My first thought was *This is the test for fags*. Ness turned away, and I looked above the mirror at the wall, where the owner had painted ALL THINGS ARE POSSIBLE. I took a deep breath and threw the rope over my head. I tried to sort of run in place and not skip to Whitney Houston, who was belting out "I'm Every Woman." I managed to keep the rope moving for about five or six rotations—with girlish double-dutch chants going through my head—before I tripped myself. Ness was talking to Geno and pointed to a ringside box with three lights—green, yellow, red. The Bell. I soon learned that The Bell runs continuously whenever the gym is open. Like a traffic cop, The Bell dictates the gym's movements: three minutes of action (green), one minute rest (red). (Yellow means thirty seconds left: better throw your punch!)

After two rounds of rope, I nodded to Ness, who sat me down and said, "Give me your hand."

I held out my right hand; he took it and then spread my fingers apart. He unfurled one of the cotton rolls Geno had given me and began to wrap my hand. It felt odd to have his big brown hand take my pale pink one and gently wrap the material—stronger than gauze, more like swaddling—between my fingers and around my wrist and across my palm. Ness explained that wrapping hands is crucial to protect the knuckles. As he wove the cloth between my fingers, stopping occasionally to test the tightness of the layers, I felt shy, as if we were on a first date.

His grip was firm but, in a way, delicate, which surprised me. He finished with my right hand and began with my left, and again, tenderness mixed with the heat I could feel coming off his body. He was preparing me, and once more he warned me about getting the wraps right: too loose, he said, and you can break your own hand throwing a punch.

Then Ness showed me how to stand like a boxer, at an angle, with my left foot planted firmly before me and my right foot skewed. You have to keep your knees slightly bent, he told me, so you can bounce easily and swerve quickly. Hold your right hand clenched and raised as if you're holding a telephone. Keep the left hand before you, as if to pound on a door. Both hands hover at eye level, ready to jab forward into the face of an opponent or to deflect a blow to the head.

"Now punch it," Ness said, holding up a padded red glove that looked like a catcher's mitt. I threw my first punch, a left, straight ahead into the red glove. *Phap*.

"Good. Again."

Another left. *Phap*.

"Good. Now give me a right."

A right hook is a harder punch, because the right hand has to travel farther across the space between two boxers in order to connect. It's a complicated move that involves turning the whole body and churning power up through the legs so that the body becomes a spring, coiled with force.

When I threw the right hook, my feet scraped the floor and my hip lurched, throwing me off my balance. I stopped midmove when I realized I had fucked up.

"Naw, man. You gotta turn, move your hip into it. Like this." Ness pantomimed the punch and raised his padded hand right to my face. "Pow," he said, "like that, turn your whole body into it. Now do it."

I repeated the punch until he said stop. I got better with each repetition. My body learned the move, my foot shifted stiffly, my hip turned, my right arm crossed the space between us, all for that connection with the red pad: *Phap*.

"Okay, C, let's do a jab, then a hook, one-two, one-two, like when you fuck."

Ness held his hands low in front of him as if he were gripping a pair of hips and gestured fucking. One-two, in-out. He grinned as he was doing this, and I couldn't believe the rawness of the move. Surrounded by men hitting leather bags or clinging sweatily to each other, he stood in the middle of it all and pretended to fuck the space in front of him. Before he could think *This white boy can't even fuck,* I started doing it too, but with my arms throwing the punches.

"That's it, C, you got it." He grinned at me. "Now let's go."

I tried to forget that I was in a room of men, that there was violence going on not only around me but inside me. I found myself bobbing to the disco beat, hypnotized by the repetition of the punches, exhausted by each endless three-minute round. And I was amazed: I was throwing punches, I was hitting Ness's padded hands, I was stalking him as he moved across the floor. I couldn't believe I was hitting something, and it felt good to connect, leather against leather, when my knuckles struck his pads hard and direct. Sweat was dripping down my forehead; so I wiped my face with my arm. My hands were clubs—I had to hit something, anybody. Ness was grinning, leading me on, trying to fake me out with his own moves. The less I thought about what I was doing, the better I got.

Maybe that's what I was after: a body that worked without thinking, without remembering what to do, a muscle moving through space. I tried to imagine the two of us circling each other in bed. Who would top? Who would bottom? Already I felt how boxing becomes sex, the heat of two men moving in need, thrusting and sparring, arms locked in embrace—how in that haze of muscle and sweat, everything else drops away, the two bodies the only reality.

But I couldn't block out the surroundings: the weighted

bags, the mirrors, and, especially, the other boxers as they moved through their workouts. Mostly black or Latino, they were young, fierce, and focused, pounding the heavy bags or sparring with partners. As Ness and I wove across the floor, we brushed against punching bags and sleek, wet bodies. I leaned into their heat, shimmering like a horizon all around me. I'd glide against a sweaty black arm or bump up against a brown leather bag, my sweat leaving a trail across the room.

By the fourth or fifth round, I was totally drenched with sweat. During a rest minute, Ness got a water bottle from a cooler by the ring. I started to take the bottle from him, but he gestured for me to lean back and open my mouth. He shot the water into my mouth, then all over my face. He squirted more than I could swallow, and the water washed over my chin and down my chest. I dropped my head and he continued to pour the cool water over me, soaking my head, as I stared down at the drops hitting the floor.

"Awright, man, that's it for today."

He led me through a cool-down of push-ups, crunches, and squats, and I did as he commanded, counting under my breath, silent and sweating, doing whatever he said.

Downstairs, alone again in the locker room, I sat on the single bench and felt the blood rush through my body. I stripped and stood in front of the floor-to-ceiling mirror. I was dripping with sweat, and my limbs were pink and bright. I grabbed my right biceps and was surprised at its hardness. Is this what "pumped" felt like? I felt leaner, meaner, and I wondered what Oscar would have thought of my body. Did I have what it takes to be a fighter? Was my body a weapon? What things could it do?

As I entered the shower, I could hear the music from upstairs, the clear note of The Bell every three minutes. And I imagined Ness up there, working on another boy, turning him into a man, a machine of muscle and speed. Maybe it was all about contact, the touching, the way Geno draped his thick arm around my neck, the way Ness wrapped my hands, then showed me how he fucked. Maybe what I wanted from Oscar was his touch, the pummeling he could offer—what touching him, even in violence, would mean for me.

The water was hot, adding to the heat of my body as the blood stayed near the surface of the skin. I lathered my chest with soap, then foamed up my groin. I was hard, my balls as tight as the speed bag upstairs, which I imagined a Latino boy pumping with his fists. I started to jerk off, my rhythm copied from the boxers I had watched, one-two, one-two, finding a rhythm and letting my body take over.

When the bell sounds, Oscar approaches me from across the ring, the EVERLAST of his red satin shorts all I can focus on. I can't look at those eyes yet, but I can see his red gloves hovering before me. I take a defensive stance, then begin circling him. He throws a left jab, which I block, and his lips protrude over his mouthpiece, like a child pouting. My hook catches him off guard, my glove grazing his chin. His hairy chest damp with sweat, he moves closer, and I back away. He follows me as I dodge his punches, trying to gauge how long I can last before he hits me again.

Backed into the corner of the shower, all I hear is the slap of leather against muscle—hard, then gone. My first curls around my shaft, one-two, one-two. I back away, but he's there, leaning into me, dancing me into the corner, where I'm all his, and I bite into my lips to draw blood to spit in his eyes. I can see his fists coming at me, and I want to break that smile that's haunted me. His hands are on my ass, spreading my cheeks apart as he plunges all the way into me. His strokes are hard and quick, and he leans into the spray to kiss me. He pumps harder, never taking his mouth from mine. We breathe like swimmers, gasping whenever our tongues break the surface of the water pouring over us.

As he fucks me harder, my cock swells. Pinned to the tile, I'm up against the ropes, and he continues to pump me harder and harder. I hold my arms up to defend myself, against his chest crushing me, and I am stroking faster and his look is fierce, his brown legs spread wide as he squats and rises, drilling me into the corner. His right hook against my thigh, his left jab pounding my pec, I'm twisting against his blows and the sweat blinds me, his face a blur, water and salt and hair against my lips. His voice comes from the water, *Sí, ahora, sí, ahora,* and he bites his lower lip, his perfect shining white teeth like a tourniquet he loosens, releasing his jism into me. When I shoot, the cum hits his chin, but before he can lick it away, the water rinses him clean. He opens his mouth like he's about to sing, and what comes out is the language of men fucking men: syllables wet with heat, a cry opening into water.

Upstairs, there were new faces as I moved toward the door. Pulling my sweatshirt over my head, I almost ran into a young Oscar, maybe eighteen. He was warming up, stretching, throwing a few punches at a bag, and he looked at me from the corner of his eye. If we had been in a gay bar, I'd have considered it a cruise, but in this place of sweat and leather and muscle, it was more a leer of competition, checking me out. Am I tough enough? Am I tougher than he is? I wondered what would happen if we stepped into the ring together: who would throw the first punch, who would be left standing, who, perhaps, knocked cold.

HARDWICK

DEKE PHELPS

Ah, the bliss of the pumped, muscular body.

Back when Arnold Schwarzenegger, already dubbed the Austrian Oak, was the leader of the pack at Southern California's venerable Gold's Gym and on the verge of becoming bodybuilding's predominant icon, he titillatingly joked to Charles Gaines and George Butler for their 1974 book, *Pumping Iron,* that "sometimes . . . a good pump is better than coming."

And although the great Ahnawld is now a mega-Hollywood star with the added glamour of being married to a Kennedy, such is his enduring influence among bodybuilders worldwide that his boast, bereft of its tempering modifier and intended humor, is still reverentially repeated by many of them as a sacred truth.

Of course the Oak was talking about *getting* a good pump, and for all I know his remark may reflect reality for those driven true believers. I couldn't say. You see, I'm nothing more than a camp follower to the pumping-iron brethren and thus don't know how the rush of a muscle-engorging pump actually feels. But I know very well that for me and my fellow muscle sluts, the worshipful rite of *seeing* a handsome ironman peaked at full pump, especially when he's nude, can surely be a transcendent thrill surpassing even that of orgasm.

Whether we're the brothers masterfully getting or their acolytes slavishly seeing, however, we're all united in devotion to pumped muscularity, the divinity incarnate enshrined in the sanctuary of bodybuilding. Never mind my ilk's routine con-

signment to rear pews while the closeted faithful are inter-
spersed at the front of the nave and among the contest-ready
priests leading the congregation's liturgy of praise and suppli-
cation from the elevated chancel. The Word made flesh for all
of us, to be specific about the essence of our devotion, is that
transfixing wonder for which the muscular body intensified
with a pump is implicitly a metaphor: a big, throbbing phallus.

But given the ingrained blue-collar stereotypes and hetero
essentiality common to bodybuilders, the majority of them
would probably scorn this signifying as smart-alecky fag talk
from a four-eyed pencil-neck who's read more books than are
good for him. And as I have ample reason to know, the most
vindictive would be the largish silent minority who are at least
experimentally bi.

Think I'm kidding? Nosiree, not by a long shot.

Witness the numerous professional pumpers who compete
in the Mr. Olympia contest and other bod matches with cash
prizes who also star on the elite gay international hustling cir-
cuit, leaving their wives and girlfriends at home; and the lesser
champs who show up in *Advocate* and *Frontiers* "escort" classi-
fieds with faces cropped from their photos; and the allegedly
straight muscle hunks increasingly side-stepping into gay video
porn after contest spotlights have dimmed for them. (Ever
watched *The Wild Ones,* featuring Bull Stanton, the cloaking
name for a former national heavyweight-class winner? If not, I
highly recommend it.)

But despite these stellar examples of fluid sexuality within
muscledom, the bodybuilding magazines have erected a wall of
silence around the realm's gay aspects that remains virtually
uncracked—except, most notably, for lip-smacking innuendo
in their gossip columns when those establishment mouthpieces
want to get rid of a brother who, once his gay bent becomes
known beyond the realm's cocoon, is deemed to be no longer
a selling attraction.

I know this, because I was once a writer for all of muscledom's
magazines. Having watched them destroy reputations, I know all
about their smarmy antigay tactics. But I also watched drop-dead-

gorgeous Bob Paris become a favorite coverman even though the magazine publishers, editors, and staffs were aware he was gay. And I watched a hot duo of mag faves put on a smooching and lap-sitting show (at a party following a national contest one of the macho beauties had just won) while their wives, attending judges, and other journalists turned their heads.

Bob Paris, regardless of his Mr. America and World Body-building Championships (Mr. Universe) wins, lost his high standing when he finally outed himself. But the less forthright twosome, lionized as "family men" and "lady-killers," graduated to pro stardom, countless more covers, and celebrity among gay men, closeted or otherwise, who worship muscle.

To be candid, I was one of those worshipers (and I know my competition!). Soon after the future national champ's smash-ing debut on the contest trail, I interviewed him and detected that although married with toddlers, he was somewhat more than "gay-tolerant." And when the interview appeared in print, he told me I was right-on by sending me a photo of himself, quite cordially signed, "To my buddy and favorite writer, you can worship me anytime you want to!" So at his next contest (from which wifey stayed home with the kids), I invited him to my hotel room and did just that, to our mutual delight.

Ironically, that night of rapture nudged my fall and eventual banishment from bodybuilding's sanctum sanctorum. As the massive hunk and I stepped into the hotel elevator the next morning, we ran into a judge from the contest. And while the judge chatted up my dominator with schoolgirlish flattery, he gave me only an icy stare. Unbeknownst to me, I had been pegged by him and his peers on a governing board of inquisi-tors as a candidate for the next round of periodic purges to re-move publicly revealed queers from their fiefdom.

If I had been on my toes, I would have seen I was in danger; their self-protective homophobic vengeance was not exactly a secret. But this was the early eighties, and still under the liber-ating influence of Stonewall, I preferred to think that their star chambers had been left in the past. Of course they hadn't (and, if less blatant now, still haven't). In addition to my work for

bodybuilding magazines, I was writing under the same byline
for many gay publications. This moonlighting hadn't gone unnoticed by the inquisitors. To them, it simply validated the ru-
mors I had sparked when I'd offered financial help to a
superbly structured young Adonis preparing for his first major
contest, an offer he confided to the owner of the gym where he
trained.

But although my generosity had no strings attached (honest!), the gym owner, who was also a national judge, assumed it
did and relayed his assumption to the board—for which I also
have only myself to blame. A former competitor who had managed to win a few leading amateur titles but sank as a pro, this
gym owner and I had had a tawdry, mutually frustrating tryst
when he was sexually adventuring in his pre-wife-and-children
days. Later, from a closeted buddy employed in his gym, I
heard he had posted a "no queers" policy.

Nevertheless, my buddy told me that the gym owner showed
obvious favoritism to delectable dudes and bragged he had
"the best looking lifters" of all the gyms in town. That, together
with the disgruntled/guilty memory of tricking with me, most
likely aroused his fear that I was moving in on the turf where
he was cock of the walk. And to capsule a long, sordid story, the
rumor he spread, supported by the so-called evidence of the elevator scene (termed "compromising" in the letter of censure
I received) and my appearance in gay magazines, resulted in
my being shorn of bodybuilding press credentials, forced to
stop the sanctioned newsletter I published for bodybuilders in
my home region, and removed from the roster of accredited
judges.

Kind of puts a weird twist on the all-in-the-family ideal, eh?
Yes indeed, bodybuilding tolerates many sexualities intramu-
rally. But woe be unto the queer (or even queer-friendly) in-
sider who crosses the line and is thereby judged to mar the 110
percent heterosexual image the realm's self-perpetuating pa-
triarchy so assiduously guards.

In spite of my official black-sheep status, however, I still have
many friends and playmates inside muscledom, so I better shut

up and not test their patience any further. Frankly, I couldn't bear to lose the access I've somehow maintained for my furtive servicing of the brotherhood. If word got out among them that I'm a sissified snitch, they might shun me altogether.

On second thought, maybe I'm being a nervous Nellie needlessly, since—with few exceptions—the brothers read only their fan mail and the muscle mags. Moreover, judging from the buddy-to-buddy phone calls and contest-time solicitations I still get on a regular basis, it seems my reputation remains intact. Not to preen, but I'm greatly respected for my ability to empower bodybuilders—from beginning amateurs to polished pros—with a competitive mental edge by convincing them that without doubt they are indeed supermen in every way.

In fact, I'm proud as hell that for the past few years a top Mr. Olympia contender has summoned me to his hotel room on the night before bodybuilding's biggest annual event to review his posing routine (another of my perfected services) and boost his conquering spirit. Sure, we both know this is a quid-pro-quo arrangement. But we each profit from the deal—he with a supremely confident mind-set, me with the year's most soul-shattering fuck—and what's wrong with that? In any case, that night is the highlight of my year, as well as the only time this superstud and I get together except by occasional phone hookups.

There are other times, with less sublime brothers, that are almost as rewarding, however. And I'm damn proud too that they continue to come to me for the unrivaled (or so I'm often told) jollies I offer, of which nude exhibition with nothing beyond my verbal praise is superseded in demand only by, in ascending order of popularity, my solicitation of a hard, stern fuck from a dirty-talking top man, ravishing him with my apparently famous blowjob, and kneeling in homage to lordly masculinity while gazing at his stripped, flexing body and bringing myself to climax.

Now, I'd be lying if I denied that monetary transaction ever takes place during these twilight devotionals. But, in truth, that seldom happens; outright hustlers learned long ago that more

fertile fields to plow lay elsewhere. The salient fact is that regardless of the form of worship the brothers seek from me, the
main thing they want is my validating adulation. (I ought to sue
the goddamned Army. No disrespect, sirs, but "Be all that you
can be" was one of my choice psyching-up litanies before you
soldier men spun it as a recruiting jingle.)

And believe it or not, the orgasm I sometimes help the brothers muster is in most cases merely a bonus for them. In this way
we're sort of soul mates, since bringing off my own Big O is
secondary to giving pleasure in the acting out of my faith. Nevertheless, I'm well aware by now that anything beyond a slam-
bam, thank-you-Sam relationship with them is rarely going to
happen. And the holy nights with my Olympian master anoint
me with revelations of heaven unlikely at my age (even if I'm
not *that* old) to come again.

Even taking into account the unpleasantness bodybuilding's
officials inflicted upon me, I'm truly blessed in another way
too. While most of the brothers even now will give me only a
standoffish glance when they know establishment loyalists are
watching, this coolness is directly opposite to the heat we continue to generate together in private. To retain this confiden-
tial intimacy is a reassuring triumph and has freed me to
pursue without qualms what was always my primary interest in
bodybuilding anyway. Indeed, ever since my worship of the
brothers was cut loose from its essentially extraneous professional involvements and distilled into unadulterated sex, I've
been sitting in the catbird seat.

I can't explain more than superficially why a literary and artis-
tically inclined queer like me became so immersed in a hereto-
fore subterranean brand of quasi athleticism that, although it
was recently legitimized as a sport by the International Olympic
Committee, has historically (quoting again from Gaines and Butler) "advertised itself with consummate tackiness." Still, I'm certain I was headed that way from birth: my childhood scrapbook
is filled with my drawings of muscular cowboys and other studly
types, pictures of hulking Samsons clipped from Bible story
books, and cutouts of hunky movie stars.

Some time ago I interviewed a novelist who's also a well-known boxing fan, and when I asked him about his passion for pugilism, I was struck by his answer. "I don't know what's in my psyche that draws me to a sport called brutal," he said. "Nor can I defend boxing. I can only say I enjoy watching it and associating with boxers and sometimes writing about it."

Notwithstanding its nasty politics and admittedly bothersome underground traffic in anabolic drugs, that's what bodybuilding is for me—an unapologetic source of abiding personal pleasure. Indeed, a new world was opened to me when, after tiring of the campily coy little physique mags stealthily ordered by mail, I discovered the bodybuilding magazines sold at newsstands. And heeding the wise advise of the celebrated mythologist Joseph Campbell to "follow your bliss," I decided in the first of my coming-outs to go for it, a quest I've pursued diligently ever since.

But there's something more that you must also know about me. When I first headed out for the Promised Land, my first major heartthrob from afar was Mike Mentzer, a Mr. Universe who was expected to succeed Arnold as the next Mr. Olympia. Unfortunately that didn't happen, but, more happily, Mentzer and I eventually became semi-buddies (if not of the sexual sort I longed for), and later he asked me to write for a training magazine he edited. In addition, I helped publicize a bodybuilding guide he authored for a major New York publisher and showcased him as a guest poser at the state championships I promoted.

Those highlights from our association, though, are superflous to the reason I've introduced him in my confessional. I really brought him up because ever since I laid eyes on him in his prime, his spellbinding combination of darkly mustachioed facial beauty, exquisitely defined and shapely legs, and overall conformity of aesthetically developed muscularity has been my masculine ideal.

(And no, in case you're wondering, my lordly once-a-year Olympian bears no resemblence to Mentzer. But he so powerfully personifies another archetype of muscular manliness that when I'm with him, Mentzer is blotted from my mind. I'm not *that* picky.)

Thus, throughout the two decades since Mentzer's heyday as a popular superstar, I've searched contest lineups and muscle magazines for look-alikes. And just when I was beginning to think my mission was in vain, I not only found a near duplicate but was rewarded with the added serendipity of seeing him announced relatively soon thereafter as the newest addition to Colt Studio's corral of exuberantly masculine dreamboats.

The virtual reincarnation of my ideal man, who'd previously gone by his real name (which I won't divulge), was identified now as Carl Hardwick. And as if I needed an extra inducement to immediately call in my order for photographer Rip Colt's debut photo sets of him, the announcement brochure pictured him tantalizingly nude—a state in which I was never lucky enough to see his prototype. If you think I had the feeling that at long last my cup had runneth over, you're absolutely right.

Just as some folks never forget when they got the news of the John Kennedy or Martin Luther King assassinations, the arrival of those two photo sets was a landmark in my life. Mercifully, it was raining that day and I was wearing a trench coat, so I didn't embarrass myself with the erection I sprang when I removed the Colt packet from my post-office box and impatiently opened it. There he was, in wonderfully tactile color, at the pinnacle of his Mentzer-like competitive shape, and, as promised, anchored by a long thick dick that was hardened in some photos and flaccid in others but in all truly staggering.

Double mercifully, I live near my P.O., so I was back home shortly, my prick still pronged, and intent on taking a much longer look despite a pressing deadline. Rushing to my bedroom while awkwardly whipping off my clothes, I aligned the twelve dazzlers in two equal rows at the edge of the bed, knelt to seal each with a consummating kiss, and, with my lusty eyes roving over them, jacked out a climax of an intensity the brothers would cite as "totally awesome!"

Unsurprisingly, Mr. Carl swiftly became Colt's most popular model, a top-stud status he's maintained ever since then. Following his introduction as a prime-time bodybuilder shaved of his luxuriant body hair, he's gone on to star as an unshaved bear in the woods and, more recently, a bestubbled and lesser (but still amply) muscled leather daddy chomping a cigar on the cover of a magazine fittingly titled *Fantasy Men!* And in fealty to his commanding magnificence, I've amassed Colt's entire Hardwick line of photo sets, slides, magazines, calendars, greeting cards, and videos. Hell, I've watched his two solo videos in the studio's Legendary Bodies series so constantly that I'm now on my second pair of tapes after wearing out the first.

Oh dear, I can hear the twitters: another poor schmuck who's fallen hard for glamorized images of a stunner he could never hope to meet in the real world. Sorry, guys; I'm a slut, not a fool. Not only have he and I met at regional and national contests, but we had some very friendly phone chats just prior to his discovery by Colt.

Furthermore, although a pal of mine at gay-oriented Colt swears Mr. Carl is not himself gay (and I've never discerned that he was during the times I've basked in his presence), I was almost certain when we talked long-distance from the gym he manages that he intuited I was gay and precisely why I was calling. But that didn't seem to be a problem for him, since when I called initially and reminded him we'd met through mutual friends at his latest contests, he began by saying in his oh-so-sexy, cowboyish voice that it was terrific of me to remember him.

And as is usually the case with bodybuilders, he relished talking about himself. So with me supplying leading questions, he told me on those occasions about his training, a part-time construction job roofing houses, a young daughter he was smitten with, upcoming contests for couples he and his bodybuilder wife were considering, and his own contest plans. In other words, I came to know him fairly well, thanks to AT&T, and was totally captivated in the process.

If I was then on the brink of being swept off my feet by his ballsy great looks and bod, the clincher was his wry humor and aural seductiveness. Neither did it take long to confirm my hunch from watching him in action on contest stages that he was self-assuredly at ease with his spectacular manliness and needed none of my "Be all that you can be" coaxing. But my trickster's bag holds other devices to get what I want, and during one call I got so horny that I deviously prompted him with a convoluted question, then muffled the phone mouthpiece and, with my free hand, jerked off as he cooperatively strung out his answer.

Giving no indication he suspected what I was doing, he ended this most memorable of our connections by urging a return call anytime I wanted. No doubt he sincerely meant it, because the next day he sent me two photographs: one, a modeling portfolio–type image, was inscribed "To my body-building buddy and greatest fan, in appreciation of your kindest support," and the other, a standard bodybuilding pose, "To my best fan, with thanks for your loyalty and belief in me as a Top Man." Aha, he *had* pierced my subterfuge and exactingly plumbed the heart of my attraction!

Thus began my enduring obsession, a life force for me that burst into full bloom when I received his initial photo sets from Colt and has flourished ever since. So, Mr. Carl, if by chance you read this, sir, please know that while I'll go on pleasuring the brothers who seek me out—and can't give up my Olympian until he no longer has any use for me—thine is the kingdom, the power, and the glory I worship most devotedly, world without end. Amen.

FIELD OF VISION

STEPHEN GRECO

All I know is what I can see, so let me start by describing the apartment.

"C'mon in and watch your head," Jack said. "Can I ask you to take off your shoes?"

Ducking under the low stoop of the nondescript, turn-of-the-century building in New York's West Village, I entered a front room that apparently serves as both gym and art gallery. I dropped my jacket on a bench-press machine and perched on a Donghia side chair to remove my sneakers. On the opposite wall hung a series of cheesy, Russian icon-like paintings of naked men, each in its own pin spotlight. The whole place was so dark that it took a moment to figure out that both floor and walls were covered in industrial gray carpeting. Gray, black, and silver were the predominant tones: the rack of iron dumbbells, the stripped steel physician's cabinet, the mountain bike stowed on a wall mount. None of this was exactly decor news.

Jack gave me the tour. A long hallway led past the bathroom to the living room at the back of the house, which gave onto a large yard with statuary that I could see, even in the fading late-afternoon February light, included quite a few startlingly priapic figures.

"The garden looks better in the summer," Jack said—a hostly apology doubling as a reminder to stop peeking through the blinds and pay attention. He was telling me where in India he had found the stone lingam displayed in a glitzy, mirrored, circular niche, also spotlighted. My God, I realized, it's just as he promised on the phone: there are cocks everywhere. But if part of me was wondering whether this man could be a little crazy—the sum total of my experience with him amounted to one chat session on America Online, three e-mails, plus the phone call—I realized that he was obviously so house-proud that there was no question of mucking things up with body fluids leaking out of a drugged or murdered visitor. Everything here was scrupulously maintained, not at all like some of the makeshift, spare-room dungeons I've seen that could pass for crime scenes.

On one side of the living room were a few pieces of contemporary black leather furniture arranged around a giant video screen in what some shelter magazines call "a conversation group." On the other side, where anyone else would have put a dining table, Jack had a large, black vinyl-padded massage table neatly punctuated with two holes—one where your face would go, if you were lying facedown on it, and the other for your cock. I noticed that the table had been prepared with a fresh, folded, black terry-cloth towel near the upper hole.

"I keep the smaller equipment here," Jack said, dramatically throwing open a set of louvered doors to reveal a walk-in toy closet custom-fitted with shelves, racks, and pull-out bins of dildoes and butt-plugs; lubricants and oils; condoms and latex gloves; straps, harnesses, cuffs, clamps, chains, rings, ropes, and other necessities. Beyond, through the galley kitchen and spare, tiny bedroom (the door between which featured another glory hole), was the office. His appointment book sat open on the desk, with a dozen or so names penned in for the week. (And there I was, down for Sunday at five.) The computer screen was flashing pictures of cocks, both naked and in various stages of bondage.

Though I found the design of the place downright tacky and old-fashioned, I did think it interesting how the residential aspect blended seamlessly with the commercial—or should I say blended *shamelessly,* since in addition to the lucrative consulting position he holds with a German corporation, Jack uses his place as the site of a discreet body-grooming business. He shaves and trims some of the city's most pubically public men.

"I started the practice because I love playing with cock in a very focused way," he explained. "And I only like being with guys who are also obsessed with their cocks—hustlers, porn stars, party boys, professional masters, et cetera. I have those guys coming over here all the time now. I hardly have to go out anymore, which is okay because I hate bars and the whole late-night thing. I have to be up early to talk with London, but by afternoon their business day is over, so I'm done and have the rest of my day."

He chuckled.

"My friends call me cock-crazy. And I agree with them."

I'd asked Jack if I could see his place because I was scouting. Having written for *Elle Decor* and *Casa Vogue,* I'd been asked by the editor of a gay style magazine to do a series on people who work at home. Jack's was the first place I had looked at. But as we sat there in his office, talking about his "practice," the idea of my writing about the place as design seemed pretty much out of the question. This is a boys' clubhouse, I remember thinking; I won't have anything to say about it. An author I knew uptown had a "Louis Louis" showplace that would make a much easier assignment.

But I said that I'd have a drink before going.

"This way," Jack said.

He made a point of showing me the bathroom again. This time I went in. There was the usual sink, commode, and tub. Then I noticed that off to the left, beyond a glass door etched with mermen, was a slate-tiled steam room large enough to seat eight.

In the living room, Jack poured me a vodka and settled into a chair opposite me. A fiftyish guy with hair too long and wavy for its thinness, he was not particularly hot by my standards, but he seemed nice enough. He was dressed for sex the way men his age do if they haven't kept up with trends in sexwear: in gray sweatpants and a plaid sleeveless shirt. I'd met Jack through another guy I know from AOL—a Philadelphian with a mammoth, tattooed penis that Jack assured me is famous.

I knew a little bit about Jack's obsession, because, for one thing, he had mentioned that in his spare time he was writing "a cock-worship Hagaddah," a user-friendly pamphlet with step-by-step instructions and commentary, for use among small groups of like-minded men. But I hadn't realized how persuasive exposure to his obsession might be. As I sat there on that leather couch, growing more relaxed, I think it was the fact that all those hustlers and porn stars had been there before me that produced a palpable pulse between my legs—the idea that their asses had dented the leather seat that my ass now occupied, that their freshly shaved balls had rested, or hung, or bounced, in the space where mine were now. It was funny to think that I could be seduced as much by the house as the man, yet the more I looked around at the glory holes and custom-made equipment, I couldn't help fixating on the point of it all: penis traffic.

I pulled off my jeans and started fondling myself. He came over and settled on his knees in front of me. With a smile meant to encourage me to lean back, he began handling me appreciatively, apparently by way of overview, to get the weight and density of the thing. Then he began licking and sucking, sometimes stopping simply to look at it and beam, sometimes giving voice to some inner, spiritual laughter.

A few minutes later he rose and suggested we move to the table. I mounted it facedown—rather, with my face to one side, cradled by the towel; my cock hanging through, feeling not so much hard as full. Jack got underneath and seated himself in some way I couldn't observe. After some adjustments he was sucking again contentedly. Half an hour earlier I might have been tempted to ask if he knew whether it was Louis XIV or Louis XV who had commissioned a special *chaise d'amour* to be built for a certain royal act. Now, though, I was silent, except for a low, intermittent moan.

It occurred to me after a while that I wanted to be looking at something. Pornography, maybe. There was that big, empty video screen and, nearby, a videocam on a tripod.

"Uh, would it be possible for me to watch somehow while you do that?"

"Why not?" Jack said after a second or two. He emerged from under the table. "It'll just take a second to set up."

Moments later, Jack was back down below and I was watching myself star in an impromptu porno movie. This was kind of a dream come true for me, because one of my favorite porn movies is a seventies opus in which a guy named Tom sucks an endless succession of great-looking cocks presented through a plywood glory hole. There's something about the film's tight, unvarying focus that makes it easy for me to project myself into it as the guy being sucked, which always amps the feeling of connection with my own cock. Now it *was* my cock in front of me, and I was decidedly connected. Though I have always liked my cock, seeing it up there on the screen for the first time made me unexpectedly gaga for it—in love with its beauty, proud of its performance, desperate to please it.

"All those photos on the computer—you took them all?" I asked when we took a break.

"Sure did," he said. "You wanna see yours?"

At the computer, Jack prepared my stills and displayed them on the screen. Nearby was a stack of zip discs, all labeled with men's names and hometowns: John from Dallas; Henry from Boston; Tom, Ray, and Paco from New York; Sammy who had just moved to Florida from Connecticut; several Steves whom I would now join. Many of the photos looked like portfolio shots, advertising his trimming business, about which he told me more.

"I don't need the money," Jack said. "But when guys are paying for it, they'll sit still longer and be more passive. Even though I call what I do 'service,' I work from a top energy. I really like when guys let me take control of the worshiping process, especially when I get into bondage with straps and rope."

He paused.

"I could do you, if you want," he said, scrutinizing my crotch.

"You mean . . . a trim?" It took me a moment to understand that my weekly, self-administered ball shave might be horribly inept by professional standards.

"C'mon. Let's see what we can do."

He showed me back to the living room couch, dimming the

lights as we entered the room. As I sat back, I discovered there was a pin spot above, aimed to highlight a client's pubic area like the site of a miniature formal drama.

"I'd bring that trim line down a bit closer to the shaft," he said expertly, pressing the shaft down, then moving it from side to side, fluffing the hair a bit. "And I'd definitely take down some of this volume." He disappeared for a moment and came back with a pile of towels and a slender, cordless beard clipper. Chattering like a small-town beautician about other clients, he knelt down and began swiping away at the hair above my cock, between my legs, and under my balls, pausing occasionally to brush it away lightly with his fingers or blow it away with little puffs of air.

"Of course, whenever Morrie's in town"—the guy from Philadelphia—"I invite a few people over to watch me groom him. It turns into quite a little scene. Sometimes we all go out for Thai food afterward. Morrie's a great guy. You really have to meet him."

He knelt there chatting, clipping, pausing occasionally to consider his work. "Ready for some vapors, then?"

He'd already switched on the steam room, and it was there that my little day of beauty came to a climax. Now, I've visited lots of public baths—sweated with patriarchs in the tiny, tiled cubicles of the Russian baths on Manhattan's East Tenth Street; soaked with off-duty army officers beneath the soaring fourth-century arches of a *hammam* in Cairo's Old City; showered with Navy boys in the strip-mall splendor of the Jacksonville Club—and in these places I have done my best to allow the effect of their design to work itself on my entire body: to release it from everyday tensions and concerns and expectations, or at least to shelter it from them; to suggest, if you will, that in ritual attention to the body we can discern the reflection of a state of existence we might call godliness. But no place was so effective in this as Jack's steam room. The impulse to create it had clearly come from something as deep as the faith of medieval cathedral builders, and it gave me, as I sat there—naked amid hot, wet clouds and the scent of expensive rosemary-olive oil soap—more loving permission to feel divine than I'd ever felt before.

Jack positioned me on the slate banquette, my back to a tinted-glass window into the living room (!) that I had mistaken earlier, from the couch, for a full-length mirror. My limbs had gone almost limp with relaxation, and Jack manipulated them with great care, like a nurse, spraying, soaping, and rinsing me. Kneeling in front of me, he massaged my legs, spreading them gently, kneading the tension from my feet, then working up to my calves and my quads, then easing back down to the toes, to which he devoted elaborate ministrations. Woozy with comfort, I found myself following his lead and massaging myself—the inside of my thighs, my pecs and shoulders. He ran his hand over my abdominals and brought my hand over them as well. He kissed my biceps, one at a time, then held my arms up so I could kiss them, too. He gathered my hand around my cock, and together we squeezed and released, squeezed and released.

His gaze remained on my cock as I masturbated. His voice reverberated in the chamber, over the hiss of steam vents.

"Yeah, Steve. Be an orgy, man."

His wet feet and butt slapped on the floor as he repositioned himself for a better view.

"Look at that. *Look* at that!"

As I stroked, he cock-ringed me with his hands, the pressure of his thumbs just under my balls turning into a slow massage of the perineum. I could feel the valleys between my fingers go electric as he whispered details of the last party he hosted, at which guys playing in the living room watched guys playing in the steam room.

"Look at that," I breathed.

"Yeah. Orgy for me, Steve."

My grip weakened, my erection ripened into something rubbery, I was doing little more than holding myself in a cupped hand.

Before long, I had finished building and spent some moments experiencing that state of fully charged calm beyond the horizon of everyday language. Then, almost casually, I asked if he wanted me to shoot in his face. His face gave me the answer.

"Then this is for you," I gurgled.

I half stood. I did little more than slide my cock forward in my palm. It was more like peeing than shooting.

I released everything, even the duty of seeing. During the massage, he had tenderly removed my glasses and set them aside—an intimacy I always perform for myself, before bed. I am so nearsighted that my cock marks the farthest distance from my eyes at which I can make out something clearly. I have worn glasses since the third grade, and even while they sharpen my view of the world, they have come to enforce my distance from a certain reality. Jack knew, I guess, that I had gotten to a place where there was nothing I needed to see that couldn't better be seen without correction.

Okay, maybe there's a story here after all, I thought as I got dressed. What's funny is that Jack and I had been positioned in roughly in the same way as the two people in an old photograph I noticed he had pinned to his bulletin board: a small boy helping a handsome young man build a tool shed in the backyard of a suburban ranch house. The man is dressed in baggy khakis and a sweaty, unbuttoned shirt whose rolled-up sleeves show off steely forearms. The boy's head is exactly level with and a foot away from the man's crotch. It was obvious that these were Jack and his father. It made me smirk to remember that I have practically the exact same picture of my father and me, only we are raking leaves. Jack told me that his picture was taken in 1952. That's maybe three years before mine was taken.

The following Sunday, Jack phoned to see whether I might be free. I was glad he called, since I wanted the opportunity to look more closely at some of his artwork, walk around in the garden, maybe see what it was like to get my cock tied up. . . .

"Morrie's in town," he said. "I want you to meet him. He *really* gets into cock. Next to him, I'm an amateur."

I was back at Jack's door within an hour. Even before knocking I was breathing more deeply. Beaming, too. I pulled off my glasses and slipped them into my shirt pocket, at which point all I could see was that silly door knocker in the form of a naked man sporting—I hadn't noticed this the first time around—a boner.

STARING BACK AT CHINA

PHILIP GAMBONE

There's a bar where I sometimes go to have a beer and watch the guys shoot pool. It's a small, sociable place, dimly lit but upbeat, one of the few gay spots in Boston that can rightly be called a neighborhood bar.

Although it's my preferred stopping-off place, I don't show up at The Eagle often enough that you'd call me a regular. Occasionally I'll run into an acquaintance, but most evenings I don't recognize anyone. And no one recognizes me, or bothers to look in my direction. There is, I've learned, a hierarchy of neighborliness, even at this most neighborly of bars. Pushing fifty, I seem not to elicit much notice or interest anymore. Most evenings, in fact, I'm pretty invisible.

Lately, however, a couple of Chinese guys have caught my attention. They look like kids, though I guess they're in their mid to late twenties. I like watching them—their boyish faces and small, delicate fingers, almost feminine in their daintiness. I like their high cheekbones, their almond-shaped eyes, their silky black hair. In the dim light of the bar, I watch the way they shoot pool, the way they move around the table, the way they handle the cue, even the way they stand around and wait their turn. I watch how they interact with the white guys they're playing with, and how those guys interact with them. I watch how invisible they, too, are to most of the patrons.

The first time I noticed these boys, I assumed they were newcomers. I'd never seen them at the bar before. In fact, I'd never seen any Asian guys at The Eagle. But times were changing,

I reminded myself. The gay community in Boston was becoming more ethnically diverse. And here was the evidence: two Chinese kids who had finally mustered up the nerve to walk through that door. I wondered if they came from Chinatown, less than a dozen blocks away.

Still, it struck me as oddly coincidental that they should appear at The Eagle so shortly after my return from Beijing. I'd been teaching there for a semester and, to the extent that a Westerner can, pretty much carrying on the daily routine of a native resident of China's capital city. I commuted to work on a rickety, Chinese-made bicycle, did my marketing in the local shops and food stalls, had my hair cut every other week at the barber down the street.

My first days in China were some of the most challenging I'll ever experience. Everywhere I went, I was confronted with situations that were confusing, distracting, bewildering. Gradually, however, I overcame my sense of disorientation, enough so that by the end of my stint the city was beginning to feel like home. Indeed, my reentry into Boston brought on another case of disequilibrium. Where were all the Chinese? I asked myself. Where were the congested streets, the tidal waves of bicycles, the noise, the smells, the tastes? Where was the sexy allure I'd come to love about Asia? Everything around me suddenly seemed . . . well, so bland, so *white*.

Over the next several days, while all around me Bostonians were bustling about in preparation for Christmas, I made forays into Chinatown. I ate Chinese food, tried to read the Chinese signs (dozens of those once meaningless characters now made sense to me), and generally took notice for the first time of what a beautiful, thriving Asian community was all around me.

That's why, on the night I spotted those two Chinese boys at The Eagle, I had second thoughts about whether they were, in fact, newcomers. Maybe they'd been coming all along, and I'd just never noticed. Before I went to China, had they been as invisible to me as I was to most of the bar's patrons?

*   *   *

As a young person growing up in the late fifties and early six-
ties, I had little experience with anything Chinese beyond the
occasional "Chinese dinner" my mother fashioned out of
warmed-up cans of chop suey, fried noodles, and water chest-
nuts. I remember enjoying this respite from our usual diet of
Italian cooking. But my maternal grandmother, who lived with
us, would always loudly protest the appearance of Chinese food
on the table.

"Mi fa schivare!" It makes my stomach turn, she'd declare,
shuddering with disgust as she pushed away her plate. And
then she'd deliver a veritable thesaurus entry of denunciations.
Pig food, slop, dog meat, vomit! The Chinese were filthy, she
insisted. They ate rats.

Nana's vociferous xenophobia was mirrored in the complex-
ion of our town, a heavily Catholic, working-class community
ten miles north of Boston whose only citizens of color were a
"black" family of Azorean descent. If, by the mid-sixties, when I
graduated from high school, my consciousness was being
raised about the existence of black Americans and black culture, I was still woefully ignorant of Asian Americans. The images and impressions I received were limited to what could be
gleaned from Charlie Chan reruns on TV and the sound track
album of *Flower Drum Song.*

In college, I tried a course in Chinese history, but it was so
impossibly crammed with dates and dynasties and weird-
sounding names that I stopped doing the reading halfway
through the course. My heart just wasn't in it. As for the few
Chinese Americans I encountered, they struck me as a rather
innocuous bunch: quiet, studious fellows who had none of the
sex appeal of the boys I was attracted to. The affairs I had in
college—and the additional dozens of fantasies that kept distracting me from my studies—all involved blond, preppie
types. If any of my Chinese American classmates were gay, I
didn't let myself notice. My sexuality, and my own ethnicity,
made me alien enough. The last thing I wanted was to hitch my
romantic wagon to someone who seemed even less desirable,
socially and sexually, than I.

From the time I graduated college until the time I went to China, a period of about twenty-five years, I learned all the right intellectual connections between my marginalization as a gay man and the marginalization of other minority people. I'm sure that this empathy, theoretical as it was, extended to people of Asian descent, but in reality, I still had no exposure to—and not much real interest in—Asia or Asian culture. In my mind, China was reduced to "Red China"—a Communist country halfway around the world that was, even after the death of Mao, a brutally repressive regime, most recently notorious for the massacre at Tiananmen Square. As for the Chinese, all 1.2 billion of them, I saw them only as a single snapshot from the days of the Cultural Revolution: masses of them in their drab Mao jackets, identical, unidentifiable, and sexless.

But I went to China. Why? Maybe for no other reason than to take a break from my life at home. I was single and feeling stale at work. I wanted an adventure, and Beijing seemed like as good a place as any to pursue one. At the time, I suppose I would have preferred a chance to teach in Europe (the Dutch and Czech boys I'd slept with on a recent trip to Amsterdam and Prague had rekindled my passions for blonds), but China would do, I guessed.

My gay friends were skeptical. "What'll you do for sex?" they demanded incredulously. "You'll be arrested if you even try!"

Only half-jokingly, I told them that part of my adventure in China would be to live for four months without sex.

During my first days in Beijing, everything, even activities as ordinary as crossing the street or buying a bunch of bananas, became a challenge. I was both exhausted and exhilarated by the overload of sights and sensations. To one friend I wrote, "Everything I see is fascinating and totally unlike anything I've seen before."

Apparently, I was as fascinating to China as China was to me, for wherever I went, people stared. At first, their looks made me uncomfortable. I had to keep reminding myself that as rude as the Beijingers' behavior seemed, their gawking was a sign not of impoliteness but of curiosity. Of course, I wanted to stare right back, to look deeply into all these faces—I must have passed a hundred thousand of them every day—but I didn't. To look into the faces of the Chinese would have presented me with too much information, more than I could possibly come to terms with.

My living quarters were in the "visiting dignitaries" dormitory of Beishida, Beijing Normal University, northwest of Tiananmen Square and the Forbidden City. A walled campus with tree-lined avenues and lots of grass, Beishida was a tranquil haven from the bustle of the city. After teaching my classes at the high school across the street, I used to retreat to the university, where, after lunch and a nap, I would take a stroll through the peaceful campus.

Here, too, differences confronted me at every turn. Most striking was the fact that the students all looked to be about sixteen. Small and slim, with childlike faces, they seemed innocent and presexual, in marked contrast to their counterparts on university campuses in the United States where I'd taught (and occasionally fooled around with guys in the saunas at the gyms). Even the guards who were stationed at Beishida's gates seemed more like toy soldiers than real officials. They wore uniforms and caps that were too large, accentuating my impression of them as kids playing at adulthood. "It seems like a country run by teenagers," I wrote in my journal.

Even more extraordinary was the fact that all over campus—in fact, all over Beijing—I began to see pairs of friends, same-sex friends, walking along holding hands. Most were teenagers or twentysomethings, but there were some, especially male-male couples, in their thirties, forties, and upward.

"Don't worry, they're not gay," a straight American colleague assured me early on, before I'd come out to him. I suspect that for him this observation—straight guys in China hold hands—was simply a bit of tourist information, a cultural factoid to be noted, cataloged, and filed away. But for me, finding myself in a country where same-sex affection could be expressed so openly was thrilling.

Every time I came across two students holding hands—or leaning on each other, one resting his head on the other's shoulder, or walking with their arms around each other's waist—I forced myself not to stare. I didn't want to call attention to their behavior, didn't in any way want these beautiful young men to think there was something out of the ordinary about what they were doing. I also didn't want to get caught staring. Not yet.

One Sunday morning, early in the semester, I ran across a group of undergraduates, boys and girls together, in a small plaza on campus. Sixty or so in number, they were apparently members of some student club. As one of them waved a large red flag emblazoned with gold characters, the others gathered around and introduced themselves. Then they formed a circle, and with the leaders of the club calling out numbers—*"Yi, er, san!"*—they learned a folk dance. Under the pretext of correcting papers, I sat at a nearby picnic table and watched. In their youthful innocence and exuberance, they seemed like a gang of kids in an early Mickey Rooney movie.

The male leader of the lesson immediately attracted my attention. He was clearly into dancing. His movements were graceful and precise, almost balletic. Each time he demonstrated a step, he would stop to push back the long, black bangs that cascaded over his brow. As I watched him, I couldn't help but think that in America his mannerisms would be considered gay. But here, how could I tell?

That night, a warm September evening, I rode around the campus on my bike. I was feeling lonely and, for the first time since I'd arrived, rather horny. The campus was dark, poorly lit by the few streetlamps along the paths and avenues. I pedaled into a dark, lonely grove, the kind of place where if I'd been back in America gay men would surely congregate for outdoor sex. It was empty.

Finally, I stopped to rest by a compound of dormitories—barracks, really. Inside I could see long rows of cots and bunk beds on which young guys wearing nothing but undershorts were lounging about, studying. Some lay on their backs, their heads propped up on flimsy pillows, exposing their hairless, boyish chests. Others were on their stomachs, the thin cotton of their shorts hugging their small, firm buttocks. A few lay side by side, sharing a bunk.

Hidden by the shadows, I stood for the longest time, peering in at this bivouac of undergraduate boys. I studied their bodies, their skinny limbs, their delicate fingers, their pale, smooth skin. In America, I'd never gone for the big, buffed look. Thin, lanky guys turned me on. And now here was a dormitory, a campus, a city, full of lanky boys. I focused on one in particular—a reading lamp lit up his face and torso—and wondered what his thighs would feel like under my caress, what it would be like to kiss his lips, to run my fingers through his black, bristly crew cut.

As the days went by, I began to make eye contact with people on the street, to smile at them, and to smile even harder when they smiled back. I wrote in my journal: "Today on the subway, I realized that I am beginning to look at the Chinese as individuals—this one, that one—with an individual's look, personality, character, and, in some cases, sex appeal. As I stood next to one guy—a young man who was wearing Western-style shoes, his shirt open to reveal a hairless chest, smooth as porcelain—he more than once looked at me. Why? Curiosity? Or was I being cruised? I don't have the language—either Mandarin or, it seems, the language of gay-speak."

Then one night in late September, at a dinner party given by a straight expatriate friend, I met three gay men, including one gay Chinese man, Duan, the first openly gay Chinese I'd met. The trio told me that after dinner they were going to The Half and Half, Beijing's one and only gay bar. Did I want to join them, they asked. Did I!

The bar was small, cozy, and surprisingly stylish, its walls painted in bright, bold abstracts. Except for the fact that almost everyone in the place was Chinese, it might have been a chic little bistro-bar in Boston's South End.

Besides Duan, my other two companions were Australian,

and the three of us, almost the only Westerners in the place, were the objects of much attention. I caught one guy looking directly at me. He had a round, moonlike face and thin lips that rose into a bashful smile, but when I returned his gaze, he demurely dropped his eyes. Nevertheless, after being stared at so often on the streets of Beijing, it was a giddy experience to be looked at here at The Half and Half, even briefly, and to recognize the unambiguously sexual implication. I began to work out in my head what the logistics would be if I picked someone up.

Around one in the morning, more Westerners started arriving. Duan explained that they were coming from a disco called Night Man, a popular, gay-friendly place. I watched these seasoned gay expatriates work the room, greeting their young Chinese friends with relaxed, hearty banter. I watched how the whole mood of the place was suddenly enlivened. The Chinese boys, who until now had pretty much confined themselves to quiet talk and card games, began to flirt and camp and carry on. They were as happy to see the Westerners as the Westerners were to see them.

I stayed another half hour, just letting the whole show pass before my eyes. It was, like so much in China, more than I could take in at one viewing. I caught a cab back to the university, crawled into bed, and, for the first time since I'd arrived in the People's Republic, masturbated, to the image of the guy at the bar with the bashful, moonfaced stare.

Duan had told me about a public park that was very cruisy, one that had not yet been taken over by hustlers—"money boys," as he called them. If I went there, Duan assured me, I was bound to pick up a gay boy. It took me a couple more weeks to screw up the nerve to try.

On a lovely Sunday afternoon in October, I made the half-hour walk from my dorm to the park, which was located just off the Second Ring Road near one of the surviving gates to the old, now-destroyed walls of the city. I wandered around for a while, familiarizing myself with the lay of the land. Like many

Chinese parks, this one had been designed as a kind of miniature landscape: there were groves of trees and open places,
rocky outcroppings around which meandered walkways and
paths, a hillock surmounted by a small gazebolike pavilion,
and, near the center of the park, a shabby, dried-up lily pond.

At the far end of this pond, a dozen or so men, a percussionists' club of some sort, had gathered. They were conduct-
ing their Sunday-afternoon practice session, banging drums
and striking gongs and cymbals in a wonderful, syncopated ca-
cophony. Joining several other people, all Chinese, who had assembled around them, I listened for a while, pretending to be
nothing more than another Sunday stroller. But every time
someone looked at me, I wondered if I was being cruised.

After a few minutes I moved on, retracing my steps, memo-
rizing the twists and turns of the paths. Maybe nothing would
happen that day—it looked as if most of the people there were
straight couples—but I promised myself I would return some
night when, surely, the composition of the park's visitors would
change. I made note of all the places where, if this had been
America, gay men might loiter and cruise.

As I was walking back toward the gate, a young man on a bicycle passed me, going the opposite way. We made eye contact. I
walked on a little way, then turned around. The guy had stopped
as well, twisting around on his bike to look in my direction. Casually, I wandered over to a rocky place across from the pond
and perched on a boulder, pretending to listen to the percussionists across the water. The guy stayed put, continuing to look
in my direction. Then he turned around and slowly headed
toward me. As he passed, our eyes met again and I gave him a subtle nod. He biked on, then stopped a little ways away. He might
have been listening to the percussionists, too. Or maybe, I reasoned, he was simply curious about this Westerner who had acknowledged him. Or maybe . . . I got up and walked toward him.

"Ni hao," I greeted. In broken Mandarin, I introduced myself. He reciprocated, but even after five weeks in Beijing, I was
not fast enough to pick up what he'd said. I smiled. Shyly, he
smiled back.

I guessed him to be in his late twenties, maybe thirty. He was shorter than I but well built, with broad shoulders and a full, square face. In his dark blue suit, a white shirt open at the collar, and a pair of soft white loafers, he had clearly dressed up for his solo outing in the park. I sat down on the rock next to him. He began to talk to me in Chinese. Although I didn't completely understand the words, from his inflection I gathered that he wanted to know where I was from.

"*Meiguo.* America." He nodded. We were communicating!

Rummaging through my backpack, I found my Mandarin phrase book. "*Wo shi jiaoshi.* I am a teacher." He nodded again, then motioned for me to pass him the phrase book.

Scanning the page headed "Occupations," he pointed to a word on the list: *gongren.* He was a manual worker, a factory worker.

In this way, passing the book back and forth, we continued "talking," pausing every now and then to smile at each other, smiles that acknowledged both how frustrating and how much fun this was.

When it seemed that we had exhausted the resources of my phrase book, my new friend—his name was Ming Bao, "Bright Treasure"—motioned for us to walk a bit. Perhaps up that hill? He nodded toward the little gazebo. Perched on a high point overlooking the park, it seemed like exactly the wrong place to pursue any intimacies. For a second the thought crossed my mind that he might be planning to mug me up there.

We climbed up to the gazebo, sat down, and "talked" for a while, our halting sentences cobbled together from the phrase book. Occasionally, as we held the book between us, our fingers would touch. When I let mine linger against his, he did not pull away.

After each pair of sentences, there were long pauses of silence, but Bright Treasure did not seem to mind this awkwardness. He seemed perfectly content just to be with me. Gradually, I relaxed into these conversational lulls. "Go with the flow," I reminded myself, the essential Taoist maxim. And so, for long stretches of that waning October afternoon, we did nothing but sit quietly, sometimes looking out over the park, sometimes looking at each other.

I tried reading his face for cues. Did he want me to touch him, take his hand? What would he say if I suggested he come back to my place? And how could I possibly communicate that to him?

"I wish I knew what you wanted," I said in English, knowing he wouldn't understand a single word.

In reply, he said something equally unintelligible. At last, I got him to write down his name and gave him my card in return. I pointed to the telephone number.

"Wode," I said. Mine.

The sun was beginning to set; it was getting chilly. Not knowing what else to do, I indicated that it was time for me to go. As we shook good-bye, I held on to his hand for a long time. Again, he did not seem to mind.

A few days later, he phoned me. We tried to have a conversation, but it was useless. In the long silences, I frantically looked up words in my phrase book, trying to piece together a sentence: *Meet me in the park tomorrow.* But I couldn't make him understand. The conversation unraveled completely, and he hung up. Later that week, he called again. And again there was the same breakdown in communication. It was the last time I heard from him.

After a few days, I returned to the park. This time I went at night. The place seemed deserted, but as I parked my bike and walked around, I began to notice other men emerging from the shadows, strolling and milling about, silent as spies. At first, I just kept walking, trying to look like a tourist, but all the while I was taking stock of where one might go to have sex.

As my eyes got used to the darkness, I slowed my pace and began to study my fellow nocturnal compatriots more closely. Some looked like laborers and factory workers; others were younger and better dressed, students perhaps. A few returned my glances, but I was too scared to make a move. Then I caught sight of one guy who, even in the dark, was so adorable that I decided I had to start something. He must have detected my interest, because suddenly he stopped walking and waited for me to approach.

"*Ni hao,*" I said. He returned my greeting. So far, so good. "Do you speak English?" I asked.

He shook his head. "*Bu yao.*"

It was clear our conversation would be limited, but I smiled, determined to hold his interest with good old American winsomeness. He smiled back. He had high cheekbones and a shock of thick black hair that fell over his forehead and into his eyes. His lips were full, deliciously puckered. I guessed him to be in his mid-twenties. I motioned for us to walk. He nodded.

As we strolled along, I quickly exhausted the few phrases I could muster, but Zhang—I'd managed to get his name— seemed perfectly content just to be silent. I found this very erotic and felt my penis stiffening. But when I directed us toward a bushy area, he shook his head. Instead, he motioned for us to continue down the path we were taking. Soon we were at the park gate. Letting him take the lead, I followed him to the canal that marked the southern edge of the park. When we got to an underpass, he stopped and leaned against the guard rail, looking out over the dark water. I stood beside him, as close as I dared.

By now I was fully aroused. For a few minutes, we did nothing but lean against the railing, our shoulders touching, my erection pressing against my jeans. Every once in a while, the *click-click* of footsteps on the concrete embankment announced the approach of a nighttime stroller. As each walked by us, I tried to hide my face, uncertain what Beijingers would think of a Westerner loitering under a bridge at midnight with a Chinese man.

A lull in these pedestrian intrusions gave me the chance to reach over and touch Zhang. I began to stroke his arm. He turned and ran his fingers over the open collar of my shirt.

"*Mao,*" he said. Somehow I knew he was saying that I was hairy.

I pulled back a little and undid another button. It was then that he noticed my erection. The phrase "he squealed with de-light" may be a cliché, but that's exactly what Zhang did. He reached down and fondled me. Making sure no one was nearby, I unzipped and pulled out my cock. Zhang grabbed it and again squealed with pleasure. His excitement aroused me even more. I indicated for him to unzip, which he did, releasing his penis. I felt him. His erection was smaller than mine, and thinner, too. And while a fleeting wave of disappointment passed over me, I was so turned on to be finally touching a Chinese boy's cock that my arousal became excruciating. I wanted to touch him all over, explore every inch of his body, cup his small, firm ass in my hands, taste those delicious lips, bury my face in the wiry bush of pubic hair that I was now riffling with my fingers.

Suddenly we heard footsteps. I stuffed my prick back into my jeans and leaned against the railing, resuming the pose of a tourist looking out over the canal. Zhang followed suit. When the pedestrian had passed by, we resumed our groping, but now continued to lean over the railing, fondling each other through the iron bars.

A few times I came close to coming, but I held back. I didn't want the evening to end, not there. I indicated that I'd like to take him back to my place. With the limited Chinese I had, it was difficult to convince him that it would be safe, but eventually he got the idea. We walked back to where I'd parked my bike, he jumped onto the back (Beijingers are adept at sharing bicycles), and off we pedaled, with Zhang's arms wrapped around my waist.

Once in my room, we quickly fell to kissing. His breath smelled lightly of savory spices I couldn't identify. I wanted to eat his tongue, ingest every morsel of his foreignness. I unbuttoned his thin cotton shirt and ran my hands over his chest. Hairless and lightly muscled, it reminded me of the days when, as a virgin teenager, I would lie in bed at night and caress my own chest, then so bare and boyish.

Having long since exhausted the few phrases we could speak to each other, we made love silently. Naked, his body seemed

even more like a teenager's. It was small and wiry, easy to maneuver around my narrow twin bed. I licked his armpits, drank
in his navel, lifted and spread his legs, sniffing his balls, his
cock, his bush. Again, that indeterminate, spicy aroma filled
my nostrils.

He resisted my attempts to fuck him, even though I had produced a condom. In fact, he refused all my efforts to get him
off. But when I came all over his chest, he once again squealed
with delight. Accustomed to American tricks getting up and
leaving immediately after sex, I wondered what would happen
next. In the chilly, unheated room, he hustled to the bathroom, where he took a quick shower. Then, toweling off, he
clicked on my television set, tuned to a late-night show—a his-
torical soap opera set in the Ming dynasty—and came back to
bed, curling up in my arms.

For the rest of the fall, Zhang would periodically show up at
my room, unannounced. (With my limited Chinese, arranging
dates was virtually impossible.) We'd spend the evening cuddling on the bed and watching television before falling to lovemaking and sleep. Because weeks would go by when I wouldn't
see him, I would often bike over to the park to find other guys.
While some of these visits amounted to nothing more than a
bit of quickie sex in the bushes, most of the men I met wanted
to talk and, when I invited them, to come back to my place for
the night.

That fall and into the early winter, I met Jeremy, who worked
in an import-export business; Guo Yang, a graduate student;
Shici, a chemical engineer; Xiao Cai, a businessman; Hong, a
physician; and Tang, an art student, who took me back to his
unheated one-room studio in an old *hutong* near the Drum
Tower. Some of these guys I saw several times; others only once.
All of them loved to cuddle and kiss.

Often I would think about my boyhood, when, during Mass,
we used to pray for "the starving people of China." Thirty-five
years later, I was discovering just how many gay Chinese were
still starving—not for food, but for a few snatched up hours of
private affection.

*   *   *

In the last weeks of November, I made friends with Skip, a young gay American who was spending a year traveling through Asia. The two of us decided to check out an all-male bathhouse we'd heard about. Reports from friends indicated that while it wasn't officially or exclusively a gay place, many gay Beijingers went there.

Following the directions that a friend had given us, we took the subway to the bathhouse, paid our fifty cents, and went in. It was a huge place, shabbily but adequately fitted out with a locker room, showers, a pool, a sauna, and several cots where some of the men were napping or receiving massages. As we entered the locker room, all eyes fell upon us. We were the only Westerners in the place.

We undressed quickly, put on our rented rubber sandals, and flip-flopped over to the shower room, where we waited for our turn to shower. All the guys washing themselves were in their twenties and thirties. Some stared at us, some ignored us. A few caught our eyes and smiled. Some of the guys were washing each other, lathering up backs and chests. One or two had erections.

At last two guys moved away and we took their places. We soaped up, rinsed off, then, not knowing what else to do, soaped up again. As we lathered up for the third time, Skip and I kept up a steady stream of conversation. It was nervous babble, noise to counter the anxiety we both felt. Not knowing how much cruising was permitted here, I tried keeping my eyes to myself. Still, it was hard not to notice that Skip and I were the only circumcised men in the place.

After showering, we walked over to the central pool, an area about as large as two or three American hot tubs and almost as deep. Although the water, a dirty gray soup, was not particularly inviting, several of the guys lounging in it were. Overcoming our squeamishness, we abandoned our towels and eased ourselves in.

Once again, Skip and I resumed the pretense that we were having a casual conversation, but all the while I kept vigilant to detect what customs, conventions, and etiquette applied here.

The whole place, I imagined, was what an American YMCA from the forties or fifties must have felt like: loud, hearty, fraternal, and very secretly cruisy.

Of the perhaps twenty of us in the tub, about half were young guys in their twenties, the other half older men, upwards of fifty. One man had brought his two sons—both under eight—who were lounging and splashing and checking us out. In such a heterogeneous environment, it was hard to feel that I could be sexual.

"There's a guy staring at you who is really adorable," Skip said.

Slowly I turned around. Skip was right. The guy was a cutie: dark, bright eyes; high, sculpted cheekbones and a smooth, hairless chest. His two buddies were equally lovely. All three of them were cozied up together, staring, then whispering, then tittering like three young queens. We made eye contact and smiled.

"This is so weird," Skip continued. "We can say whatever we want, and no one will understand a word."

The cutie moved toward me and reached out to examine the beaded necklace I was wearing. He fingered it tenderly.

"It's Navajo Indian," I said, knowing he wouldn't understand a word of this. "*Meiguo*. American." He was standing now, the water only up to his navel. He motioned for me to give him the necklace. When I shook my head, he pouted and returned to his friends.

Suddenly, the smile disappeared from Skip's face.

"One of the guys next to me is touching my dick."

"Which one?" I asked.

"I think the older one," Skip said.

"Well, are you enjoying it?"

Skip chuckled. "I want it to be the other one."

"Oops, me too," I said, feeling a hand caressing my cock.

Nearby, about two feet away, a young man was looking at me. I could tell from the way his arm was extended under the murky water that he must be the one.

"Yum," Skip said, expressing his approval. He moved away

from the guy who was feeling him up. "But you're getting all the young, cute ones, and I'm only getting the older guys."

I suggested it was time we check out the sauna.

As in the pool, the guys in the sauna kept looking at us, smiling, commenting, and occasionally chuckling.

"How many of the guys in here do you suppose are gay?" Skip asked.

"From the looks they're giving us, I'd say all of them."

"I can't believe this!" Skip said. "All these yummy rice cakes, and me a rice queen, and—"

He was interrupted by the steam that rose as one of the guys poured water onto the sauna's hot coals. The heat became almost unbearable. We decided to take another plunge in the pool.

As we got back in, a Chinese man asked us in perfect English if we were Americans.

"I'm Lee," he said. "Is this your first time here?"

It was, we said. Lee was in his late thirties, bright-faced and solidly handsome. He said he'd been to the bathhouse only once before, the previous day. He was from Hong Kong, a visiting scholar. He introduced his friend, someone he'd met at the bath yesterday. We began comparing notes, but out of the corner of my eye I couldn't help but notice that the boy who'd been eyeing my beaded necklace was still looking at me.

"You like him?" Lee asked.

"Yes, I think he's beautiful," I said. "But I think he's only after my jewels." Lee didn't get the joke. The boy smiled at me again and said something to his comrades. I decided it was now or never. I moved closer to him, reached out under the water, and fondled his dick. He cried out rather theatrically and moved away, an outraged, offended queen.

"Didn't like it, huh?" Skip asked.

"Well, he could have fooled me," I said.

The rest of the guys in the pool seemed unruffled, even amused. Whatever breach of etiquette I'd stumbled into hardly seemed to cause much of a stir. The boy resumed his seductive leering at me. It was then I noticed that the water level in the pool was going down.

"They're draining the pool for cleaning," Lee explained. "I think it means they're closing for the evening."

Skip and I got out and found a free shower head. Even more than before men were sharing showers, taking turns washing each other. The erection count seemed high.

"Let's come back tomorrow," Skip said.

As we toweled off and got dressed, I wondered if we'd missed any action, but I doubted that much sex went on at the bath-house, other than a lot of touchy-feely stuff underwater. Never-theless, these gay Chinese, ever resourceful, had managed to create a place for themselves where, as Walt Whitman once put it, "the dear love of comrades" could prevail.

My last Saturday in Beijing, I stopped in at The Half and Half to say my good-byes to friends. It was a bittersweet evening, full of reminiscing and embraces, posing for snapshots and prom-ises to keep in touch. Unlike Skip, who laughingly called him-self "a slave to the yellow man," I hardly thought of myself as having an exclusive passion for Asians. And yet, the romantic, physically affectionate way I'd been treated by most of the Chi-nese guys I'd met at The Half and Half—and the ones I'd picked up in the park—seemed far more pleasurable than the experiences I'd had with American guys back home.

Around eleven, I decided to call it a night. Making my way to the men's room, I passed a striking, mustachioed guy, a Chi-nese man in his early thirties, whom I'd seen at the bar on a few other occasions. We began to talk, and soon I was inviting him back to the university.

In the cab, we held hands. He began to tell me his story: he was a doctor from another province, on a research grant in Bei-jing, married and miserable. He had tried to tell his wife, who still lived back in their home province a thousand miles away, that he was gay, but she had only laughed and refused to be-lieve him. They had a daughter.

Back in my room, we made love. As with so many of the Chi-nese men I'd slept with that fall, reaching orgasm seemed in-cidental to the tender hour of caressing, kissing, and cuddling that we enjoyed. Eventually he fell asleep, softly weeping in my arms.

Early on during my semester, one of my Australian friends, a man who had lived in Beijing for several years, had warned me, "Watch out for these Chinese boys. You could easily break their heart. They'll fall in love with you at the drop of a hat." Ironically, as I was packing my bags that final morning, I realized it was *my* heart that had been broken, several times over.

It's been a year and a half since I returned from China. These days, when I'm out with friends, they remark on how I seem to be attracted only to Asian guys. "What have you become?" they ask. "A rice queen?" They are afraid I've gone overboard, afraid my attraction to Asian men has turned into an obsession.

It's true that I tend to pay more attention to Asian guys than others I pass on the street. I can spot them from far away. There's a distinctive profile—the high cheekbones, the graceful sweep of the neck, the boyish silhouette of the arms, the thin waists. I seem to have developed a sixth sense for picking up on it. But when we pass and I try out the same smile I used in Beijing, most of them don't notice. Most of them avoid making eye contact with me. Maybe they think white guys wouldn't be interested in them. Or maybe they've become too Americanized, and have already adopted the American obsession with youth. Maybe I am as invisible to them as they were once invisible to me.

Lately, I've been asking myself a lot of questions. Could it be, I ask myself, that what I'm really attracted to—perhaps even obsessed by—is the innocent trust I found (or thought I found) in the arms of so many of the Chinese men I slept with in Beijing? Or could it be that I was, and am, attracted only by the foreignness, the exoticism of Asians, the mystery of them? And what about those boyish bodies, those faces that look like teenagers' faces? Is *that* what my newfound passion for Asian men is all about? There's the fact, too, that most of my verbal interactions with Chinese guys were so limited. Did I prefer that our communication was fragmented? What exactly was I projecting into those long silences, those halting, misshapen sentences? Am I, I ask myself, incapable of intimacy with someone I can talk to fluently? Am I afraid of *that*?

I wrestle with these questions, these doubts. Sometimes my concerns seem accurate to me: the voice of reason, cold, dispassionate, logical. At other times, my questions seem like just so much cleverness: smart psychobabble that ignores the beauty of what I felt in China. I listen to the way my doubts belittle and diminish the memories I have. I listen to the way they betray my fears.

In a city, in a culture, where, more and more, I feel sexually invisible, I can recall that Chinese "boys" gave me back my erotic visibility. The way they spoke to me, held me, the way they made love to me—it reminded me of what it is I most deeply want in life: intimacy. I want to be stared at, want to be *seen*—deeply, lovingly, completely. And I want to stare back, unafraid. I want to look into the deep, dark eyes of another man—yes, right now my fantasy is that he'll be Asian—with the same intensity, the same vulnerability, the same courage, that so many Chinese showed to me.

Chinese "boys" broke my heart because they were men, because they were unafraid to look at me and to give their hearts to me, even for a little while, even given the impossibility of our situation. In the face of their limited prospects for happiness, the courage displayed by my gay Chinese friends has emboldened me to ask other questions, too: Do I have the courage to hold on to my dreams? Do I have the daring to keep looking for the guys I fancy, even if they're so much younger than I? Do I have the guts to refuse the erotic invisibility that my culture keeps foisting upon me? In short, am I man enough to keep expecting love?

RATBOY

JEREMY MICHAELS

On March 19, 1991, on my daily walk around a small lake in the local city park in Carthage, Missouri, I noticed a kid watching me from a picnic shelter. He looked about nineteen. As I walked by, he'd run from one side of the shelter to the other to watch me. On my third lap, he stepped into stride beside me and began walking and talking as if we'd been friends a lifetime.

He was, as it turned out, fourteen. He talked up a storm about his life and asked if I'd be his big brother. He was a troubled, disturbed kid, and I inferred from his stories that he had had an unstable home life, and was abused by various stepfathers. I found out later that his brother had been sent to prison the day I met him.

Ratboy, as I dubbed him, and I never spent much time together. During the next couple of years, we saw each other only occasionally, in passing. He invited me to a school concert he was performing in, and I went to show support. He came to a couple of parties at my house. Then he moved to Dallas for a while.

In March 1993, when he was sixteen and a half and I was exactly twice his age, I invited Ratboy on a road trip to New York City with me and my best friend, Dusty. I didn't think he'd go, or that his mother would allow it. They both surprised me.

In Illinois, at a rest stop, after consuming a two-liter bottle of Mountain Dew and a whole box of Little Debbie cakes, he bounded out of the car and onto the roof of a picnic shelter. He stood there flexing his muscles, puffing out his brown, hairless chest. He was wearing nothing but a tight pair of jeans. No underwear, no shirt. His long brown hair fluttered in the night breeze. He had grown into a tall, gangly, energetic, outgoing young man.

As we approached New Jersey, Ratboy began roughhousing with me. I was in the front passenger seat, he was in the back. He would pick on me, touching me constantly in one way or another, his eyes full of unasked questions. Dusty, driving, shot us glares of annoyance.

At a motel room in Newark, we had our first no-holds-barred wrestling match. He attacked me without warning and tested all kinds of moves on me. I fought back as valiantly as I could, but I was no match for him. He had studied wrestling since grade school.

The gleam in his eyes betrayed him, indicated he was turned on by dominating me. But he wasn't nearly as turned on as I was, being thrown around a motel room by a hyperactive, sweaty, tall, brown-skinned, brown-eyed, sixteen-year-old boy with a drop-dead smile.

He pulled my hair, and I pulled his. He bit me several times. He'd bite, grind his teeth back and forth, and hang on. It hurt like hell, but I didn't want him to stop. I cherished the resulting souvenirs, the angry red teeth marks on my arms, chest, back, and shoulders. The soreness would last for days.

Every wrestling match in that motel room ended with my arms pinned above my head and him shirtless, sitting astride my chest, his denim crotch in my face. I wanted him so bad, but I was terrified of his youth, afraid he would freak out. So I played rag doll and let him make all the moves.

Ratboy sent my heart into overdrive. I was astounded by the magical, electric hot feel of his young skin on mine. I felt euphoric when he stretched the length of his body over mine. I lived for each wrestling match, for each time he would pin my arms above my head, his naked chest on my face, a nipple innocently pressing against my lips.

In New York City, we stayed with a poet friend of mine and slept beside each other on the floor. While Dusty dozed, Ratboy and I talked all night. He was typically curious about sex and asked every question about gay sex he could think of. I answered as honestly as I could.

He told me he enjoyed inflicting pain on people and that he liked the taste of blood. I asked if these feelings were sexual, and he said no. He kept telling me he wasn't gay.

Somewhere in Pennsylvania, on the way home, we encountered a horrific blizzard and were forced to stay at a motel for two days. The first night we stayed up late, talking and wrestling on one bed while Dusty sprawled across the other bed, sound asleep and snoring like a freight train.

When Ratboy and I decided to go to sleep, I asked if I could share a bed with him instead of with Dusty, as I usually did. I promised to stay on my own side, and he said it would be okay, but I could not touch his "o-zones." After the lights were off, he unashamedly wrapped his arms and legs around me, pressing his body as close to mine as he could, and went to sleep. He said, "I feel so safe with you." Nothing in my thirty-three years had ever felt so right as having this boy wrapped around me. I didn't even think about sex that night. All I wanted was to hold Ratboy and keep him safe, to remain in that hot, tight cocoon forever.

From then on, we slept in the same bed. Dusty raised an eyebrow but said nothing.

After we returned from the road trip, I called Ratboy every day, oblivious of what his mother might think of this thirty-something smitten queer guy constantly calling her teenage son. He spent several nights with me at my home. We went on a rampage of getting to know each other. And then, only weeks later, Ratboy moved in with me and the three gay friends I lived with. Though he was supposed to be living in the basement, he crawled into bed with me every night, and most of his belongings were in my room.

At my request, an astrologist friend of mine who lived near San Francisco cast a compatibility chart for Ratboy and me. She wrote back a hysterical letter ordering me to "get away from him! His Saturn sets on your north node!" This meant, she said, that we had lived thousands of lives together and that every one had been fraught with violence. Our past lives involved black magic, sexual abuse, and murder. In every life he had murdered me. This lifetime was the one in which we were to resolve all the issues of our past ones. The only way to resolve them was for me to walk away, in peace, without looking back.

I'm skeptical about astrology and all things New Age. And I knew I could not turn my back on Ratboy.

In May, after Ratboy had been living with us about three weeks, I came home one evening and found a note that said, "I joined the carnival. Be cool to each other." I felt as if I'd been punched in the stomach.

For three days I didn't know where he was or how to contact him. I was a basket case. I realize now that he needed to get away from the intensity of our friendship and that I should have let him go. But my obsession with Ratboy blinded me to the obvious.

I found out where the carnival was and visited him there. When it moved to Springfield, Missouri, about an hour from my home, I spent a weekend in a motel there. Ratboy and his carny friends used my motel room to shower and party. The last day, Ratboy got upset with his boss, called me at the motel, and said, "Come and get me." I picked him up and we went home.

Ratboy had one girlfriend during the time we were housemates. He would have sex with her in his room in the basement. When it was over, he'd leave her down there alone and come up to my room on the second floor to sleep and cuddle with me the rest of the night.

After a couple of months, he made his first sexual move, which scared the shit out of me. We'd had a rowdy wrestling match, ripping each other's shirts off in the process. He bit me repeatedly, sucking my blood. He shoved my face into his sweaty armpit and held it there. The pungent musk of him sent me into a tailspin. I felt drunk. I threw my arms around him and squeezed as hard as I could. He ground his crotch into mine. My heart was beating triple-time.

When the wrestling died down and we turned the lights off,

Ratboy slid into bed beside me. He picked on me a little more, pinching and biting. I told him to stop because I had to get up early in the morning for work. He said, "Shut up or suck my dick!" I replied sanctimoniously that I preferred to shut up. He said, "No. I'm serious. Get busy." He was still only sweet sixteen and I couldn't bring myself to do it, though by then all in the world I wanted was to please him. I reminded him that we had to wait until he was eighteen. He murmured "Okay" and fell asleep with his head on my chest. I didn't sleep a wink and went to work a zombie that next morning.

A few weeks later, one of our wrestling matches took an especially erotic turn. We were wrestling at my friend Veronica's house, both of us wearing loose-fitting sweatpants. I somehow got the best of Ratboy and sat on him, straddling his pelvis. He grinned and thrust his pelvis up, lightly inserting his flaccid dick between my butt cheeks. I gasped and jumped off him as if I'd been shot, exactly as he'd known I would! He would do *anything* to win a wrestling match.

He attacked me again and held me flat on the floor, face-down. He mounted me and lay with his entire body stretched over mine. He pinned my right arm behind my back, pried my legs apart with his knee, and began thrusting his pelvis fast and hard against my ass. Though we were clothed and he had no erection, it was sweet torment enough—until he sank his teeth viciously into my back, just below my neck, and began tearing like a wild animal. He flipped me over, saw the stunned, euphoric look on my face. He smiled and said, "You *liked* that, didn't you?" I murmured, "Well, yeah, kinda . . ." He was very pleased with himself.

Our favorite thing to do was to buy a case of beer and spend the weekend in a motel room, watching TV and wrestling. Ratboy would do backflips from one bed to another. We almost got thrown out of one motel room for making so much noise, banging each other's heads against the walls. We also broke a lamp (which I glued back together).

One motel excursion turned ugly after we both drank a little too much. Around two A.M., Ratboy became angry over something silly and walked out, saying he was going to hitchhike to his mother's. He was wearing only jeans—no shoes or shirt (he never wore underwear). I was barefoot, too, but followed him out the door and across a busy four-lane highway. He was headed for the interstate, which was on the other side of a six-foot wooden fence. We were in the middle of a wheat field behind the motel. He tried to climb the fence. Each time he'd get a leg up, I'd grab the back of his jeans and pull him down.

After about six tries, he sighed and said, "I'm going to hit you if you do that again." He got another leg up, and I grabbed the back of his pants and pulled him down again. He looked daggers at me. I said pathetically, "Please don't go."

He began screaming at the top of his lungs, and so did I. A police car drove by, scanning the wheat field with a spotlight. We ducked down into the wheat. We started giggling, realizing there were other people in Springfield and we had disturbed their peace. The cops left, and we stumbled back to our room. I fell asleep with Ratboy's arms around me, his head nestled on my shoulder.

After five months of living with my friends, we moved into a place of our own. I couldn't bear to share his company with anyone else. I was convinced that everyone else in the world wanted him and would take him away from me. We rented a small, cheap motel room—with one bed, of course.

One evening I was lying on the bed, talking on the phone. Ratboy attacked me as I talked and began biting my neck. He started rubbing his body all over mine. He was wearing thin shorts and no shirt. I continued talking with my friend as if nothing was happening. Ratboy kept humping me and I continued to ignore him, only to hear him exclaim, "Goddamn! You gave me a hard-on!" He jumped off the bed and went outside while I finished my conversation.

We lived in that room for a month, and then moved into a one-room cabin in my parents' backyard in a small town nearby. He was seventeen and a half now, and still trying every night, once it was quiet and dark, to seduce me. I kept refusing, terrified over his age. One night he decided to sleep naked. He told me that he was attracted to me. I told him I wanted him as much as he wanted me, but that we had to wait until he was old enough. Every night he slept cuddled as close to me as humanly possible.

But by day, he was a raving heterosexual. With his friends and family, he showed no evidence of his gay side. It was absolutely forbidden to talk about "it" or to hint at "it" in any way.

On March 9, 1994, we had a terrible fight about something, I forget what. I wouldn't speak to him. Ratboy could not take it when I was mad at him for any reason. He cajoled me until I forgave him and started talking to him again.

This is what I wrote in my journal:

Stayed up talking with [Ratboy] all night and around 6:30 A.M. he started talking about sex and asked me to suck him off and started rubbing himself all over me like he has done a million times before. I said, "I'm tired of telling you 'no,' [Ratboy]—I'm not going to anymore. . . . So if you don't mean it, don't say it!" He said, "Then don't say 'no.' I'm serious." I said, "You'll have to do something to let me know you are serious." He took my hand and put it on his dick, which was hard. . . . I said, "You're serious!" I played with him through his clothes for a while to make sure he wanted to and his hands started exploring me. I pulled his clothes down and went down on him and got him off. He is so beautiful, so sexy, I really never believed I'd have him this way. I do not feel the least bit guilty—I love him so much, making love with someone I'm in love with was the most satisfying experience ever. I know he was only experimenting and don't want to push him too far. We were both awkward and inhibited, but it was still good. He was real quiet afterwards, but he did smile and say, "Hmmm . . . ! I'm bisexual now!" Then he rolled over and went to sleep. Needless to say, my emotions are on the rampage.

After that, he wanted sex once every two months, and I obliged. In the intervals, I would suffer from wanting him, but he made it clear that he preferred to be with, and *was* with, other lovers—all female.

I often wondered if he really enjoyed our sex, or if he did it only because he thought he owed me something. I got my answer one night after I had given him a pair of silk boxer shorts that he had worn all day. At lights-out he said, "I'm so goddamn horny! I'm never wearing these things again!" He stripped, flung the shorts across the cabin, and then attacked me. I blew him; then, when my mouth got tired, I used my hands to jack him off. While I was doing this, he started bucking like a horse, moaning "Oh God, that feels so good!" over and over. I stopped using my hands, and he said, "Keep doing that twisty thing you do with your hands." I did "the twisty thing," and he resumed moaning and ended in a loud happy orgasm.

One night, shortly after he turned eighteen, he showed up at the cabin with a pair of handcuffs. We were watching a movie, and he decided he wanted to put my hands behind my back and cuff me. He told me he would take the cuffs off after the movie. I didn't resist.

After the movie, he said, "I'm tired," and turned off the TV and light. I said, "*Ahem* . . . what about the handcuffs?" He said, "Leave them on all night." I said, "No." He said mockingly, "Well, then take them off!"—knowing I couldn't.

He began tickling and pinching me. He bit my chest, arms, back, stomach, and neck. He pulled my shirt up over my face and started rubbing his hands on me. He took off my sweatpants. I said, not very sincerely, "Hey, put those back on." He said, "No," and went down on me.

I'd never thought he'd go that far in his curiosity. I was pleasantly surprised, to say the least. He was embarrassed, which I guess is why he covered my face at first. But then he took my shirt off as much as he could, mounted my face, and assumed a sixty-nine position. He was so excited by total domination of me, and I was just as excited to be completely at his mercy.

Having all-out sex with Ratboy signed and sealed my obsession. In my mind, now he was *mine, all mine.* Of course, teenage Ratboy had different ideas about commitment. His idea was that he should have sex with anyone and everyone as much as possible. Every time he met a girl (or guy), I would be insane with jealousy, unable to concentrate on the things that had once been important to me.

I neglected friends and family, breaking promises, and lashing out when I was angry or frustrated about Ratboy. I quit two jobs to spend more time with him. Trying to meet Ratboy's endless demands, I went bankrupt in January 1995. In order to feed my Ratboy obsession, I was teetering on the brink of losing everything that meant anything to me.

Eventually, as his curiosity was satisfied, our sexual encounters became few and far between. He began using me for financial support only. Anytime he had other friends or girlfriends, he would completely disappear, only to reappear when he had used them all up.

He began to use the cabin as a place to flop between parties and lovers. A safety net. A last resort. I served utilitarian functions and nothing more. I was good for transportation, buying cigarettes and beer, and feeding him.

I lived with that bullshit for more than a year.

When Ratboy decided we should move to St. Louis, I agreed, and we drove there to find jobs. When he was offered a job working with the mentally disabled, I told him to go for it and promised to join him later. I never did. My sanity returned like a long-lost friend. I was on Pepcid and Prozac. I'd let my life fall into ruins trying to keep this lean, sexy, beatific, rough boy pleased and in my life. But he wasn't happy with me. And I was as miserable with him as without him.

One August night in 1996, a month after he'd started his job, Ratboy returned to pick up his belongings. He'd bought a nice used car. He was wearing clean, new clothes and had cut his hair. He was as handsome, vivid, and kinetic as ever, all smiles, chattering to me and my family in the driveway about his job, his new girlfriend, and his friends in St. Louis. He didn't stay long. He put his things in the car, hugged me, and left. I waved to Ratboy as he drove off into adulthood.

ODE TO BOY

ALLAN GURGANUS

I Sing how their socks fall down.

I Sing the amount of mousse you can get on hair this short and have it make absolutely no difference. I sing how plain they show their secret worry with their hair, touching its sides, checking in every glass storefront. They cruise their mall. I sing their defeatist loyalty to others, 11–14. I sing how they groan, a chorus, when the mother picking them up in the station wagon from the Chevy Chase flick says, "Was the movie cute?" I sing their satiric vision of those governing lumps, the rest of us. I sing how wrong they are about the rest of us; I sing how right.

I Sing how they need a belt because there's nothing extra keeping Levi's up, nothing on the hips but hipbones (O, at forty-four years old, the miles I've jogged, knowing I will never run back that far, ever!).

I Sing how their socks are still falling down: bucking the tide of how everything else is so often standing up.

I Sing the contents of the pockets of that blond one, The Boy on the Left. In his linty P-coat pocket: a single house key chained to a blue Grandpapa Smurf he's owned and loved since age three; eighty cents' worth of grape bubble gum; one peek-a-vu stolen from his father's dresser that, if lifted toward daylight, or mall skylights, shows Jayne Mansfield with her nipples retouched in a red that's lurid beyond most any other red this side of blood or fire departments; his mother's work phone number written on blue lined children's school paper; ninety-seven cents in change; plus a single condom, mint-flavored, user-friendly.

I Sing how I, at fourteen, I tucked one condom in my wallet and kept the damned thing safe right there till college; I sing how this kid's mint rubber is his third replacement one since Thursday; I sing that, their unawareness of my early suffering.

I Sing their valor in the video arcades, a valor resented by parents (one quarter at a time), a valor admired by their own sort, esp. that dufus who's at the next machine for ten minutes and has scored only eight hundred points at the next machine. I sing their short attention spans at school, short for anything beyond each other. I sing their not quite needing to shave yet, though their mothers nag about the mingy silver-blond mustache. I respect their child-reticence at committing to any daily deodorant: I sing their scent—part wet puppy, part vanilla extract, add one drop of motor oil, part snakes, part snails, part stone, and partly stick. A smell now bitter as a child on waking, but some days bloomy milky as a bride, lying down.

I Sing how girls their age turn heads and literally stop traffic in the mall's vast lot, esp. those girls who're prodigies at makeup. I sing how same-age boys live hidden, grouchy under tent-size khaki coats, eyes safe back of bangs like purposeful awnings; and beneath bangs, behind the best of their extensive sunglass collection, they themselves lurk, formulating, a stern and groggy hibernation as they come to reproductive life. Or, having arrived there, decide what to do about it . . . The new beauty is a secret even from the mom of each. (Except recently, when she forced him into a blue blazer for Sis's graduation and everybody oohed so much about the handsomeness it made The Boy, like, barf.) I sing an unwillingness to change the bedsheets, ever. I sing the hatred of underwear and especially pajamas. And how quick socks bag out on you. The NO TRESPASSING sign, emphasized by an I LOVE THE DEAD decal, nailed to his bedroom door, that I also chant.

I Sing boys' worship of usually worthless heroes: "Bruce" means Bruce Lee, "Sly" or "John" means Stallone/Rambo, hopeless, wrong heroes, big-chested, low-cerebellumed, visible and lumberish as totempoles of lats and pecs—target GUYS. I sing how heavy and how light boys are.

I sing the five swiped porn mags hidden underneath The Boy's bed and the uses of the magazines and his knowing them, like catechism, page by page. I sing how the woman bending over on the bottom of page 46 is named Verna. Because The Boy decided. And then what could Verna, like, say?

I Sing the boys' contempt of any pop music except bootlegged Liverpool or Hamburg working-class-inspired heavy metal. The heavier the metal the better, with decibels as the one sure proof of artistic seriousness. And yet I sing their singing something else. I sing how, grouped piratelike near the mall fountain and goldfish pond, they can utter nothing for twenty minutes, beyond "Weed?" (when requesting a Joe Camel) or "Fire?" (a Bic lighter). Only nodding toward the backview of young housewives busying their strollers and their credit cards all morning in tight jeans, often a fashion mistake. Then The Boy will suddenly pitch into a Whitney Houston ballad. And his whole gang, despite their professed disgust with slick market-research pulp trash, his whole gang joins in, eyes closed from so knowing all the words. Crooning whole choruses, they hardly notice doing it. Their falsettos hope to make their usual come-and-go-soprano-blurts seem sent up there by choice. I sing their singing like forlorn alley-animals in some Disney animation; they choirboy over the fakey fountain's real roar.

"If God so filled my heart with stars,
He musta meant me as all yours."

I sing how the cartilage is stretching him on a rack marked ADULT SIZES. I sing how rapid growth can make your joints ache; I sing how growth, like, hurts him.

Plus it makes his socks fall down again, goddammit.

I wish to sing their love of parents but really probably cannot, just yet; I wish to sing their future promise but that too, from this mall, seems sometimes sketchy. I wish to sing their skill at drawing, table talk, or knowing more than the four chords re-

quired to play the rudiment plumbing of so-so garage band rock;
I can't promise. They know about all Hendrix; they know whole
pages of *How the Grinch Stole Christmas;* they know about oral sex
tricks (when in doubt, breathe through yer nose); about a kind
of African music called ska—part reggae, part tribal drums, part
French pop, and that's supposed to really be drop-dead cool: but
they can't get the mall's jerk-off CD store to order any (partly because the boys don't know the name of any artist or recording of
it, of ska; but they know it's outstanding, probably). They know
who sells your best dope in hitchhiking distance. They slouch
around the mall, unpopular with merchants, waiting to be discovered, not having yet discovered what it is they'll be discovered
for, but patient in a fatalistic herding way.

At home, behind the NO TRESPASSING/DEAD sign, The Boy's
bedsheets feature Captain Marvel doing wondrous lifting
chores and projects involving flying, etc. These same bedsheets
were requested when The Boy was nine, just four years back.
He wanted them in earnest and for real, because—with their
canary-yellow background and the "Pow" "Zap" in jagged
speech balloons—they seemed just plain old Great. In the years
since, these sheets have become a source of shame, have gone
through being so out of it they're like ultra-in once more. Captain Marvel sheets now seem an arch put-down of just what
made them seem so rad and right, way way back then. The
sheets haven't changed (except colors' slight sun-fading, plus
some sudden scallop-edged stains that no detergent, not even
Captain Marvel himself, could lift out). What has changed is
four years' way with the body of a child.

His pals' Doc Martens brogans rest on these sheets now,
friends slumped here in early dark, no lamp lit. Door is locked,
and they are waiting for something, waiting for something
other than themselves, to happen. The buddies will sometimes
mud their way through the house and back here, grabbing
cracker boxes and drinks as they traverse an unsuspecting
kitchen. The Boy's mom still at work. Plush dinosaurs still
crowd every ledge but all wearing sunglasses now. The tyran-
nosaurus rex sports, beneath its granny glasses, a mint-flavored

ribbed rubber that masks its cartoon smile, that binds most of its crook neck. Somebody pulls out the skin-mags and shows Verna and others and a gross three-way involving two guys in (then out) of postmen's uniforms, men who look no better or worse than your average old guy in a postman's outfit, sad— men the boys' dads' ages, 39–41, sick-o. Pals situate for a smoke or a talk or a nap before heading back out to do . . . what? to see what's going on at Big Elk Browse 'n' Buy Mall or the little woods beyond it, back and forth, forth and back . . . tiring.

One guy goes: "Nothing to do down here in Nowheresville. Earth to Captain Tommy, no, Earth to, like, Earth, come in, Earth? Earth, where's the party? Verna? Earth? Party-animal earth, come in, please?" (Laughter.)

One poster, found in his dad's attic footlocker, then Scotch-taped to The Boy's wall, shows a group called Three Dog Night(!). And they're, like, sitting in a 1945 house trailer, guys with their hair blown dry but trying to look ruff anyway; and they're in these aqua corduroy bell-bottoms whose bottoms are wider than any woman's skirt since *Gone With the Wind* times and then real tight at top so their crotches are strangled up into knots you can't miss, and probably with socks stuck in to poke it all out more bosslike, and their arms are crossed in T-shirts to show off their pretty-dweeby biceps, and they're thinking they are the hottest shit, ever. (Deeper, longer laughter.) And the trailer is pathetic (leopard throw pillows! dig it) and The Boy and his friends can get stoned and sit here and just collapse with cackling. "Look at this dickbreath, with his mouth like . . . and his arms like *boing boing* and his prod trying to get in the picture and thinking that women will do an instant-wet from being, like, even *near* this," and they keel over and sometimes, if feeling full of incentive, will take the poses themselves and then check out the poster and just crack up to see if they got it right. I sing their righteous contempt for the hype of bygone ages; but is there any glory in their own, beside the joke of hypes past?

(I also wish to sing the fact that, even when this particular group was popular when I was these kids' age, I never bought even a 45 by Three Dog Night. Dig it?)

I Sing the mall that serves as blank frame for Youth that notices only itself, and makes jokes at the expense of everybody
older and everything else, till more Youth comes along. I wish
to sing their desire, a force making them feel even larger than
their own enlarging frames predict. Marvel is the Captain; they
are flown, not piloting. Puppies get judged by paw size, and
those two seated there on the end, though just eleven, wear size
13 Converse All-Stars already.

I Sing the crazed appetites that fuel their bitter jokes and I
sadly sing Time itself. The time that will turn these critics into
the bottom-heavy middle-aged men they mock. "Catch a load
of Mr. Forties in Sweatpants—real jock, right? He must be dangerous, why? Because he's got on gray sweats priced to, like,
move at the fuckin', like, Gap! Yeah, real Olympic medal winner, going for the gold in 'Having a can bigger than his wife's,
even' and look at the lard bouncing on her one! Yschhh." I sing
the snobbish Yschhh of a kid eleven who could eat the earth
and remain innocent of weight-gain. I sing that metabolism
and wish for it. I even sing the hope that singing may itself
prove calorie-reducing.

I Sing how, at eleven, you don't know that you're in Gravity
or Time. And I blessedly lack a Republican wish for them to
find that out fast. "Abstinence till marriage," say the millions of
aging male amnesiacs who hate the young so much they act as
if they never really *were* boys first. I sing a wish for these kids to
stay free. And free to hang out, do nothing, learn rock lore and
fuck lore via word of mouth; I want them to stay safe from the
gravity and time that now has me.

I Sing their shoplifting of fine-grained sandpaper and then
retreating to the mall parking lot, back by the Dumpsters, to
stand there as a group and sand the crotches of their new
Levi's; to show everything good off good. I wish to sing the
thirteen-year-old, owner of the Captain Marvel sheets, our host
recently, who, four months ago, stuffed a sock in his Jockeys so
everything shown off would look like more of a good thing.
And I really wish to sing the fact that last week, he put the same
sock on his left foot, no longer needing it elsewhere. But, over-

doing as boys will, while being boys, he soon sanded at his front so much, tore right through. Had to go back and heist a whole new pair of jeans and start over, a lot more gradual, a little more loving.

I Sing these overlooked ones, in their black and khaki, grouped like crows on backless (don't get too comfortable) benches at their mall. They drift around here because they're now too old for their backyard swing-sets. (They've grown so big they bent the swing's crossbar last time they trooped out, on a mom's dare, and sat there, but only as a goof.) They are too young to get driver's licenses. They are waiting, between.

I resist knowing how they too must someday become, like me, citizens of mere matter and occupant time. Look, must they balden like me? Must these children thicken as I have, as I am, work out though I do, sometimes? Will biology and clocks force even these marginally wild ones to someday choose a favorite chair, seek tax shelter, stay home more, even weekend nights?

I fear I must sing Yes. And yet, ex-boy myself, how readily I recognize my fellow scrawny mongrel beauty outlaws.

The young, it is said, look forward.

The old, it is said, look backward.

And the middle-aged, I say from my chair in my sweats, we look around.

So, even from here, I see them around, unnoticed or ignored. I see them looking forward to something and managing to expect it, and even at The Mall. But they know to expect only in side glances, the way they check out their own hair, savage with mousse, using the mirrors and plate glass that, if you're vain enough (young enough), can turn even a mall into a reflecting chamber, a walk-in closet's wraparound view of you.

I, ex-boy, ex-snot, ex-punk, former-scourge, ex-shoplifter, ex-backtalker, ex–sex pistol and curfew buster, former fever blister, ex–hex perpetual, ex–eternal boner, am still here, mostly.

I yet recall the purifying rage of being so new here and this impossibly sexy (was it possible to be, if not this sexy, then this sexed?) and yet so utterly overlooked. I, grown, overgrown, stride past their bench in Gap sweats. Hoping nothing jiggles much. They are visible to me because I am invisible to them. But some founding sixty-eight pounds of me, the boy starter culture, still knows. Can still guess each guy's name and rep. Still wants to hang with them. Still fears they will outscore me at the arcade, still hopes to get my initials up there in lights forever: Highest Scorer, this machine, this mall, like, ever . . .

And finally I sing how, when they leave each other, even to go and snag some unwatched pizza wedge at The Mall's International Food Court, they mumble to each other, "Later?" "Later."

If they only knew how true that is! (Thank God, they don't.)
"Weed?"
"Fire?"

I sing socks fallen down so long, so far, they've taken socks off.

At forty-four, I sing how it can all fall down, how it all comes off (you know that too, don't you . . . well, thank God you can briefly forget).

How light and heavy boys are.
"If God so filled my heart with stars . . ."
From where I sit, to where they loiter, I just sing just Them— all glum, tough and touchy, the cherubs posing as Hell's Angels, untamed, terrified, each one Captain Marvel's chosen sidekick-mascot though less powerful than he, but loyal—suddenly a major eater, a product and a product defacer, nonwasher except the hair, a sneer disfiguring a dimple, so smugly doomed, but, in side glances, hoping.

For all those boys who are All Boy,
But not, alas, for long,

I sing.

I AM GOING TO EAT YOU

SCOTT HEIM

There were no secrets at my small-town Kansas high school. Everyone knew everyone else—their addresses and birthdays, their fathers' occupations. Here, tiny Here, the appearance of a new face meant gossip, fluster, a flurry of shut and shattered hearts. But I doubted there were any faces, new or old, that could ferry me away from the things I loved: my close-knit group of friends, my obsessions with New Wave music and horror films. Oh, I was wrong. Because that year, 1983, the new face was Brad. I've written about him before, calling him Bill once, Rex another time, but in truth his name was Brad and I've never been as ferally obsessed with anyone, anywhere, before or since.

He arrived anonymous in Little River, cast out, we imagined, by his drug-fiend parents, or so ran the rumor, sent to endure the remainder of his teenage years with his tottery edge-of-town grandparents. His skin was paper-pale, his hair ink-dark. He kept the hair long, bangs level with eyebrows that locked above the bridge of his nose. He wore jean jackets and untucked short-sleeved Ocean Pacific shirts, and even from far off the veins on his forearms branched visible. Rocklike knucklebones; farm-firm calluses on his palms; a garnet class ring shimmering devotion to some school in the opposite corner of Kansas. Most days he sported a Trans Am belt buckle. And, like his male classmates, cowboy boots—but Brad's boots scarred arcs on the floors, ashy slashes of rubber, evidence of his bandy-legged heel-toe misstep. I could tell when Brad had moved close by: he was the first in our school to wear Polo cologne, that suffocating musk from the palm-size emerald bottle, thumb-dabbed to his clavicle between classes. I watched and watched him, his lanky self-conscious gait, and when he passed I breathed the air, that smell delivering me, if only for a moment, from all people and classes and end-of-period bell bleats around me. It was the smell I would soon raise to my nose at night, from my own Polo bottle bought discount at the city mall, a smudge to the wrist and a long-clinging breath and then Brad, Brad, his face hovering behind my pinched-shut eyes.

"He's so beautiful I can't look directly, making him like the sun: I only stare somewhere to the side of his perfect face." Or so went a sentence I wrote, that year, in the journal I'd previously devoted to lists of favorite horror-film directors and actresses and murder scenes but now devoted to him. Another: "His smile is a bow arching invisible arrows to my heart." And another: "He's a shining meteor God dropped on this colorless town."

Had an actual meteor fallen on me, halting my life, my mother and stepfather would have found this Brad-obsessed journal. Worse yet, they would have discovered all I had saved. For at home, in the dresser that housed my collection of videotapes, I had begun constructing a shrine to him, a microcosm kept in my bottom drawer. I had accepted Brad as unattainable and therefore wanted the things, the pieces of him, I *could* have: loving not him, exactly, but rather the things saved in his honor. Brooding, green-eyed, with an aw-shucks grin as heartstoppingly rare as rainbow: just conjuring his image now reminds me why I, pimply and thin in my silly clothes and sillier spiked haircut, would tuck myself deep into this manic collecting.

The shrine's inception was innocent enough. All I wanted, initially, was pictures. Just weeks into my junior year, I signed up for yearbook staff to master the intimate, intricate rules of the darkroom. Brad had recently joined the basketball team, effortlessly acquiring first-string status with the rest of the jocks, and inside a manila envelope of negatives marked SPORTS, I found my bounty. Late and later after school, squinting into a

loupe to search the strips of monochrome negatives: every
thirty, forty frames, I'd strike gold and recognize some part of
him. Black-lashed, glistening eyes. Impossibly outsize shoes,
double-knotted with red laces. His knobbed and freckled el-
bows. The darkroom's November chill brailled my arms with
goose bumps, made every breath visible, but I unwound each
film roll quick as ticker tape. Here he stood, number 22, his
white-and-red tank top displaying more forearm veins, a sinewy
biceps and shoulder, the clove of his Adam's apple. The crinkle
to his eyes when he concentrated on a shot; the long hair not
quite disguising prominent ears; his astoundingly square jaw.

   Wasted hours, wasted photographic paper. At home, my
dresser drawer made a rustling hiss when opened, the curl-
edged basketball snapshots piling like leaves. But soon I
wanted more than merely these photos. Throughout that winter, my collection grew more refined, idiosyncratic, bizarre.
Brad himself could not fit in the drawer. But his detritus, the
throwaways he didn't want, could. One afternoon, cafeteria
hour, Brad ate everything on his plate except the smiley-face
sugar cookie dessert; I fished it from the garbage, then trans-
ferred it to a plastic bag. Scanning the library's weekly overdue
list, I learned Brad's favorite books (*The Catcher in the Rye;* antique-
car encyclopedias; Zane Grey), and soon slid the check-out
cards from their back covers, his left-slant signature repeated in
varicolored ink. I found boot tracks of dried farm mud. Stole
his American History paper, graded a red C-minus, from Mr.
Douglas's desk. Hovered in rest rooms after Brad's exit, lifting
brown paper towels from the trash in hopes the damp-wiped
grime was his. An adhesive name tag; leftover screws from his
shop project; a shirtfront button near his locker. A pencil
welted and ridged with teeth marks. I became the mastermind
spy, the secret agent, unearthing each clue from the catacombs
of our school. One especially auspicious morning, slipping tiptoe into the rest room after Brad, I found a toilet bubbling gold
with someone's unflushed urine. Hoping, deliriously dreaming
it his, I stole a test tube from the biology lab and dunked it,
stoppering it with a cork and saving the piss in my pocket until

later, at home, when I could center this treasure amid the rest of him.

Brad wore wristbands during basketball games, white cuffs of terry cloth to sop his exquisite sweat as the coach barked "Give it a hundred and ten percent!" and Brad leaped God-ward for the rebound. I wanted those salted bracelets; even one would do for my collection. After dallying around the gymnasium's lockers—painted scarlet and black, our school colors—I determined which was his. I wriggled a screwdriver into the slats of number 103 (same as his hall locker, no need for memorization, and stickered bottom to top with Dole and Chiquita labels from banana peels), finally curving a slot wide enough to stab a wristband. At home, before securing my new item in its proper place, I held it against my nose and mouth and breathed. Then against my tongue to suck what hint of liquid I could. At last I double-wrapped the wristband around my dick and squeezed my eyes tightly enough to picture him sailing, in living, breathing color, through the cheerleader-powered air as his hook shot sank its single breezy whoosh and I came and came.

Always the unrewarded obsessions prove the worst. The deepest and darkest, never requited with sex, not even a simple kiss, they therefore linger the longest, spilling the most body fluids, telling us astonishingly terrible things about ourselves. Would my obsession, I wondered, follow this unrewarded route? Nightly I folded myself into this perpetual worry. There had to be something, anything, I could do to make Brad want me. Alone in my room in our outskirts-of-town two-story, I ignored my mother and stepfather and heated frozen pizzas, dumped most of them away uneaten, and devoted my time to the boy I loved. I crouched on the floor beside the dresser, the ache in my stomach unraveling as I scribbled across another notebook page, hundreds of adolescent "poems" I'd later crumple and sidearm to the garbage. I gawked at Brad's photos until my eyes glazed with star-struck tears and the images seared on my memory. Incredible: his awkwardly shaped skull,

rush-jobbed by God. Glorious: a mole round and black like
peppercorn, so black it seemed a health hazard.

In our school there was no art room, no space for the yearbook staff. Little River's art and yearbook instructor was a
portly, eccentric woman named Ms. Beckett, who abandoned
her frothy-jowled St. Bernard in her pickup during classes; who
secured her hair bun with a paintbrush; who gave salted-in-the-
shell sunflower seeds to her black-sheep students, which we
spat defiantly to the floor. Ms. Beckett's classes, since we had no
convenient room, were conducted on an often-unused stage
where each spring students performed the school musical. The
art and yearbook staffs shared a world of three grungy walls
plastered in charcoal drawings; our fourth wall consisted of a
heavy hanging drape, a burgundy curtain dropped perma-
nently on that disremembered stage.

My theory went that Brad hated art; he had enrolled, I reasoned, only to escape some course like Physics or Trigonome-
try. But in truth he drew quite well. Sometimes, post–basketball
season, he would remain after the end-of-day bell, shuffling
back inside from the parking lot and its ten to fifteen minutes
of sweet, clumsy pot smoking with his cronies (Curtis, Patrick,
a pair of Mikes), to work on sketches. I spied on him once; by
that time I'd grown so stealthy and meticulous I doubt he
would have discovered me even if unstoned, if suspicious. I co-
cooned myself in a far fold of stage curtain. Brazen, my mind
and fingers numb, I slipped both bony shoulders, the harp-
curve of my hip, into the deep drape of the curtain's flutes
until only the side of my face, one glittering, yearning eye,
peeked precariously forth.

Brad's drawing was a still life of random objects positioned
and repositioned by Ms. Beckett for a semblance of aesthetic
appeal. A battered table lamp, an unabridged dictionary, a
Coke bottle, three rattleseed gourds. The still life was ridicu-
lous, and seeing Brad sitting there, intently sketching, lower lip
folded into his front teeth in concentration, would have made
ordinary spies giggle. But I was zealous, relentless: no ordinary
spy. I watched with trapped breath and heartbeat sloppily rising

in my throat—hours, it seemed—until Brad finished. And
when he finished, I saw him stand, pause, turn over the drawing
as though ashamed, and tiptoe across the room—the stage,
I mean, Brad now the Romeo and I the audience—toward Ms.
Beckett's desk. He kept his gaze on the stage door to verify that
no one was approaching. Then he crouched to the file cabinet
beneath the desk and opened it with one swift pull. Inside, I
knew, were the teacher's pencils and brushes, her hundred-odd
tubes of paint. As I watched, as I leaned a hairsbreadth closer,
Brad twisted the caps off a pair of paint tubes, lifted them to his
nostrils, and, with slitted eyes and furrowed brow, inhaled.

Suddenly I swelled so hard it seemed my dick would shatter inside
my pants. My chest throbbed from the breaths held there,
but I waited. Waited longer. Slowly he continued, slowly, sniffing.
The paint fumes clouded the room, but there, too, was Brad's
musk; hidden in the curtain I longed to unbutton his polo shirt,
sky with sea-blue collar, and nuzzle close to his clavicle, his chest,
breathing to know what scent, beneath that cologne, he truly
gave. Still I waited. After sniffing the odors of a few more colors,
Brad lay back against the floor. Because I could not risk discovery
I stayed there, stayed until he rose and left the stage.

Of course I hurried to Ms. Beckett's desk and examined the
site for charcoaled fingerprints, stray hairs, any tiny puddle of
drool. Of course I stole pocketfuls of paint tubes (chrome yellow,
cerise, lapis lazuli, satin white) for my drawer at home. In
the coming weeks, I would sniff these paints as I did the bottle
of Polo, but instead of carbonating my brain, the fumes only
made me hard. Day upon day I swore sexual allegiance to
paint. Anything resembling their alkaline odors would work.
My stepfather's gray-grained cake of pumice soap; fumy leaded
gasoline I pumped into the tank of my friend Deb's Gremlin;
even the sweetish hint of glue from the flaps of every envelope
I sealed but did not send: those wounded lovelorn letters I
wrote to him, beautiful Brad, in worship.

Sure he owned a terrific car. It was a Pontiac GTO, nightmare-
blue and devastating, sleek as sharkskin, the only convertible in

the students' lot. According to rumor, Brad had received the car from his mysterious parents: gift of guilt for all the hassle and woe they'd caused. When I thought of this disastrous father/mother pair, I fantasized Brad hating them as deeply as I thought I hated mine, tears on his furious scarlet face, revving his motor and racing into the night. I imagined him leaning toward me, allowing me to kiss away those tears, but before I could imagine anything further I was coming once more, quick too quick against my skinny stomach. . . . Again I shut the drawer.

The single time I rode in his car seems a dream now, something I invented as part of my steady fantasy, yet it actually happened. By then spring had arrived full-bloom, my drawer was crammed so deep I could hardly secure it shut, and I had landed a role in Little River's spring musical, *No, No, Nanette*. Evenings, I'd rehearse with the rest of the cast, flubbing lines, skewering the melodies of solos, tripping through the tap-dancing number that was supposed to be our showstopper. And Brad, along with one of his basketball-star pals, had undertaken the duty of light and sound manager. He didn't seem to watch as we sang, as we brush-stepped and ball-changed across the stage. But I kept content in knowing he hovered just outside the auditorium, nursing his rabbit's-foot pot pipe in the parking lot, his daydreamy eyes drifting somewhere else.

Often, between school's final bell and the start of play practice, groups of us would drive to the town's lone supermarket for nightly sugar rushes: candy bars, candy-nugget necklaces, fruit pies, twenty-nine-cent sodas with glimmery generic labels in grape, orange, cherry-cola. Brad drove sometimes, and this once, this specific once, I got to ride front-seat, brushed beside him, crowding with other cast members and stagehands. Again I remember his scent, his ever-present foresty musk that smelled, now, like my pillow at home. I remember that the radio, as he gunned the engine, played some smash-hit ballad none of us liked, and I remember Brad gesturing for the glove box to offer me, *me*, the choice of the cassette tape. Inside I found two condoms, and my heart nearly, neatly, stopped.

I pretended not to notice and, instead, uncovered tapes mostly by headbanger bands (Motley Crüe, Ozzy Osbourne, Twisted Sister); also one by the Cars, a band I adored. Naturally I chose this, hoping Brad and I would be the only ones who knew the songs. The stereo slot swallowed the tape, he upped the volume, and the Cars rattled his car. And right then he smiled (straight row of teeth, slightly big, slightly squared; his mouth crooking higher on the left; the snuggled inkling of a dimple on the chin). That smile was for me. It was mine.

What would Brad have done if I had confessed then the details of my dresser drawer? What would he have said—or how brutally, how exquisitely, would his fists have struck—if I had mentioned the top-ten list I had made of his basketball photographs? The way I molded my masturbation rules around them, as impetus to study harder—how an A on a test allowed me to jerk off to my favorite photo; a B-plus, my second favorite; descending the ladder toward the out-of-focus tenth favorite for a D-minus or, most horribly, no picture at all for an F? Would Brad have cringed, would he have hurled me from the GTO, had I recited each memorized stanza from the journal devoted to him? "I want to be the rubber ball/you habitually squeeze during class/to strengthen your forearms." "The chalk-orange baby aspirin/you chew to cure each hangover." "The bedside lamp/by which you read your western books." Instead, I spoke none of these. I let the music swell its splendor through my ears and glanced cautiously, now and again, at superstoned Brad, smiling Brad, as he drove toward the store, four, five, six quick streets, the spring sun leveling red behind us.

My favorite Brad fantasy began immediately after that ride in his GTO. I dreamed him revving top-down into our farmhouse driveway, some sultry night, to escort me to the city's single drive-in theater. My mother would look concerned and my stepfather would threaten, but Brad and I ignored them. The drive-in was showing another horror triple feature, and he had asked me to accompany him! Would you like some popcorn, Scott, he'd ask. Butter, salt? And what about those favorite dark-

chocolate toffee bars your mom used to buy in the days before
the stepdad? I imagined Brad rushing for the concession stand,
swift as a superhero, boots crunching the theater lot's gravel.
Upon his return the first of the films would begin, and together
we would ease back in the seat, his slenderly stony knee bone
nearly touching mine, as the blood gushed on-screen and ac-
tors screamed their insect voices through the window speakers.
He would hold a bottle of one of his favorites (Jack Daniel's, I
knew, but usually the cheaper Coors or Bud Light), periodically passing it to me. Both boots kicking free to air his sweat-
socked feet. One hand fixed in arrogant ownership on the
steering wheel. And, after crescendos of suspense or particularly gruesome deaths, Brad would glance cross-seat, all
untrimmed bangs and crack-corner grin, to check my reaction.

Yes, I kept this fantasy rational; although I masturbated while
thinking it, although my mind stayed focused on this scene, in
truth I knew that Brad wouldn't reach to take my hand,
wouldn't kiss me, wouldn't unroll a hidden condom from his
glove box and spread me facedown on his mud-flecked backseat to writhe, thrust, undulate, hammer. . . . Instead, I was content to imagine him simply asking me to the drive-in: just an
innocuous night with a friend. He liked horror films, I knew;
not many others in our school did, so was my fantasy all that im-
probable? I waited for the week, that May, when the drive-in
premiered *Zombie,* an Italian gorefest in which the undead
trampled through towns, obliterating all obstacles in pursuit of
human flesh. Maybe Brad would want to go. What could I do to
drum up his interest? From a movie catalog, I mail-ordered a
T-shirt emblazoned with the film's infamous image: flesh-
rotting, fang-toothed zombie, a clotted knot of worms oozing
from one eye, over the film's blood-dripping title and the slogan WE ARE GOING TO EAT YOU. Despite the disapproval of Ms.
Beckett and the other teachers, I wore the shirt twice that week,
hoping Brad would take the hint.

He didn't. *Zombie* lasted seven nights, and soon a new film, a
romantic comedy, opened at the drive-in. They wouldn't show
another horror triple feature until the summer; by then, school

would be out and Brad would be gone. I would go and watch
those movies, crowded in the Gremlin with Deb and the rest of
my unloved, outcast girl friends. We would gorge ourselves on
chocolate and link all eight hands together in a flowerlike
front-seat clump. We would halfheartedly scream. And
throughout the night, during all three films, I would wear that
shirt in Brad's spirit. I still have it today. The zombie's face has
faded, but the words spell their warning.

The last day of that school year was the last time I saw Brad.
The upperclassmen, after final bell, had driven thirty miles to
Kanopolis Reservoir for our annual beer-soaked party. We settled on a rocky lakebank beneath a hot pale sky and whispery
cottonwoods just beginning to split their pods. Summer had
opened like a premature blister; soon I would be a senior, and
Brad would be graduated, gone. I lazed on an outstretched
blanket with my minuscule clique and watched him, on the
bank's north end, doling beers to his senior friends. "We are
fuckin' *history*!" I heard him yell. His arms had tanned and his
hair had leavened to a dirty warm-weather brown, but still he
was beyond beautiful.

All I had wanted was to be wanted by Brad. It mattered not if
he was drunk or stoned; he didn't have to recognize my face or
tell me boy from girl. Even only a glint, a matchstroke mis-
judgment or error: all I needed was that desire in his eyes, brief
circuitry directed toward me. Nothing else mattered. But the
school year was over and I had failed. As the afternoon hours
blued into evening, my friends and I grew more and more
drunk. A group of partiers splashed in the sun-scalded water,
and soon I found myself there too, dog-paddling far and farther, although I hardly knew how to swim. Brad stayed onshore,
blitzed, unaware of me. I was a failure and Brad was disappearing into adulthood, a job, real life. Deeper out, the water was
chilly, and I outthrust my head like a setter's, thinking of him
with each desperate kick.

I drifted past the shallow smears of moss, and soon my toes
could not touch bottom. My head had spun so drunk that now

even the water seemed boozy, littered with empty beer bottles in green glass and pale amber, bobbing and glittering under the remaining sunspikes. Farther away, remote from him. I thought back to only weeks before, the final performance of *No, No, Nanette,* my feeble shot at small-town stardom. I remembered tap-dancing to "I Want to Be Happy," awkwardly perched on that ramshackle stage, my eyes searching the auditorium for Brad, I Want, searching still as I belted the words, to Be Happy, knowing he wasn't watching me.

Far, far out in the whiskey-colored water I felt the first cramp. Pain seized my left leg and, swiftly after, my right. In panic I clawed both hands at the water. I struggled to raise them into a steeple, tried yelling for my cluster of friends, but they could not hear. Onshore, Brad dialed his GTO stereo louder; lobbed another bottle at the lake. Had he shielded his eyes from the sunset and looked, I would have seemed a redheaded speck, a thorny obstacle inside his blurred vision. I was going under: the muscles in my legs deadened stone, two knots clenching in my lungs. This is it, I thought. The waves made a singing sound and I could feel them gushing through my ears, filling my throat. Tiny stars in the water, explosions of green as I tried screaming help help with wave after wave pushing through me. This is it.

In one flickering, fragile second I imagined being saved by Brad. For someone had seen me after all; in those last moments a figure came diving, rushing, to the soft black whirlpool where I twisted and kicked. Was it him? Just perhaps, that tiny second, I believed it was: Brad's muscles against mine, his wet-sharp strands of hair in my eyes. His mouth on my mouth and every breath breathed in loving rescue. His two arms holding me. His smile.

These thoughts of Brad passed in a single moment; suddenly my head ripped free from the weltering skin of water and my fantasy disappeared. Another arm—not his, I knew; just by its touch I knew—pulled wildly at my hair. A leg coiled ropelike at my back. The water went smooth, and someone—a girl, I saw at last—towed me slowly toward the shore. I could feel the sun beat against me once again. I could feel the jagged rocks and smell the gingery tangled green of moss.

The swimmer who hauled me back was Laura, a senior with hair pinned back in pink barrettes who was so fuddled by Boone's Farm Strawberry Hill she would later remember zero of the event. Overdramatically, I collapsed at her feet. Brad didn't notice. While I was coughing, running a towel through my hair, and accepting Laura's offer of beer, he sprawled shirtless with his friends on the indifferent shore, below the trees, near his parked GTO. I swallowed away the deadwater flavor and watched him—he had almost killed me, I remember thinking, it was all his fault—as soon the shadows gathered heavy and Brad grew too blue to see. Stung with sunburn, still breathing back the cough, I turned away. Downed a seventh beer, an eighth. My muscles hurt. My chest, and my heart inside it. I lay my head on someone's lap; it didn't matter whose. I stayed on the blanket, far from the water's edge, apart from him.

The party, terrible day, ended just after sunset. Into the drawer at home went a limestone rock, a cicada shell my friends and I found clamped to a tree. But I strayed from my usual obsessiveness and refrained from assembling anything more lyrical, meaningful: no ashes from the bonfire where Brad and the other seniors torched their history notebooks; no beer can stained with the memory of his heat-chapped lips. For on that day of the near drowning, I had begun to surrender. My muscle cramps would loosen and sunburn would fade. Summer would slip swiftly that year, easing into autumn, my final days of school. As a senior, I would fall for an absurdly slow-witted sophomore from the football squad, the only boy who accepted the head coach's dare and ran the forty-yard dash with a slab of raw calf's liver in his mouth to prove his manhood. Still later, weary of Little River and school work, I would dye my hair a rebellious white; I would be banned from the house by my stepfather and live four days with my real dad. I would slit two shallow lines in my wrists and wear long sleeves for a week.

During all this, I wouldn't, couldn't, forget Brad. School wasn't the same without him. Life wasn't. At home, I would

open the bottom drawer less and less, but his effects, his drawings and signatures and mummified mud tracks, continued to
linger there. I'd never before prayed to any sort of God, but
now, in bed at night, I began begging. *Please let me see him again,
just once. Oh please, this one special night, let him visit in a dream.*

A classmate of mine—not Laura; not Deb or any of my sad
soul mates—briefly dated Brad. This girl's name was Amy, and
in high school she had helped lead the volleyball team to
Kansas state victory; had worn frilled tube tops and loitered between classes at her locker mirror to apply frosted pink lipstick.
I would have forgotten her fleeting attachment to Brad if she
hadn't reminded me, more than a decade later, in a letter. Amy
had contacted me out of the blue, I had written her back, and
for three autumn months we exchanged generic pages packed
with small talk, a correspondence that ended as elliptically as it
had begun. At some point, I asked about an old boyfriend of
hers. In a surprisingly long and detailed answer, Amy revealed
that she had not, as was the rumor at Little River, yielded her
virginity to Pete, but rather had given herself—impulsively, for
one "promise you won't tell anyone" evening—to Brad.
    Without hesitation I demanded every detail. And she told:
Brad had parked his GTO on a back road, not far from his
grandparents' farm. He had backswung his arm from the steering wheel to her shoulder, checking his unskilled grin in the
rearview before trying it on Amy. He leaned in closer; the hand
dropped from her shoulder to her breast; and Amy—who confessed to me that the date went exactly as she'd secretly
planned—succumbed. Brad's kisses were characterized by an
acrobatic tongue and, she claimed, "too much spit." When she
unzipped his jeans and tried to lower her mouth on him, he
pulled her face back to his and kept kissing. Thoughtfully, he had
brought condoms (she didn't have to tell me where he kept
them; I remembered, I remembered), and he didn't have to
ask: Amy slowly wriggled her way horizontal on the seat, her
head canted back, both eyes steady on his white leather top-
down hood. "His dick was super big!" she wrote: that, only that.

While he fucked, he wouldn't look into her face, but instead buried his mouth in her neck. Amy tensed her own mouth against Brad's ear (and I recalled, with torture, those ears, almost translucent, oversize yet delicate as a girl's, the lobes soft cusps of blood). When she arrowed her tongue into his eardrum, Brad jerked his head away, ticklish.

With Amy's letter it all flooded back. By then I lived in New York, far from Kansas and my teenage life, that blaze of obsession. I no longer collected things—who has time or space to collect in New York?—and hadn't revisited home in years. I had barely thought of Brad. But suddenly, after Amy's words, I could smell him again. I could see his sleepily luminous smile, the veins in his arms, his unruly chop of bangs. For a moment I wanted more: What about the cum, the condom? What followed afterward, what drive home, what swollen silence? I couldn't ask. Already I knew more than I needed; already I felt something fizzing in me, something long ago abandoned. Until now, Brad had remained eighteen forever. An unrequited mystery, a perfection. Now I knew, at least in part and sketchily, what sex with him was like. To imagine it was unbearable. And unbearable, even more, to picture him in the present day, an electrician somewhere maybe, a school custodian. He would be prematurely aged, I supposed; he would have a diligent wife and delinquent, awkwardly stunning children. He still would wear the garnet ring, his resplendent forearms now riddled with fading tattoos.

In my reply to Amy's letter, I told her about one afternoon that summer, mere weeks after our end-of-school party. The day was silver and balmy, a day off from my job at the city softball complex. I had visited my father at his farmhouse. I was bored, I told her, and began to wander through the far sloped field where my father's cattle grazed. By the barbed-wire fence I found a broken, corroded pocketknife. I headed for the oak tree in the center of the field, an ancient thing of childhood legend, a knurled explosion of branches and leaves from the bomb-stalk of its trunk. As I carved, I imagined Brad pressing himself behind me, punishing, pushing my face into the tree so that the imprint of bark would scar forever, the scent of its wind-worn must, its shriven sapless pulp on my tongue as he forced himself against and into me and the force became love. His breaths white fire on my ear. His skin shaming mine with its flawlessness.

But this was only fantasy, and on finishing the reply to Amy I saw how foolish it was, all of it. I never sent the letter. Yet writing each feverish sentence had brought me back, had changed and haunted me anew. I could clearly picture his hands again, his hands and his boots, the smoke-clouds from his mouth. I could hear the leaflike rustle as the drawer opened; the feeling, warm as home, that tingled through my fingers, up my arms, as I lowered myself to all I'd collected. He was only Brad. Just a boy I loved who would not love me back. Never again did I ride in his legendary car. Never did I sniff paint fumes with him; shoot hoops against his grandparents' garage backboard; or read aloud, page after page of Zane glorious Grey, as he drifted, so heartbreakingly soft, to sleep. And never, ever, did I eat him. Never. If my father's oak tree still stands—if it hasn't yet fallen from lightning or wind, hasn't eroded into the black midwestern loam—then out there, still, are the initials I carved with my teenage fist. The S and the H. The clumsily cut B; clumsily followed G. At last the plus sign to link me with him. I remember trying to draw a heart around it all, but even in this minor effort I failed. The knife slipped. I cut my hand. I walked back to the farmhouse, bleeding, trembling. But *this* tremble, the resulting ache I feel now, is worse: here, at the keyboard, miles and years later, just typing his name.

CONTRIBUTORS

MICHAEL LOWENTHAL is the author of a novel, *The Same Embrace,* and editor of many books, including *Gay Men at the Millennium.* His short stories, essays, and reviews have appeared in *The New York Times Magazine, The Washington Post, The Boston Phoenix, The Kenyon Review,* and in anthologies such as *Best American Gay Fiction 1, Queer 13,* and *Men on Men 5.* He has edited the *Flesh and the Word* series since 1994. He lives in Boston.

TOM BACCHUS's work is findable in many forms and forums. Zines: *PUP, for men who need to be on a leash;* collected works: *Bone, Rahm* (in Spanish as *Sueños de Hombre*); anthologies: *Happily Ever After: Erotic Fairy Tales for Men, Best American Erotica 1998, Stallions and Other Studs;* and art: MetaPorn (visual art that mythologically sexualizes superheros and celebrities), shown in New York, Los Angeles, and San Francisco.

KEITH BANNER lives in Cincinnati, Ohio. He has had stories published in *Christopher Street, Minnesota Review, Men on Men 7, Best American Gay Fiction 3,* and *The Kenyon Review,* among others. His first novel, *The Life I Lead,* is being published in 1999 by Alfred A. Knopf.

PATRICK BARNES is a songwriter/performer from New York. His essay "Fantasy/Reality" appeared in the anthology *Two Hearts Desire,* and his lyrics are in *What I Meant Was,* published by TCG. He is currently composing the score for an opera, *The Wolf of Gubbio*, and a musical, *Scarlet Street*.

BRIAN BOULDREY is editor of *Harrington Gay Men's Fiction Quarterly* and the annual *Best American Gay Fiction* series. He is associate editor of *"lit."*, the literary supplement for the *San Francisco Bay Guardian*, and a frequent contributor to that paper. Recent fiction and essays have appeared in *TriQuarterly*, *Sewanee Review*, *Zyzzyva*, *Harvard Review*, *modern words*, *Flesh and the Word 4*, *James White Review*, *Fourteen Hills*, and *Gay Travels*.

CHARLES FLOWERS is a freelance editor and writer living in New York City. He received his M.F.A. in poetry from the University of Oregon, and he is the co-author of *Golden Men: The Power of Gay Aging*, forthcoming from Avon Books. "In This Corner" is his first piece of erotica, and he hereby offers to take on Oscar de la Hoya, anytime, anywhere, as long as his boyfriend can be referee.

MACK FRIEDMAN was castigated in kindergarten for spending too much time looking at maps. He is co-editing *Strapped for Cash*, a collection of sex-work narratives, which will be published in 1999. He lives in Pennsylvania.

PHILIP GAMBONE is the author of *The Language We Use Up Here*, a collection of short stories. His essays have appeared in numerous anthologies including *Wrestling with the Angel* and *Boys Like Us*. His latest book is *Something Inside: Conversations with Gay Fiction Writers* (University of Wisconsin Press). He teaches at The Park School in Brookline, Massachusetts, and in the writing program at Harvard Extension School.

STEPHEN GRECO is editorial director and a founder of Platform, the urban youth culture network at www.platform.net. A former senior editor at *Interview* magazine, Greco writes frequently on the arts and entertainment for magazines and newspapers in the United States and abroad. His short story "Good with Words" appeared in the first *Flesh and the Word*.

ALLAN GURGANUS is the author of *Oldest Living Confederate Widow Tells All*, a novel, and *White People*, a collection of stories and novellas. His latest novel from Knopf is *Plays Well with Others*. *Oldest Living Confederate Widow Tells All* won the Sue Kaufman Prize from the American Academy of Arts and Letters; *White People*, a PEN/Faulkner Prize finalist, was awarded the *Los Angeles Times Book Prize*. Gurganus's political essays often appear in the *New York Times*. He cofounded Writers Against Jesse Helms and has been a vocal opponent of homophobia and censorship. Gurganus has taught at Duke, Stanford, and Sarah Lawrence. He now lives in a village of twenty-four hundred souls in his native North Carolina.

SCOTT HEIM is the author of two novels, *Mysterious Skin* and *In Awe*, and a book of poetry, *Saved from Drowning*. His screenplay adaptation for *Mysterious Skin* won a Sundance Fellowship, and he recently spent the autumn teaching writing in England through the London Arts Board. At present he lives in Brooklyn, New York, and is completing a second book of poems and a new novel, *We Disappear*.

ANDREW HOLLERAN is the author of three novels, including, most recently, *The Beauty of Men*, and a book of essays, *Ground Zero*. He lives in Florida.

MICHAEL KLEIN is the author of *Track Conditions: A Memoir*, and *1990*, a book of poems. He has been nominated for three Lambda Literary Awards and has won two of them. He teaches writing in the MFA program at Goddard College in Vermont and as part of the Summer Writing Program at the Fine Arts Work Center in Provincetown. Michael is currently working on a book combining fiction and nonfiction, which includes "The End of Being Known."

ADAM LEVINE, a loyal member of the Central Branch of the Philadelphia YMCA, is an avid gardener and garden writer whose work has been widely published. A previous essay, "Roots," appeared in the Preston/Lowenthal anthology *Friends and Lovers*. He lives in Rose Valley, Pennsylvania.

KELLY McQUAIN recently won the *Philadelphia City Paper* Poetry Award. His fiction has appeared or is forthcoming in *Best Gay Erotica 1997* and *1999*, *The Inquirer Magazine*, *The James White Review*, *Kansas Quarterly/A Kansas Review*, *Harrington Gay Men's Fiction Quarterly*, *Best American Erotica 1999*, and *Wilma Loves Betty*. His nonfiction has appeared in *The Journal of Gay, Lesbian and Bisexual Identity*, *The Philadelphia Inquirer*, *Philadelphia Gay News,* and *Art & Understanding*, where he serves as contributing editor. He is completing a novel and a collection of short stories.

JEREMY MICHAELS lives in Missouri. He has had poems published in numerous literary journals and has had eight books of poetry published.

DEKE PHELPS (a pseudonym) contributed "The Man I Made: A Bodybuilding Memoir" to *Flesh and the Word 3*.

KEITH PIERSON is a writer and editor living in San Francisco.

D. TRAVERS SCOTT is the author of a novel, *Execution, Texas: 1987,* and editor of an anthology on public sex, *Strategic Sex*. His writings on sex and culture have appeared in *Harper's*, *PoMoSexuals*, *Steam*, *Gay Men at the Millennium*, *Women & Performance*, *Best American Gay Fiction 2*, *New Art Examiner*, and *Best Gay Erotica 1996* and *1997*. He lives in Seattle.

REGINALD SHEPHERD was raised in the Bronx and miseducated at numerous institutions of higher learning. His first book, *Some Are Drowning*, was published by the University of Pittsburgh Press as winner of the 1993 Associated Writing Programs Award in Poetry; his second collection, *Angel, Interrupted,* published by Pittsburgh in 1996, was a finalist for a 1997 Lambda Literary Award. His third book, *Wrong,* is due from Pittsburgh in 1999. He lives in Chicago and talks back to Prozac.

MATT BERNSTEIN SYCAMORE now has a sink with sharp edges. His writing has appeared in various publications, including *Best American Gay Fiction 3, Flesh and the Word 4, Queer View Mirror* (1 and 2), and *Quickies.* He is currently editing a nonfiction anthology, *Tricks and Treats: Sex Workers Write About Their Clients,* to be published by Haworth Press in 1999. He is also working on a collection of short stories, and lives in New York City.